Praise for *The New Apologetics*

"Ian S. Markham has a natural gift for writing fresh, engaging, and lively theology. His work is always pertinent for the churches and public theology, and in this brilliant book he focuses on the urgent task that faces apologetics in our age. With sciences and secularism seemingly in unassailable ascendancy, what is the future for spirituality, religion, and theology? Markham marks out new terrain for the engagement of theologians, and in the process, stakes some striking new claims for faith that can form the basis for a renewed public theology. This is a fascinating book from one of the finest exponents of contextual public theology." —Martyn Percy, dean, Christ Church, Oxford

"Reverend Ian Markham presents an intriguing argument focused on a new approach to supporting Christianity. Specifically, his argument in favor of a spiritually-infused universe offers a different perspective on the connection between the fields of science and religion. As a science and religion scholar, I am pleased with how he carefully outlines the perceived conflict between these two fields and am optimistic that his argument could push this dialogue into a new and fruitful direction." —Ian Binns, University of North Carolina, Charlotte

The New Apologetics

The New Apologetics

At the Intersection of Secularism, Science, and Spirituality

Ian S. Markham

LEXINGTON BOOKS/FORTRESS ACADEMIC
Lanham • Boulder • New York • London

Published by Lexington Books/Fortress Academic
Lexington Books is an imprint of The Rowman & Littlefield Publishing Group, Inc.
4501 Forbes Boulevard, Suite 200, Lanham, Maryland 20706
www.rowman.com

6 Tinworth Street, London SE11 5AL, United Kingdom

Copyright © 2020 by The Rowman & Littlefield Publishing Group, Inc.

All rights reserved. No part of this book may be reproduced in any form or by any electronic or mechanical means, including information storage and retrieval systems, without written permission from the publisher, except by a reviewer who may quote passages in a review.

British Library Cataloguing in Publication Information Available

Library of Congress Cataloging-in-Publication Data Available

ISBN 9781978711341 (cloth)
ISBN 9781978711365 (pbk)
ISBN 9781978711358 (electronic)

I dedicate this book to my nephews
Timothy, Arthur, William, James, Andrew, Alex, Nicolas, Gareth, Ollie,
and Stephen

Contents

Acknowledgments		vii
Introduction		ix
A Thought Exercise		xiii
1	Living in the Shadow of Deism	1
2	Superstition: The Concept and the Weapon	17
3	A Spiritually Infused Universe	35
4	The Necessary Prologomenon: The Legitimacy of Trust	61
5	The Incarnation and the Trinity: Theological Reasoning in the Christian Tradition	91
6	Sacramentality: The Basics	117
7	Apostolic Succession: The Authority	139
8	Angels and the Communion of Saints	163
9	Inclusion, Justice, and the New Apologetics: Objections and Replies	179
Concluding Reflections		189
Bibliography		193
Index		207
About the Author		217

Acknowledgments

In 2016, the Board of Trustees of Virginia Theological Seminary (VTS) determined that I was permitted to have a sabbatical for one calendar year. The year was an extraordinary gift. I traveled—to the Dominican Republic, Hong Kong, China, Oxford, and Germany. I reconnected with old friends. And I worked on this book.

There are many to whom I am grateful. Bishop Shand was the chair of the board; Melody Knowles became the acting dean and president for 2016. The senior team that heads up the Seminary was, in 2016, Heather Zdancewicz, Katie Glover, and Barney Hawkins; I am grateful to them all. Since returning from sabbatical, the senior team included Jacqui Ballou, Linda Dienno, and Jim Mathes. All were helpful in the process of writing this book. Martyn Percy and Emma Percy read chapters of the book and allowed me the privilege of staying in the Deanery at Christ Church. Parts of this book were delivered as sets of lectures at King's College, London (thank you to Richard Burridge and Meg Warner), and Hong Kong (thank you to Gareth Jones). A Conant Grant made much of this possible. At VTS, we have Meade Seminars where faculty can share drafts of chapters: the hospitality of Melody Knowles and the conversation of Stephen Cook, Kate Sonderegger, and Tim Sedgwick were precious gifts. In stimulating conversations with John Knight at the "Grape and Bean," I clarified the argument. I am grateful to the director of the library, Dr. Mitzi Budde, who has ensured that I have the materials necessary to support my writing. Shannon Preston was my research assistant at the beginning and did a fabulous job starting the project. Leslie Roraback became my research assistant and helped get the manuscript into appropriate shape for publication. And my entire professional life is managed by the talented gift of Cassandra Gravina, my executive assistant. For her help, I am deeply grateful.

My good friend and colleague Barney Hawkins, who is probably the finest writer I know, sat with the manuscript for many hours and help improve the flow of the text. I am deeply grateful for him, for this gift, and for our friendship.

It was Michael Gibson at Lexington Books/Fortress Academic who signed this volume for the press. It has been an honor to work with him. I am grateful to others who assisted in bringing this book through to production, namely Neil Elliott, Gayla Freeman, and Lisa Dammeyer. Katherine Malloy and Alison Malloy did a fabulous job on the index. For this, I am grateful.

Finally, my wife Lesley and my son Luke are extraordinary gifts in my life for which I am grateful daily. And my family, of which my nephews are a lively part, bring joy and fun. It is to my nephews that I dedicate this book.

Introduction

My mother died when I was nineteen. For a good two weeks, I was furious with God. Indeed, I resolved to be an atheist. My only difficulty was that I was an atheist who prayed. Granted, these were prayers of torment, anger, bewilderment, and sadness. But they were prayers, nevertheless. My atheism dissipated.

Doubting the existence of God has been hard for me. Perpetually, there is this sense of God constantly at the edge of my experience. A thought exercise might help: Imagine that you are in a restaurant, perhaps with a group of friends, engrossed in a conversation. Imagine further that there are other diners at other tables farther way. As you engage with your friends, you are conscious at the edge of your experience of these other diners. You know they are there. When a group at a table leaves, you might focus for a moment on those now departing diners, before refocusing on the conversation with your friends.

This is my sense of God. God is those diners at the other tables. Much of the time, it is a comforting embrace. It is an awareness that we are in a universe intended, surrounded by a spirit presence that enables all things to be. The sense of the spiritual is part of my every conscious moment. Fortunately, the presence projects warmth: It seems to tolerate the moments when I am less than I should be; and it seems to share my moments of joy and even pride when things go well. It is not spectacular—no glossolalia, no intense mystical visions, and no voices. It is just a steady, unrelenting, and inescapable presence.

In the same way that as the other people in the restaurant arrive or depart, they are suddenly more visible and impinge rather more on your immediate experience with your friends, so there are moments when the spiritual presence (which from now on I will call God) is more visible. To walk into an old church building, where countless women and men have been exposed before God, is to experience God in a much more visible way. Suddenly, I am aware that this place has been changed by the countless prayers—some of agony, some of joy. Unlike a modern office building, this space feels different. When the choir sings "Panis Angelicus," God again becomes more visible. As one closes one's eyes, the divine impinges in a deeper way. There is almost a tangible connection with the divine in a place painted with prayers.

This rather mundane experience of God does not involve talking to an invisible person sitting just above the clouds. It is not that along with tables and chairs there is also a God "object" in the room. Everything I experience is embraced by the spiritual presence. One feels as if the whole living moment is dependent on the spiritual. Even tables and chairs depend on this spiritual presence for their existence.

Given this experience of the world, the so-called "problem of evil and suffering" is now more complicated. As I discovered at nineteen, the sense of God does not reduce or change the numbness and shock of loss. Interestingly, living within the pages of the Bible illuminates extremely well the tragedy and pain of being human. At the heart of the drama is a young man dying at the hands of an occupying power. On every page, death and illness are documented. Living is difficult; lives are fragile. All of this is captured in the text of the Bible.

Learning to see the whole of life is the challenge of apologetics. In the same way as a specialist in art history can help you see dimensions to paintings that are otherwise invisible, so the church needs to help others see the dimensions to life that are otherwise not noticed. Caravaggio's fabulous painting, the *Beheading of Saint John the Baptist*, is on one level a rather imaginative depiction of the killing of John the Baptist in the prison yard. On another level, it is a graphic portrayal of death as the knife starts to sever the tendons and skin of the neck. With a guide who knows Caravaggio's work, the full power of the painting can be seen.

The "new apologetics" is a call for the church to reconceive the challenge of evangelism. Ever since Richard Dawkins's *The God Delusion*, there is a deluge of books defending the faith. Yet, there is very little evidence that the skeptical are being persuaded to faith. This book argues that the difficulty is our expectation. Our expectation is that faith is a matter of rational persuasion. Building on the work of Charles Taylor, we (and by "we" I mean the author and the reader—we are making this journey together, even if you completely disagree) will see that the problem with faith in the Western world is less to do with arguments and more to do with "mood." I coin the word *anafühl* to describe this mood. Our horizons and self-understanding have changed such that we no longer see the universe as spiritually infused. The need is for the church once again to invite women and men to see the world in a different way—as spiritually infused.

There are two elements to this argument. The first makes the simple point that a spiritually infused universe is plausible. Discoveries in modern science do not support materialist reductionism; the witness of the faith traditions and non-Western cultures provides evidence for a spiritually infused view of reality. However, this leaves us with a generalized spirituality but very little content. Therefore, the second element makes the case that it is appropriate to trust a revelation that informs us about the nature of that revelation. As a Christian, the argument in this book is that the disclosure of the spiritual is captured in the eternal Word made flesh, Jesus of Nazareth.

Building on these two elements, the book then invites us to affirm the rich description of the spiritual realm, as advocated by the church. Four elements are explored in detail: a sacramental view of reality; the apostolic succession; angels; and saints. In each case, these aspects are defended within an Anglican ecclesiology. It is a deliberate attempt to defend Catholic doctrine with a mainline sensitivity. By this, I mean an ecumenical generosity, a historical sensitivity, and an acceptance of the extraordinary insights derived from a scientific worldview. Part of the argument of the book is that a spiritually infused universe, which affirms many insights traditionally taught by the church, needs a mainline disposition. To caricature for a moment: This worldview cannot be commended simply on authority—trust the church or trust the Bible. The apologetic also needs to be compatible manifestly with the insights we are learning from other traditions. In that respect, it is a liberal defense of theological traditionalism.

This project is not simply intended for those outside the church but also for the progressives inside the church. Theological traditionalism is viewed with considerable suspicion by many "liberals." Herein there is a sad irony. We have worked hard to ensure that women are able, rightly, to participate as a priest at the Eucharist. We are celebrating the recognition that a lesbian or gay person can be allowed their integrity to love and, at the same, enjoy their full participation as a priest in God's church. And at the same time, progressives, who worked so hard to make such participation possible, have also diminished their account of the priest—sacraments are simply a memorial, or the apostolic succession is pure superstition—that one wonders why they put so much effort into persuading the church that women and gays should be included. A secondary, yet important, part of this project is to defend a richer theological account of the world so that inclusion really means something.

The picture of faith that I am commending is one that has the following shape. It invites women and men to look at the world and "sense" the presence of God. It rejects a crude materialist reductionism completely (e.g., there is nothing more than physical atoms). It sees texture in the world around us. It is a faith that can "feel" the prayers of the faithful in a place of ancient worship. However, there is more: As Christians, we trust what we learn about the spiritual realm from Jesus Christ and the tradition inherited from the Christ of faith and the Jesus of history. Jesus Christ talks about a creation that is inhabited by angels. Therefore, let us affirm the reality of angels. The tradition teaches that those who have gone before are resurrected and in the presence of God: So, let us ask the saints to pray for us. However, there is even more: We believe the church is a divine institution. We believe that holy orders really are a setting apart of sinful women and men to become vehicles of divine grace to others. Therefore, there is a connection—with the laying on of hands to the apostles—for those who are serving now the church. It is through touch—the very tactile act of laying on of hands—that grace is mediated through the sacraments to the people of God.

This sounds "magical," and perhaps even "superstitious," but these are the implications of this argument. Down to the very touch of a vessel by a priest, God's grace is meditated. We are a long way from materialistic reductionism. This is an enchanted mystical world of faith that sees a spiritual realm intertwined with the immediate world of science. Flowing through, in, and all around us are the spiritual realities revealed and taught by the Christian tradition.

This then is the primary goal of this book. It is to challenge our contemporary skepticism, which is widespread both inside and outside the church. It is an apologetic for a rich worldview that takes the discourse of the spiritual seriously—in an objective, realist sense. The goal is to help others to see that Christians have a very rich understanding of the spiritual realm. Given this, the task of apologetics is to take the hands of the seeker and invite them not simply to see the world as spiritually-infused but as inhabited, alive, and open with the intersections of the spiritual seen everywhere.

A Thought Exercise

Inspired by the thought exercise at the start of Alasdair MacIntyre's *After Virtue*,[1] let me offer a thought exercise of my own. In the late-twentieth century, no one realized the damage that "screens" did to the eye. Everyone used a computer; but as time passed, people also used a laptop, an iPad, a cell phone, and an ereader. No one knew about the mysterious rays emitted by the screens that, in a barely perceptible way, were damaging the eye's capacity to see colors.

However, by the start of the twenty-second century (yes, I am looking ahead), many people had a diminished capacity to see colors. The world was becoming a blur; primarily, sight was confined to a limited range of colors—black, white, some blues, and some greens. But different shades of a particular color had gone. With this change, art galleries became curiosities; programs about art history were struggling to survive; and specialists in great art provoked bemusement and confusion. One leading biologist at the University of Oxford insisted that all specialists in "great art" were speculators on nothingness.

The good news was that the damage to the eye was not permanent. If people put down their screens, went for long walks in the country, and started to meditate afresh in front of great art, then slowly the eye corrected itself. Slowly, different shades of red became visible. Slowly, the achievement of a great painting could be seen. But it was hard. The challenge was this: How do you encourage a range of practices that create options for experiences a person cannot imagine when they start those practices?

The argument of this book is that we are no longer seeing the textured nature of reality. We are no longer seeing the world in color. The paradigm of reductionist science has so distorted our experience that we are really starting to see nothing but "complex bundles of atoms." Our sense of God—

of the spiritual—has almost vanished. Even all those pointers to the spiritual realm—our sense of love and morality, our appreciation of great music and art—are increasingly seen as just immediate material experiences. We are no longer seeing the depth in reality. It is analogous to technology robbing us of the capacity to experience the world in multicolor.

There is hope. It is partly an act of will. This is an invitation to sit and experience the world as a place that is textured. The very act of trying will help us see that it is so. We need to recover certain practices. For those outside the church, the New Apologetics is an invitation to discover Christian practices without actually having any confidence in the experiences that will be opened up to them. This is not an invitation to the spiritual in the abstract.[2] The argument is made that there is a place to trust that God has spoken: We have been told what the spiritual realm is like. In short, this is spirituality grounded in the revelation of God as seen in Jesus Christ, the eternal Word made flesh.

NOTES

1. See Alasdair MacIntyre, *After Virtue* (Notre Dame, IN: University of Notre Dame Press, 1984), "A disquieting suggestion."

2. Medi Ann Volpe understands the need to link practices with a tradition and, also, explicate the details of the doctrine underneath practices. Her pioneering work in practical theology is the best example of good theology connecting with spiritual practices. See Medi Ann Volpe, *Rethinking Christian Identity: Doctrine and Discipleship* (Oxford: Wiley Blackwell, 2013).

Chapter One

Living in the Shadow of Deism

The gift of faith is fragile. The capacity to trust that the universe is intended and that there is agency at the heart of everything that is loving and good do not come easy. The task of the church is to create afresh the option of faith for an age that cannot even begin to see how faith is possible.

This chapter starts with a statement on the problem. Building on the insights of Charles Taylor, I suggest that we need to confront the challenge of a mood, which I suggest could be called *anafühl*. Then we look at the primary strategy that has dominated the response of the church since the rise of modern science: This strategy has made propositional arguments central and tended towards deism. Instead of inviting people to see how the spiritual infuses the entire universe, the option has been a remote God at the end of an argument.

THE PROBLEM

Skepticism abounds. Certain parts of the world are resolutely secular. If you live in western Europe or on the coasts of the United States, then believing is difficult. Taylor's question has real force: "Why was it virtually impossible not to believe in God in, say, 1500 in our Western society, while in 2000 many of us find this not only easy, but even inescapable?"[1] Just 500 hundred years ago, faith was assumed. Atheism was hard. Now the situation is reversed: Skepticism (perhaps atheism is too strong, more an agnosticism) is the default position. Religious confidence is seen as bizarre.

Why is this? Many proponents of this skepticism believe that we have become "enlightened." Science has exposed the errors of religion. Taylor describes this position as the official narrative of the Enlightenment. It is a narrative of "subtraction,"[2] which tells a story of the rejection of a world of angels and saints, made possible by various valiant heroes (Galileo), to a world that is beyond magical, mythical, and mediaeval thinking. For Taylor, this narrative of "science displacing religion" has two difficulties. First, he thinks the arguments made from, for example, the truth of evolution to therefore theism are false, even weak; and second, he thinks there is something deeper going on. It is as if he feels that 'arguments' are rarely the decisive factor in changing human behavior and cultures,[3] and therefore, modern secularism is less the triumph of good arguments and much more a mood.

Taylor is right. Science is a powerful narrative, but the mystery of consciousness or morality or even the origin of life itself does not exclude the possibility of the transcendent. Get beyond the media impression and there are no rational grounds for the presumption that "science has disproved religion." Indeed, modern science is too puzzling, too opaque, and too mysterious to disprove anything. As we shall see later in this book, contemporary discoveries in physics leave transcendent options open; they do not close them down.

Perhaps the problem is more idiosyncratic. Perhaps our skepticism is grounded in our personal reaction to beliefs. Perhaps we are living at a time when the "boggle threshold" of people in western Europe and on the costal United States is just lower than it was 500 years ago. Renée Hayes is responsible for the concept of the boggle threshold. The idea is this: There is a level when the mind boggles when faced with some new fact or report or idea; one finds the fact, report, or idea inconceivable. It is more than implausible; it is outside of our framework of conceivability. Often, it is "the instant gut-reaction" of conceivability about the possibility of a report.[4] For Hayes, the "boggle threshold" is analogous to the "pain threshold," which "varies from one person to another, probably from one culture to another and quite certainly in varying circumstances."[5] The factors that determine one's boggle threshold are many. A high boggle threshold means that you find many things outside your ordinary experience very likely, while a low boggle threshold means that you tend to be skeptical about any unusual things happening outside your ordinary experience. Hayes explains: "The Boggle Thresholds of those who read the 'heavies'—*The Times, The Guardian, The Observer*—will be lower in some respects and higher in others that the Boggle Thresholds of those who read 'the pops.' The former may accept sociological forecasts without adverse reaction; the latter may not jibe at the astrological predictions for their birthdays."[6] So, for example, the sociological forecast about the likelihood of incarceration among certain socioeconomic groups might be believed by readers of quality newspapers (and, therefore, in this respect, have a high boggle threshold), while astrological predictions are very implausible (and, therefore, in this respect, have a low boggle threshold).[7]

One helpful insight here is that many reactions to certain ideas are operating at a gut-reaction level. Consider the following list: mass murderers share a similar genetic makeup; a Virgin Birth; a bodily resurrection; reincarnation; ghosts; a miracle healing; alien lifeforms living among us; and the Loch Ness Monster. For the more "scientific reductionists," the "mass murderers sharing a similar genetic makeup" and "the Loch Ness Monster" are possible, although they are perhaps unprovable. All the rest of the ideas are beyond the boggle threshold. Evangelical Christians who affirm a virgin birth, a bodily resurrection, and miracle reports are perhaps agnostic on mass murders and the Loch Ness Monster and skeptical of the rest. New Age advocates might be comfortable with the entire list. It is quite literally a prejudice (a pre-judging), which is shaped by the subculture with which one identifies, and determines the plausibility of the report of the idea.

However, the problem with Hayes' critique is that it makes it all too personal. It is as if we are just evaluating the plausibility or otherwise of a belief by some form of personality reaction. The problem we are facing is bigger than this. There is a pervasive mood that underpins this skepticism.

Naturally, there are a whole host of ostensible reasons that are given. Some might cite religious pluralism: "How do you know which religion is right?" Others might cite the problem of evil: "How can you believe in a good God responsible for so much evil and suffering?" Others might focus on all the religious wars. However, if you probe these reasons, then they are often weakened under questions. So, yes, religion is a factor in certain conflicts, but Stalin and Mao were adamant atheists, and they were not exactly peace-loving rulers. Yet, the skepticism remains in place. So, what is it?

Perhaps, at its simplest, it is a sense that religion is just implausible. As an illustration, let us start with why the scientific narrative is suggestive (not as a matter of logic but of *feeling*) of skepticism. Bill Bryson, in his delightful *A Short History of Nearly Everything*, tells the story of the universe from the big bang onwards. Here he is explaining the importance of extinction in the history of the Earth:

> It is a curious fact that on Earth species death is, in the most literal sense, a way of life. No one knows how many species of organisms have existed since life began. Thirty billion is a commonly cited figure, but the number has been put as high as 4,000 billion. Whatever the actual total, 99.99 percent of all species that have ever lived are no longer with us. . . . For complex organisms, the average lifespan of a species is only about four million years—roughly about where we are now.[8]

Bryson goes on to report that there have been five major extinction episodes: the Ordovician, Devonian, Permian, Triassic, and Cretaceous. The largest was the Permian extinction of 245 million years ago, which saw the end of the dinosaurs.

At no point does Bryson make any religious observation. What do we do with his narrative? Perhaps in God's providence, the processes of extinction were operating to allow humanity (made in God's image) to emerge, and humanity will be immune from the extinction processes of the Earth. This is logically possible, but it doesn't feel plausible. We find ourselves with an impression. The modern scientific narrative of a universe 13.7 billion years old and with species coming and going makes God unlikely. Although one might concede that, logically, none of these things are decisive reasons for skepticism, religion, however, feels implausible. It is a combination of the sheer age of the world and the likelihood of another meteorite (apparently we are due one) causing mayhem again on Earth that just seems to squeeze God out. The God narrative doesn't "feel" right.

Let us take another illustration of this skeptical mood. Julian Barnes reflects on the nature of his mortality in *Nothing to Be Frightened Of*, and the opening sentence is, "I do not believe in God, but I miss Him."[9] Barnes never learns any practices; he is never taught to pray; yet, he has an endless fascination with the gift of faith as he sees it in others. Barnes confesses that his lack of faith was grounded in an adolescent fear of being watched as he masturbated. He writes:

> My own final letting go of the remnant, or possibility, of religion, happened at a later age. As an adolescent, hunched over some book or magazine in the family bathroom, I used to tell myself that God couldn't possibly exist because the notion that He might be watching me while I masturbated was absurd; even more absurd was the notion that all my dead ancestors might be lined up and watching too. I had other, more rational arguments, but what did for Him was this powerfully persuasive feeling—a self-interested one, too, of course. The thought of Grandma and Grandpa observing what I was up to would have seriously put me off my stroke.[10]

The heart of Barnes' rejection is not an argument but a feeling—or, as he puts it, "a powerfully persuasive feeling." The idea of God was beyond his boggle threshold; his mind quite literally boggled at the thought that God was there. He concedes that this was not a good reason. He writes:

> As I record this now, however, I wonder why I didn't think through more of the possibilities. Why did I assume that God, if He *was* watching, necessarily disapproved of how I was spilling my seed? Why did it not occur to me that if the sky did not fall in as it witnessed my zealous and unflagging self-abuse, this might be because the sky did not judge it a sin? Nor did I have the imagination to conceive of my dead ancestors equally smiling on my actions: go on, my son, enjoy it while you've got it, there won't be much more of that once you're a disembodied spirit, so have another one for us. Perhaps Grandpa would have taken his celestial pipe out of his mouth and whispered complicitly, "I once knew a very nice girl called Mabel."[11]

It is an emotional and gut response to the experience of the world. Barnes is not constructing a rational analysis of the arguments for and against God. Barnes just thinks it is ridiculous. And interestingly, God never recovers for Barnes. He concedes that this is not a good argument for atheism, but his atheism is now established. It is part of him. He never shakes it. Faith has gone forever.

Women and men are finding themselves thinking "Nah, I can't believe that." It is a feeling. And there are many routes to this skepticism. Scripture teaches that the Persian Empire was raised up to take out the Babylonian Empire (see Isaiah 45). Historians suspect that the Babylonian Empire under the king Nabonidus was undermined by a variety of factors. The Marduk priesthood disliked Nabonidus for his elevation of the moon-god Sin; the military disliked Belshazzar (the person appointed by Nabonidus to oversee the military) who was easily distracted by his other interests (e.g., the records of temple). Conditions were ripe for the empire to fall. In this case, the social and political narrative of historians makes the religious narrative implausible.

Taylor has provided a narrative that seeks to explain this new and changed environment. In brief, Taylor starts this narrative by identifying the factors 500 years ago that made atheism conceptually difficult. He identifies three. The first was that the natural order pointed beyond itself (i.e., human consciousness is animated by a soul); the second was that social order pointed beyond itself (i.e., the court of the earthly ruler is reflected in the heavenly realm); and the third was that the world was enchanted (i.e., there are spirits, demons, and angels everywhere). All three were institutionally supported and comprised an integrated grid.

This picture of the world is undermined in several ways. A key factor is the shift to a "mind-centered view" of meaning as opposed to the "enchanted world."[12] The claim of secularization theorists is that modernity "disenchants" the world, bodies do not have souls, and diseases are no longer demonic. However, for Taylor, the shift in meaning is more significant. It is the shift from an external world (packed full of objective and external meaning) to an internal world (where the mind is the sole source of meaning).[13] In the enchanted world, things have power. The relic of a saint, for example, has power to heal. There is a porousness, an exchange, between the world of things and our minds. In the enchanted world, things have the power to change us.

The modern self, by contrast, is buffered.[14] The external world is, for the modern, just stuff. It cannot affect my mind. As Taylor puts it: "The porous self is vulnerable, to spirits, demons, cosmic forces. And along with this go certain fears which can grip it in certain circumstances. The buffered self has been taken out of the world of this kind of fear."[15] The buffered self is a protected self. Immaterial forces outside the mind do not make a difference. In summary (and not sharing all the details of Taylor's argument), we now have, for the first time in the history of ideas, "atheism" as a natural possibility.

Taylor makes much of various ironies. The Reformation—a significant religious movement—contributes to the rise of disenchantment.[16] Some Reformers argue that the sacraments are simply a memorial; asking the saints to pray for us becomes inappropriate; and Scripture can be simply read without the setting of the Church. Taylor summarizes, "So we disenchant the world; we reject the sacramental; all the elements of 'magic' in the old religion. They are not only useless, but blasphemous, because they are arrogating power to us, and hence 'plucking' it away 'from the glory of God's righteousness.' This also means that intercession by the saints is of no effect. In face of the world of spirits and powers, this gives us great freedom."[17] The porous self is disappearing; the buffered self is emerging.

The narrative now develops by eliminating the transcendent and focusing on the immanent. Traditionally, the doctrine of providence claims that there are transcendent purposes of God. There is a telos for the moral order; there is a God transcendentally shaping the political realm. But with the emergence of John Locke and Adam Smith, this idea disappears. Locke insists that God provides a framework, but apart from that, He does not interfere;[18] and Smith identifies certain fundamental economic laws that, through the market, enable needs to be satisfied.[19]

Taylor now arrives at part 2 of his magnum opus at a chapter called "Providential Deism." This is the intermediate step towards the creation of an "exclusive humanism."[20] Taylor identifies three parts to deism that are significant for his narrative. He explains:

> The first turns around the notion of the world as designed by God. This understanding, which of course is perfectly orthodox as a general notion, goes through an anthropocentric shift in the late seventeenth and eighteenth century. I will call the upshot of this shift "Providential Deism." The second facet of Deism is the shift towards the primacy of impersonal order. God relates to us primarily by establishing a certain order of things, whose moral shape we can easily grasp, if we are not misled by false and superstitious notions. We obey God in following the demands of this order. We see a third facet of Deism in the idea of a true, original natural religion, which has been obscured by accretions and corruptions, and which must now be laid clear again.[21]

The emergence of the deists is crucial. The disenchantment of the world is almost complete. The universe is no longer spiritually infused. Instead, God's role is completely outside the machine and humans can work out the will of God from the design of the machine. We can work out right and wrong; and Christian faithfulness is following the demands of the moral order built into the machine. In addition, as with Thomas Jefferson and his version of the message of Jesus, we need to get behind the miraculous Jesus to the authentic advocate of a religion of reason. Living within the framework suggested by the deists, we have what Taylor calls the emergence of the "polite society"—a society "dedicated primarily to the arts of peace."[22]

The result is our immanent frame. We are stuck in a world where the meaning is determined by our mind (rather than found in the external world); where the natural world is largely autonomous (with God at best outside the system); providence and ethics are grounded in the design of the machine; and where our horizon is now confined to the immediate.

This narrative makes sense. The theistic worldview has been undermined on a variety of fronts. We have a changed view of the self: we have a changed view of nature. We interpret the world from a self-vantage point: The self is no longer porous but buffered. A mechanistic science has triumphed in our imagination.

While Taylor describes the variety of ways in which our experience of the world has changed, there is something more that needs to be recognized. We receive this changed experience of the world through our "Nah, I can't believe that" spectacles. God has become too neat—too convenient. There are too many ways in which we just feel God is implausible. There is an anarchic feel to this moment. God has become, for the modern imagination, a totalizing narrative that provokes intrinsic suspicion. We cannot allow the complexity and mystery of the world to be wrapped up so conveniently. Any attempt to do so is utterly implausible.

We need a word to describe this mood. I am proposing that we coin the word *anafühl*[23] (pronounced anna-fuel). It is the combination of two German words: *gefühl* and *anarchismus*. *Gefühl* is the German word for feeling. It is a word that describes all forms of feeling—from happy to sad. It is all-embracing, and other synonyms in English include emotion, sense, sensation, sentiment, impression, touch, and hunch. It is an all-pervasive reaction, which is not grounded in any arguments, but are almost part of one's personality. The other word is *anarchismus*, which is best translated as anarchism. In political theory, this is the view in which political structures are not necessary and are undesirable. Here the word is focused on the affirmation of personal liberty and individualism. God is the ultimate challenge to anarchism: It is the recognition that all human lives are governed by an overarching structure, which means a human life is answerable to an entity in some sense.

Therefore, the mood can be appropriately called anafühl. The definition is this: *the pervasive suspicion of any transcendent narrative or context for human lives, grounded in a swirling mass of impressions that makes such a narrative implausible.* It is a suspicion because it is an impressionistic feeling, often one not given to much analysis or thought. The reach of this suspicion is all forms of religion and often other totalizing narratives (such as Marxism). The swirling mass of impressions attempts to capture the sheer variety of feelings that can create this impression. As we saw in the case of

Barnes, it is the thought of God watching him masturbate. For others, it is the sheer scale of the modern understanding of the universe. However, the list is long: For others, it is the absurdity of imagining a cosmic mind knowing everything about seven billion people on Earth, let alone any other alien lifeforms. For others, it is ridiculous to imagine a mind existing without a material brain, which would be a condition for life beyond the grave. And, again, it is just ridiculous to imagine that bread and wine could, in any meaningful sense, really be the body and blood. These impressions rarely get to the stage of an argument: They are normally asserted and felt. The feeling is sufficient. It is so strong that there is no need to go any further. The result is that the narrative of faith is dismissed as implausible.

Therefore, as we think through the issue of apologetics, we need to recognize that the challenge of our age is less arguments for faith than a mood against faith. As we shall see in later chapters, the arguments against faith, especially from science, are weak. Antibiotics are amazing, but it is strange to assume that the impact of antibiotics is evidence for a scientific reductionism. We have always known that there are physical causes for certain physical changes. However, we also know that a person's disposition during illness can assist or hinder illness, that the mind can affect the body (and conversely, incidentally, the body can affect the mind), and that the mysteries of free will or consciousness seem to transcend scientific reductionism. We have not been persuaded away from faith but simply shifted perspectives and created a new construct. This new construct, as Taylor tells us, is local, immediate, and close. But herein is the irony: The immanent frame is being undermined by the science that started it. Reductionist science provides models of knowing that make no sense in the quantum mode or in the strange talk of a multiverse. Perhaps because the quantum is so difficult to understand (or even the multiverse theory) it has not thus far impacted our mood. We remain thinking in a reductionist way, even if the reductionism has been disproved.

THE FAILED STRATEGY OF DEISM

Returning to Taylor, one important part of his argument is that the combination of the Reformation and Deism created a "pre-shrunk" religion that eliminates the sacred from the world and confines the spiritual entirely outside the earthly realm. This is right. The impact of deism on modernity cannot be underestimated.

Peter Byrne's study, published as *Natural Religion and the Nature of Religion: The Legacy of Deism*, describes in some detail the impact of deism on modernity. He takes as his key people the following: Edward Herbert (1583–1648), John Locke (1632–1704), David Hume (1711–1776), and Immanuel Kant (1724–1804). Byrne's study shows that for the deists there is a natural religion lying behind all the various religious expressions, which is the pure disclosure of God. This creates some affection for Natural Theology (the view that using human reason one can arrive at certain basic insights about the nature and existence of God) and some antagonism toward all extraneous doctrine. Byrne explains:

> If any one thing unites the thinkers now called "deists," it is their readiness to question aspects of traditional, revealed religion. The volume of deistic criticism of orthodox Christianity is accordingly enormous.... [There is] a tendency in rationalist thought to locate the essence of religion in the preaching and practice of morality. [Therefore], it would not be difficult to come to believe that most of what belongs to traditional religions in their various forms is alien and distracting to this rational bedrock, since such systems of belief and practice end up by laying new injunctions on their devotees, distinct from and competing with the plain duties that pertain to self and neighbor.[24]

A good illustration of this was the disciple of Locke, John Toland (1670–1722). He complained how the "plain institution of Jesus Christ could degenerate into the most absurd doctrines, unintelligible jargon, ridiculous practices, and inexplicable mysteries."[25] So the following picture is emerging for the deists: there is a God, and this God creates the world and provides a moral framework. This pure natural religion is constantly distorted by priests and leaders of the church, whom, for their own ends, want to distort the purity of the message and create all these accretions that are implausible and damaging.

For Byrne, the primary legacy of the deists is the sensibility that religion is a human activity that can be judged and understood within the normal processes of human history. In short, the deists contributed to the environment that made possible religious studies.[26] However, he does note, "many aspects of the liberal theology that still enjoys wide appeal in religious life today are prefigured in their writings."[27] Byrne is right. The deists provide a religious argument for the disenchantment of the world. For the deists, the consistency of God requires a distinctive, settled disclosure of the moral life that is available to every culture.[28] They insisted that, following some of the themes of the Reformers, many traditional religions have been distorted by the self-serving leadership of the church. The obvious examples are the relics of saints or the saying of a mass on behalf of the dead. Taylor's buffered self is being born for religious reasons.

It was Christian Smith and Melinda Lundquist Denton who, based on the National Study of Youth and Religion (organized 2002–2003), provided an impressive survey of American teenagers. As they summarize the interviews from this survey, the authors suggest that the phrase "Moralistic Therapeutic Deism" best captures the worldview embedded in many of these interviews. They write:

The creed of this religion, as codified from what emerged from our interviews, sounds something like this:

1. A God exists who created and orders the world and watches over human life on Earth.
2. God wants people to be good, nice, and fair to each other, as taught in the Bible and by most world religions.
3. The central goal of life is to be happy and to feel good about oneself.
4. God does not need to be particularly involved in one's life except when God is needed to resolve a problem.
5. Good people go to heaven when they die.[29]

This creed is found across traditions. The authors note: "Such a de facto creed is particularly evident among mainline Protestant and Catholic youth, but is also visible among black and conservative Protestants, Jewish teens, other religious types of teenagers, and even many non-religious teenagers in the United States."[30] Moral Therapeutic Deism (MTD) focuses on the inculcation of goodness and morality, as a part of creating a good and happy life. There is very little discipline (i.e., no regular prayer or fasting or even attendance at church); instead, the emphasis is on self-growth and the attainment of inner happiness and security. God is on the edges of their experience. And it is here that Smith and Denton link the worldview with seventeenth-century deism. They write:

> Like the deistic God of the eighteenth-century philosophers, the God of contemporary teenage Moralistic Therapeutic Deism is primarily a divine Creator and Lawgiver. He designed the universe and establishes moral law and order. But this God is not Trinitarian, he did not speak through the Torah or the prophets of Israel, was never resurrected from the dead, and does not fill and transform people through his Spirit. This God is not demanding. He actually can't be, because his job is to solve our problems and make people feel good. In short, God is something like a combination Divine Butler and Cosmic Therapist: he is always on call, takes care of any problems that arise, professionally helps his people to feel better about themselves, and does not become too personally involved in the process.[31]

Naturally, Smith and Denton have provoked a lively discussion.[32] However, sociologically, a case can be made that a certain deistic outlook has become a part of the consciousness of the young. However, I want to go further by suggesting that a deistic tendency does not only describe the religion of America's teenagers but also captures much of the religion of modernity. Our default religious option in the West is deistic.

Let us clarify precisely what is meant by deistic here. Throughout the book, the key issue is the extent to which the spiritual infuses the material. The seventeenth-century deists were in awe of the remarkable achievements of science. As we shall see in chapter 3, the dominant metaphor was a machine. The mechanistic view of the universe captured the human imagination. Basic laws were being discovered that explained the machine. It fitted together perfectly, and it did not seem to "need" any agency outside these basic laws.

The modern theological tendency is to share with the deists an assumption that there is no spiritual agency in the material world. Granted, there are some evangelical and Roman Catholic theologians who recognize both the possibility and actuality of spiritual agency in the world. However, when it comes to the mainline, there is an overwhelming hostility to the idea that such things as miracles occur.

One illustration might help. John Hick is a good representative of contemporary liberal theology because of his robust clarity. He writes clearly; you know exactly what Hick believes and what he does not believe. Now Hick's particular route to a "deistic" tendency is the challenge of religious diversity.[33] He suggests the hypothesis that each culture names their religious experience of the transcendent (he cannot call it God, so opts for the term "Real," and concedes that we do not even know whether it is personal, out of deference to Buddhism) in the language appropriate for their culture. Hick, drawing on the epistemology of Kant, explains his position thus:

> I want to say that noumenal Real is experienced and thought by different mentalities, forming and formed by different religious traditions, as the range of gods and absolutes which the phenomenology of religion reports. And these divine *personae* and metaphysical *impersonae*, as I shall call them, are not illusory but are empirically, that is experientially, real as authentic manifestations of the Real.[34]

Much is attractive about Hick's pluralist hypothesis. The hypothesis provides an explanation for religious diversity (i.e., they emerge because of different cultural interpretations of religious experience); it affirms the experience behind the words (i.e., there really is an entity that is causing these experiences); and it recognizes the intrinsic validity of all the major religious traditions (i.e., they come from the transcendent and are all inviting us into an ethically focused life).

The difficulties with Hick's pluralistic hypothesis, however, are overwhelming. Hick accepts the Kantian (in terms of epistemology) principle that we cannot distinguish between different accounts of the Real. We do not know whether God is personal or impersonal. We do not know whether Christians are right to talk of God as a Trinity or Muslims are right to stress God's unity. In all cases, the doctrine is simply a cultural interpretation of experience. This means that at the heart of Hick's theology is a virtual agnosticism. There is something there about which we know very little.[35]

We can go further. It was Michael Goulder who used the term "deism" to describe Hick's theology. Goulder points out that Hick's God does so little:

> He [i.e., Hick's God] "creates" the world . . . ; and he is present to his creation, influencing for good all who attend to his loving presence. Most of the props of the traditional Christian drama are gone: there is no original sin, no election of Israel as God's people, no incarnation, no resurrection, no providence, etc. . . . It is close to the view known as Deism, which retained belief in God as creator, but dispensed with original sin, the election of Israel, the divinity of Jesus, providence and so on; the view whose most famous exponents were the French writers, Rousseau and Voltaire. John's theology has more to it than Rousseau's, but there is a marked family resemblance.[36]

In response, Hick insists that his view is different from deism because God "is creatively present at every moment of time and every point in space, so that it is in principle possible for human beings to be consciously related to him in any phase or region of human history."[37] However, Goulder still wins this exchange. Hick's theology is a version of deism. If we place traditional Christianity at one end of the spectrum and deism at the other, then Hick's theology is on the deism side of the halfway point. It is a God confined to three activities: creating the world, sustaining the world, and providing experiences of love to those who open themselves to that possibility. It is close to the MTD of Smith and Denton. It is moral (i.e., God is inviting us to shift from self-centered to Real-centered); therapeutic (i.e., God wants us to have good experiences of the transcendent); and deism (i.e., ultimately, there is a creator who sustains the universe). God does not perform miracles; bread and wine is not changed; the saints are not interceding for us; and the angels and demons have completely disappeared.

Sociologically, a theology of Hick does not sustain the church. Motivation to participate in Christian community requires more than an experience of some enigmatic reality about which we know nothing. One does not get out of bed to go and join others and sing hymns and listen to Scriptures that are simply a cultural projection onto transcendent experiences. We surrendered the natural world to reductionist science. We try hard to cling to divine cause and sustainer, but in terms of both relevance and evidence, we are on weak ground. What is the relevance of a God so far away from everyday living and life? If the spiritual realm is invisible in the immediate and local, then what reasons do we have to suppose that God is needed in the realm of macro and remote?

But more seriously, in terms of truth, the preshrunk religion of modernity (e.g., the MTD) is buying into a construct. We have not arrived at this impoverished, empty view of the world by good arguments. Contra Rudolf Bultmann, plenty of cultures believe in the electric light and demons. Empirical causation can combine with a spiritual realm. As the cultures of Asia and

Africa get shaped by the remarkable achievements of science and modernity, they are creating a fascinating blend of modern sensibility that retains much of the spiritual language of their culture. It is pure cultural imperialism to assume that such a worldview is "not facing the implications of modernity."

Skeptical modernity has a response to the beliefs that shape the indigenous cultures of Asia and Africa: It is to invoke the word "superstition." Along with deism, this is the accompanying concept that seeks to undermine a religious sensibility. We explore that concept in the second chapter.

NOTES

1. Charles Taylor, *The Secular Age* (Cambridge, MA: The Belknap Press of Harvard University Press, 2007), p. 25.
2. Ibid., p. 29
3. This is not a new insight. Both René Descartes and John Locke can be read as arguing that belief is not completely voluntary.
4. Renée Hayes, "The Boggle Threshold," in *Encounter*, August 1980, p. 94. Hayes is citing three UK newspapers here.
5. Ibid., p. 92.
6. Ibid., p. 94.
7. Now, what is interesting is that this gut reaction—this Boggle Threshold—has a complex relationship with truth. Hayes explains: "In the most primitive of all [i.e., human contexts] it can apparently be so high as to prevent people so much as perceiving something totally unfamiliar and incomprehensible; as happened when the Australian aborigines apparently failed to see Captain Cook's ship, the *Endeavour*, when she anchored within half-a-mile of them in April 1770. They completely ignored her presence, but when boats were lowered, they reacted instantly. They knew what boats were; they made and used their own. . . . Later examples of a low Boggle Threshold are to be found in those nineteenth-century doctors who confidently ascribed to 'shamming' the fact that a patient had shown no sign of pain while having his leg amputated under hypnotic anesthesia." These two examples illustrate that a Boggle Threshold can lead to a significant misinterpretation of the world. For the Australian aborigines, there really was a ship; for the nineteenth-century doctors, the human mind really can work to reduce the impact of pain on the body. The world is just more surprising than our boggle threshold would necessarily expect it to be. We should be suspicious of our initial skeptical reactions.
8. Bill Bryson, *A Short History of Nearly Everything* (New York: Broadway Books, first published in 2003; republished in 2004).
9. Julian Barnes, *Nothing to Be Frightened Of* (London: Jonathan Cape, 2008).
10. Ibid., p. 16.
11. Ibid, p. 16.
12. Charles Taylor, *The Secular Age* (Cambridge, MA: Belknap Press of Harvard University Press, 2007) p. 31.
13. This is complex, and there is a vast literature on this. However, one often-cited illustration is how, for Descartes, the sun (which from Plato onwards serves as a metaphor for God) becomes the metaphor for the human mind. For a good discussion, see Kurt Smith, "Descartes' Theory of Ideas," *The Stanford Encyclopedia of Philosophy* (Winter 2018 edition), Edward N. Zalta (ed.), https://plato.stanford.edu/archives/win2018/entries/descartes-ideas (Accessed October 3, 2019).
14. Charles Taylor, *The Secular Age* (Cambridge, MA: Belknap Press of Harvard University Press, 2007) p. 38.
15. Ibid., p. 38

16. It is true that the Reformation has many strands; and there were plenty that continue to affirm a sacramental theology; so Taylor is here alluding to the more Reformed branches of the Reformation.

17. Ibid., p. 79

18. Ibid., p. 167.

19. Ibid., p. 177.

20. Ibid., p. 221.

21. Ibid., p. 222.

22. Ibid., p. 235.

23. My good friend Max Wenzel Weber (b. 1995) coined this word for me in a memorable car ride from his home into the center of Munich on September 16, 2016. When I asked Max for possible words in German that capture this general, skeptical mood, it led to a rich conversation. For Max, the word includes the definition in this text but carries a range of additional connotations. It describes the swirling confusions that are impossible to manage inside the mind of many millennials. He links the word with the challenge of social media, vast information sources, and the resulting information overload. This creates a crisis of choice for the millennial. He feels that there is a potential political aspiration embedded in the concept. Millennials aspire to change in the world, which does not involve a traditional politics but could come about once we recognize a shared problem in anafühl. It is the quest for some sort of political, philosophical, and cultural guidelines. Anafühl is the recognition of a generational problem. Max writes, "Being an individual in the modern world is seen as an exciting opportunity, but the millennial generation is lost. Without some sort of cultural guides leading us through this weird time, we run the risk of facing the ghost of our generation."

24. Peter Byrne, *Natural Religion and the Nature of Religion: The Legacy of Deism*, (London: Routledge, 1989), p. 79–80.

25. John Toland, *Letters to Serena* (Oxford, UK: Oxford University, Garland, 1704), as quoted in Byrne, *Natural Religion and the Nature of Religion*, p. 83.

26. One can construct a range of narratives for the emergence of religious studies; Byrne gives credit to the deists; others would stress the role of Hume, Kant, and Hegel (the philosophy of religion story), and others again would stress Max Weber and Émile Durkheim (the history of religions story). But I do think Byrne is right that for English contributions to religious studies methodology, the deists were significant.

27. Peter Byrne, Natural Religion and the Nature of Religion, (London; New York,: Routledge, 1989) p.xiii

28. As an illustration of this argument, Byrne directs us to the writing of Charles Blount's *Oracles of Reason*; see Byrne, *Natural Religion and the Nature of Religion, p. 53.*

29. Christian Smith with Melinda Lundquist Denton, *Soul Searching: The Religious and Spiritual Lives of American Teenagers* (Oxford, UK: Oxford University Press 2005), p. 162–63.

30. Ibid., p. 163.

31. Ibid., p. 165.

32. For a good and contrasting account of the worldviews of American young adults, see David T. Gortner, *Varieties of Personal Theology: Charting the Beliefs and Values of American Young Adults* (Farnham, UK: Ashgate, 2013). See, in particular, his insistence that MTD does not capture the views of theodicy among young adults (p. 147ff). In addition, there are those who are very critical of Smith and Denton's methodology.

33. I focus on religious diversity, but another key reason for his deistic tendency is theodicy. For Hick, any spiritual agency (especially if caused directly by God) creates a major problem for theodicy. For if God is willing to intervene to save, say, one child from leukemia, then it would be unjust for God not to save all such children. Given God does not do so, this makes all interventions by God inappropriate. See John Hick, *Evil and the God of Love* (New York: Harper & Row, 1966).

34. John Hick, *An Interpretation of Religion* (London: Macmillan, 1989), p. 242.

35. It is worth noting that it is a virtual agnosticism; Hick believes in an objective reality (so in that sense it is not agnostic), but given all the cultural perceptions are so varied, one does not

know anything about that reality (hence it is virtually agnostic). Goulder, of course, was not responding to Hick's Gifford Lectures, but the criticism has some justification.

36. Michael Goulder and John Hick, *Why Believe in God?* (London: SCM Press, 1983), p. 87–88.

37. Ibid., p. 98.

Chapter Two

Superstition

The Concept and the Weapon

In the last chapter, we looked at how most contemporary apologetics has been shaped by deism. The key assumption is that science has largely, if not completely, explained the natural world, but God is still needed as a creator and source of morality. Even those who are not formally deists are still shaped by this attitude.

In this chapter, we look at the modern sibling of deism: the concept of superstition. This chapter has two tasks. The first is to look at the meaning of the concept and track the way the modern concept emerged. The second is to look at the continuing use of the word to describe animist cultures, especially in the two-thirds developing world, which some people consider "backward," "magical," and "unscientific." The first task is an exploration of the concept; the second is a discussion of the way, even today, the word is used as a weapon against premodern and many traditional cultures around the world.

THE CONCEPT OF SUPERSTITION: A NARRATIVE

Dale Martin, in his *Inventing Superstition*, offers the current contemporary meaning of superstition:

> What is "superstition"? To those of us who do not think of ourselves as superstitious, superstitions are beliefs or practices that presuppose a faulty understanding about cause and effect, usually by assuming notions of causality that have been rejected by modern science but may represent long-standing popular beliefs or practices. So people for centuries have believed that certain numbers are unlucky and others lucky. Modern science has uniformly rejected

beliefs underpinning "lucky" and "unlucky" numbers, but we still have buildings and elevators with no thirteenth floor. In the modern world, therefore, "superstitions" are often seen as vestiges of older popular beliefs and practices that survive somewhat out of place in modern culture, influenced as it is by modern science and its notions of what is rational and irrational.[1]

As Martin goes on to illustrate, this modern definition of superstition sets the concept against modern science. However, this was not true in the ancient world. In first-century culture, the category of "supernatural" did not exist. There was not this contrast between the natural realm and the supernatural realm.[2] Yet the word "superstition" was used.

But what did it mean? The actual word in the Greek is *deisdaimonia*; in the Latin, it became *superstitio*. Martin explains that, initially, the term had a variety of meanings.

> The basic definition of *deisidaimonia*, according to ancient writers, is "fear (*deisi*) of daimons (*daimones*)." But this is accurate only if both halves of the term are allowed a wide range of meanings. *Deisi* could refer to awe or respect rather than actual fear. And *daimones* could be taken to refer to gods or goddesses, semidivinities, or any kind of superhuman being (like "lower grade" gods, "heroes," daimons/demons, or what moderns might think of as ghosts or angels). Thus *deisidaimonia* could be a positive or neutral term, as we have seen in the previous chapter, referring to piety or the respect of sacred things that most people would have considered quite appropriate. But it could also be taken to be a term of reproach. . . .[3]

However, the term did evolve. It evolved into a contrast between popular practices and the more intellectual form of the faith. So Celsus, the opponent of Christianity and author of *The True Word,* writing in the second century, used the word superstition against Christianity because it has a view of the divine, which is capricious and inconsistent. Later some Christian apologists sought to distinguish their account of the faith from popular forms (which were superstitious). Therefore, Martin explains:

> "Superstition" was a category invented by ancient intellectuals, especially those we call philosophers. They came to believe that traditional notions about nature and divine beings could not be true, and they criticized all sorts of beliefs and practices that their contemporaries simply assumed were legitimate. The philosophers, by and large, never rejected basic religion, but they did criticize religious behavior they considered excessive or embarrassing. They argued that popular notions that the gods were capricious and immoral were false. They taught that traditional myths about divine misdeeds must not be true. They pointed out that the gods surely weren't the type of beings that could be "bought off" by sacrifices, much less by shameful or disgusting offerings. The Greek and Roman writers also mocked the hasty importation of "foreign" religious practices into their own culture, though they clearly never

halted the flow of imports and were never "pure" from foreign taint themselves.[4]

Early on, then, three contrasting definitions of superstitious have emerged. These are:

- A respect for gods or goddesses and related entities. This is the first, and probably the earliest, definition.
- The practices and piety of the uneducated, which often include elements of fear because of divine capriciousness.
- A belief that the gods are morally inconsistent or arbitrary.

Meanings continue to evolve over time. So, in the fifteen century, Bernardino Busti (1450–1513) of the Observant Franciscan order, in Milan, offers a set of sermons dealing with superstition. The purpose is to prepare the penitent for confession. The focus is the first commandment—"I am the Lord your God, who brought you out of the land of Egypt, out of the house of slavery; you shall have no other gods before me" (Exodus 20:2–3). It is a combination of conferring deity on anything other than God and the recognition of divine powers in places that are not authorized by the church. Fabrizio Conti explains:

> The *superstitiones* classified as *vanae observationes* cover sins against the First Commandment such as interpreting the future using dreams, which, interestingly, Busti considered as simple desires of the human mind; and belief in astrology or that one can be induced to do good or evil under the influence of constellations and planetary signs. Then there are the celebration of special days and months, such as the first of the year (*kalendiis Januarii*), or the fastening of green tree branches to houses on the first of May. Other *superstitiones* include: hanging up pieces of coal from fires on Christmas night to stop hail, predicting the future using the flame of an oil lamp, or the chirping of birds or the strength of the wind, or believing that a passing comet portends the death of a prince.[5]

Now, this was a significant tradition that was emerging in the church, which provides our fourth definition of superstition, which is:

- Any religious observance that does not have God as the focus: it is the inappropriate worship of God, in strict violation of the first commandment.

This view is found in both Angelo Carletti di Chivasso and Thomas Aquinas.[6] In practice, it meant the associating of divine casual powers with some other form of agency. This definition does challenge the picture of this period developed by Keith Thomas in his *Religion and the Decline of Magic.* Thomas describes holy water carriers, who would invite members of the parish to sprinkle homes, field, and animals. Holy water could resist the evil spirits in the air after a thunderstorm; and some priests were inviting the sick to drink the holy water so they would recover.[7] Now, granted, some of these practices were authorized by the church, but as Conti makes clear, the agent always had to be God. Magic, as such, was not authorized by the church.[8]

It is the Protestant Reformers who next take up the word "superstition." Helen Parish and William G. Naphy write:

> The Protestant assault on superstition had as its targets some of the most visible and tangible components of late medieval Catholic theology and devotion, sacraments and sacramental. Evangelicals theologians and polemicists saw superstition in the "externals" of Catholic piety, in the multiplication of rituals in the church, in the repetition of a set number of masses, and especially masses for the dead. Belief in transubstantiation was "superstitious." . . . The lighting of candles, the recitation of a fixed number of prayers, the consecration of physical objects and their use inside and outside the church was "superstitious." Divine power was exercised by God alone, and the church, its priests, and its holy objects and places were no more *loci* of the sacred or supernatural than any other.[9]

The Reformers had a whole host of particular practices that they found problematic. Martin Luther found the repetition of the Hail Mary as the "babbling of lips and the rattling of rosarie."[10] In so doing, he gave birth to our fifth definition of superstition, which is this:

- Misguided Roman Catholic practices.

Luc Racaut notes that this strategy of association did have an impact. He writes, "The opposition between superstition and reason has coloured our understanding of the Reformation debate since the Enlightenment. Around this time Protestantism was irremediably associated with reason and Catholicism with superstition."[11] Roman Catholic theology, with its deeper and richer sense of the spiritually infused nature of reality which certain practices can tap into, was now officially superstitious and, therefore, not rational.

Racaut also documents the evolution of a new definition of superstition, which is:

- The affirmation of "magic, witchcraft and devil worship."[12]

So, the papal bull, which was published by Sixtus V in 1586, explicitly links astrology with the devil and with superstition. It reads: "These, in a similar attempt to divine hidden things . . . openly make a pact with the Devil. . . . They beg that same Architect of Deception to show them the future or whatever is hidden . . . or they seek the truth about the future and hidden matters through that same Father of Lies . . . by means of . . . various superstitious ceremonies, and so try to foretell it to other people."[13]

Naturally, there is much that is commendable in the emphasis on the distinction between true faith and popular practices that are not grounded in the Christian tradition. However, it is worth noting the danger that is emerging. The term superstition is driving a wedge between faith in God and a variety of practices that laypeople hold dear. Even in the patristic period, the term is being used to challenge certain accounts of providence and divine agency. In the fifteenth century, it is being used to distinguish true worship of God from popular assumptions about the spiritual in the physical world. Ironically, these definitions of superstition prepared the way for the modern contrast between superstition and the natural world, a contrast seen most clearly in the thought of David Hume and Baruch Spinoza.

In this narrative about the evolving meaning of superstition, Hume is a transition person. Hume, in the eighteenth century, is the one asking all the modern questions. "How do we know if this or that is true?" A skepticism shapes his philosophy. In his essay "Of Superstition and Enthusiasm," which was published in *Essays Moral, Political, and Literary (1742–1754)*, he reflects on the social and political implications of superstition and enthusiasm. He explains that "weakness, fear, melancholy, together with ignorance, are, therefore, the true sources of Superstition."[14] Enthusiasm, on the other hand, emerges from the optimistic side of humanity and results in our imagining that we are favored by the divine. Of the two, superstition is the more problematic. It is superstition that gives power to the priest, which, in turn, gives power to the Roman Catholic Church.

Hume explains:

> My first reflection is, That superstition is favourable to priestly power, and enthusiasm not less or rather more contrary to it, than sound reason and philosophy. As superstition is founded on fear, sorrow, and a depression of spirits, it represents the man to himself in such despicable colours, that he appears unworthy, in his own eyes, of approaching the divine presence, and naturally has recourse to any other person, whose sanctity of life, or, perhaps, impudence and cunning, have made him be supposed more favoured by the Divinity. To him the superstitious entrust their devotions: To his care they recommend their prayers, petitions, and sacrifices: And by his means, they hope to render their addresses acceptable to their incensed Deity. Hence the origin of PRIESTS, who may justly be regarded as invention of a timorous and abject superstition, which, ever diffident of itself, dares not offer up its own devotions, but ignorantly thinks to recommend itself to the Divinity, by the mediation of his supposed friends and servants. As superstition is a considerable ingredient in almost all religions, even the most fanatical; there being nothing but philosophy able entirely to conquer these unaccountable terrors; hence it proceeds, that in almost every sect of religion there are priests to be found: But

the stronger mixture there is of superstition, the higher is the authority of the priesthood.[15]

He goes on to illustrate the abuse of power by attacking the Roman Catholic Church. Now Hume is a transition person because there is a sense in which this is a classic post-Reformation position. The Roman Catholic Church is identified with superstition. However, there are two other aspects that need to be noted. First, he is making a universal condemnation of priests as found in "almost all religions." Second, he is developing the modern meaning of superstition as a non-rational religious belief that affects the material world. Superstition, Hume implies, is the result of "ignorance and fear." This would imply that those who have a grasp of science will not be ignorant and fearful and, therefore, would not be superstition. We are on the cusp of our modern definition of superstition, which is:

- A belief in any spiritual causation in the material world.

Interestingly, the conceptual clarity came a century earlier with Spinoza writing in the seventeenth century. It is to him that we turn next. Spinoza was a controversial figure. The Christian Church in Amsterdam supported his excommunication by the Jewish community. In his work, the historical and scientific sensibilities are central. The historical turns the Bible into just one inspired text along with others (for example, Plato and Aristotle); the scientific undermines traditional theism and, along with that, all forms of superstition.

As Roger Scruton notes for Spinoza, "the physical world is all that there is, and it is a system bound by laws that relate every part of it to every part."[16] Spinoza still wanted to talk about God—as the self-dependent cause of this world, which is within this world. However, he was a resolute opponent of traditional religion. The obligation to pursue the truth means that we cannot retreat to a pre-scientific worldview.

Spinoza makes three claims about superstition. The first is that superstition is the result of fear, ignorance, and hell. At the start of *The Theological-Political Tractate*, Spinoza writes, "It is fear, then, that engenders, preserves and fosters superstition."[17] In a letter to Henry Oldenburg, Spinoza explains that superstition is "founded on ignorance."[18] And the fear of hell is identified in a letter to Alfred Burgh, where Spinoza writes, "Especially as I see, and your letter clearly shows, that you have become the slave of this Church not so much through love of God as fear of Hell, which is the single cause of superstition."[19] The second is that superstition is in conflict with reason. Spinoza sees superstition as grounded in emotion—in a reluctance to face the truth. He writes, "It follows that superstition, like all other instances of hallucination and frenzy, is bound to assume very varied and unstable forms, and that, finally, it is sustained only by hope, hatred, anger and deceit. For it arises not from reason but from emotion, and emotion of the most powerful kind."[20] The third is that superstition underpins religious authority, especially Scripture. The "invented" authority of Scripture is supported by superstition, "which teaches men to despise reason and Nature, and to admire and venerate only that which is opposed to both."[21]

Susan James explains why Spinoza finds superstition so problematic. James writes, "A first damaging aspect of superstitious practices lies in their capacity to create unstable and alternating hopes and fears."[22] Superstition creates expectations about the management of the world that do not succeed. The second damaging outcome is that superstition "undermines security by making it difficult or impossible for governments to maintain order."[23] The argument here is that Spinoza fears the superstition competition between different groups (i.e., my power practices are better than your power practices). Given reason cannot resolve these different claims, the result is an inherent instability in the body politic. The third problem is that "it is pacifying."[24] James writes, "The trouble with superstition is that it prevents us from staring our fears in the face by examining their causes, and thus inhibits the growth of a kind of psychic independence and strength of character that enables us to combat anxiety more effectively."[25]

For our purposes, Spinoza is stressing the conflict between superstition and science and reason. On science, Spinoza's monism, sometimes called his naturalism, means that he cannot abide causation other than the laws of nature. Michael Della Rocca explains that Spinoza had a "thesis that everything in the world plays by the same rules; there are no things that are somehow connected with each other but that are not governed by the same principles."[26] On reason, Spinoza has a narrative that explains intolerance and persecution as a result of superstition. So, Stephen Smith writes the following:

> His story takes the form of a natural history of religion. Human beings, Spinoza announces, are uniquely prone to superstition and credulity. While Spinoza is correctly known as one of the greatest rationalists in the history of thought, this did not blind him to the power of the passions and emotions in human life. Reason is weak when compared to the twin pressures of "hope and fear." Spinoza traces the origins of our propensity for superstition back to our natural ignorance. It is because we do not understand the causes of our fortunes and misfortunes that we find ourselves oscillating between the extremes of overweening arrogance and abject servility. A knowledge of the true causes of things will liberate us from these vices and allow us to live rationally.[27]

Spinoza has become the spokesperson for the modern understanding of superstition. We have arrived at a picture of the world where the physical sciences are the only legitimate form of causation. The term "superstition" has moved from an initial definition of "respect for a god" to a complete denial of any form of spiritual causation. Everything is dismissed—miracles, the Eucharist, angels, and an apostolic succession.

Deism and superstition are the two keywords that have shaped the modern apologetic for faith. They are linked. Both assumed that science has triumphed in the material realm. The modern concept of superstition was the term used to eliminate any concept of spiritual causation in the material world. Deism, then, was the response. The only Spirit needed was at the start of the entire process. God alone was the spiritual entity that could and needed to be defended.

Is the category of superstition helpful? The journey through the narrative of this evolving concept has revealed definitions that are contradictory. The initial definition (probably the one used in Acts) assumes a spiritual realm that is active and, therefore, needs our respect. The final definition seeks to eliminate any sense of the spiritual in the material world. The word became a weapon. It became a means by which popular faith practices were denigrated; and it became a way of expressing anti-Catholicism.

Generally, then, the category of superstition is unhelpful. However, there is a set of issues that the word, when used at its best (i.e., definition 4, with its focus on acknowledging the sovereignty of God over the spiritual realm), is seeking to delineate. What exactly is the spiritual realm? How do you get angels in and the lucky rabbit foot out? This is a question that will pervade later chapters.

Now we need to turn to the second part of this chapter: the way that the concept of superstition is continuing to be used as a weapon against any concept of spiritual causation.

SUPERSTITION AS A WEAPON AGAINST TRADITIONAL RELIGIONS

Returning to Thomas' classic *Religion and the Decline of Magic*, written in 1971, we find a cultural imperialism, which assumes Spinoza's view of superstition and believes that Western science has eliminated any sense of the spiritual. When Thomas is explaining the overreach of the medieval church in terms of the potential impact on society, he writes the following:

> Comparable assumptions are to be found among many newly converted African peoples today. Many of Cewa of Zambia and Malawi believe that Christians use the Bible as a powerful means of divination, and assume that conversation is a likely prelude to worldly success; indeed the prophets of the native Pentecostal Churches have tended to usurp the role of the traditional diviners. The Makah Indians of North America similarly regarded Christianity as a new means of divination and healing. In Sekhukuniland the Pedi were

attracted to the new religion by the hope of gaining additional protection against sickness, and for the Bantu the healing message of Christianity was the central pivot of evangelization.[28]

This is, he goes on to write, just like medieval England. Thomas is confident that the Western scientific narrative has made all such causal connections between the spiritual and the material impossible to justify. This is despite a worldwide witness that this is not the case.

In 2009, I was in Tanzania leading a conference for local clergy at Msalato Theological College, a partner institution of Virginia Theological Seminary. As we were thinking about the character of faith, I paused and simply asked the gathered group of clergy, "So tell me, do you ever doubt your faith?" I was curious to see if Richard Dawkins had penetrated eastern Africa. After a few moments of silence, finally, one local pastor said, "Sure." I asked: "So sometimes you are not sure about the existence of God?" They looked at me incredulously, "No way, of course, God is there." "No, the problem is the other spirits, the power of the curse—sometimes I doubt whether Jesus is strong enough to counteract them."

In Tanzania, the spiritual and the physical are intertwined. They are happy to use cell phones, go to a Western doctor, and appreciate the internet; but, at the same time, these priests (almost all of whom are farmers), who live so close to nature and the seasons, see the spiritually infused nature of reality. Even as cell phones come to Tanzania, the awareness of reality as infused with spirits is pervasive. A spiritually infused universe runs parallel with development. Reductionist scientific materialism is manifestly false: They feel the energy, the spiritual, and the way in which some people have a greater control of that arena than others.

The case I need to make is that to treat indigenous religious traditions as simple superstition is unfair. This case will be made in three ways. First, by focusing on Africa, we shall get a general sense of the metaphysic operating there. While conceding that generalizations about African religions are misleading, the argument will be made that, at a minimum, there is no doubt that the metaphysic is suggesting a spiritually infused universe. Second, by focusing on a case study in India, the experience of this spiritually infused universe is positive. Indeed, for those inside—in the case of India, a shrine-based healing system—it works; it makes sense. Third, by drawing on the work of Rita Astuti and Maurice Bloch, we shall see that there is an appropriate humility about the veracity of the underpinning narrative. It is not a blind faith.

Let me recognize there are limitations to this approach. In respect to the second and third ways, I am trusting that they are representative of certain dispositions that are found more widely. I concede that I am not in a position to establish this (partly because data of the type that could confirm that such dispositions are indeed universal among traditional African religions is not available). However, the studies cited are impressive. For the purposes of my argument, it does establish a more nuanced attitude to these beliefs than the word "superstition" would allow. This, in the end, is sufficient for the argument of this book. My goal is to conclude this chapter with the idea that exclusionary narratives are unhelpful. It is not rational simply to assume that all forms of spiritual causation are superstitious. Instead, science needs to be in conversation with the insights of indigenous religious traditions. In truth, this world is much more complicated than we often assume. We start with the metaphysic of Africa.

AFRICAN TRADITIONAL RELIGION

Generalizations about African religions are doomed. The sheer variety of description is amazing. From tribe to tribe, there are significant differences. However, the testimony I heard in Tanzania of a spiritually infused universe is typical. This is a central piece of African religious understanding. Jacob K. Olupona summarizes the basic characteristic of Africa religion well, when he writes:

> Although it is difficult to generalize about African traditional worldviews, a common denominator among them is a three-tiered model in which the human world exists sandwiched between the sky and the earth (including the underworld)—a schema that is not unique to Africa but found in many of the world's religious system. A porous border exists between the human realm and the sky, which belongs to the gods. Similarly although ancestors dwell inside of the earth, their activities also interject into human space. African cosmologies portray the universe as fluid, active, and impressionable, with agents from each realm constantly interacting with one another. This integrated worldview leads many practitioners of African religions to speak about the visible in tandem with the invisible.[29]

This is a worldview where the spirits are still causal agents. The identification of these spirits varies considerably, although the types are common across tradition. John S. Mibiti divides the spirits into primary types—nature spirits and human spirits.[30] The nature spirits divide into sky spirits and earth spirits, and the human spirits divide into long-dead (e.g., ghosts) and recently dead (e.g., living dead). So, the sky spirits include the sun, moon, stars, rain, storms, and thunder; the earth spirits include mountains, rocks, boulders, trees, and forests. The spirits who died many years ago are recollected in the tribal, national myths and are often key founding figures, while those who are more recently dead (i.e., within five generations) are the key spirits for a family. These beliefs continue to persist. Taylor's porous self is alive and well in Africa; we have a spiritually infused universe.

THE INSIDER'S POSITIVE PERCEPTION

Trying to get inside a worldview where the universe is animated by spirits is hard. Even for a Christian priest, who is sympathetic to religion, one reads descriptions of their beliefs and find them in so many ways alien. Certain studies by anthropologists can help. The study by Ann Grodzins Gold makes a compelling case that, from the inside, this animated worldview is positive. Her book, *Fruitful Journeys*, is a deeply empathetic exploration of the worldview of the Hindus of Ghatiyali. Located near Pakistan, the village of Ghatiyali is in the region of Rajasthan. Gold lived there during the early 1980s. The village has some farming, a strong dairy business, post office, lower school, dispensary, and electricity (although intermittent and expensive). It is also a deeply religious culture; this, naturally, is the focus of her study.

Shrines to various divinities are found everywhere. Lingering spirits of the dead are everywhere. Gold writes, "The houses, lanes, fields, and wastelands of Ghatiyali are inhabited by the spirits of many kinds of dead persons whose presence affects the living."[31] Trips to the various shrines were for almost every conceivable malady. Gold describes the treatments that would be issued by the shrine when she writes:

> Treatments for the problems brought to shrines are varied, multiple, and often successful. Causes and treatments crosscut many differing afflictions: an offended household deity might be the cause of sick children, madness, or poor business; and the remedy for any and all of these might involve certain offerings, acts of worship, and applications of powerful substances. Following the proper execution of prescribed remedies, healthy babies, the cessation of disturbed behavior, or financial success should ensue; and following such reversals of difficulty, satisfied pilgrims revisit shrines to affirm, celebrate, and perpetuate the boon they have received. Such celebrations naturally increase the deity's fame and are thus considered extremely pleasing to him.[32]

It is important to note that Gold's impression was that invariably trips to these shrines were successful. It is worth dwelling on this for a moment. In a predominantly scientific culture, we find a trip to the local doctor results in improvement normally. We are also accustomed, less often, hopefully, to endless trips to doctors that do not ever get to the bottom of the precise medical difficulty. The shrines seem to have a similar success rate. Now, of course, this might reflect the therapeutic power of such a journey. But it does expose a key factor in the persistence of such worldviews. Empirically, they are just as successful as Western medicine.

Naturally, some shrines do not bring about improvement. Gold documents, faithfully, the "trust" and explanations that are offered by those who face disappointment. In a sustained interview with a father whose son is described as "crazy," Gold has the father describe his various attempts to bring healing to his son. He does go to the hospital in Victoria. He also goes to many different shrines, with the best improvement being at the shrine of the deity Kanei Mavalya Mataji. The father explains, "No change came at any place, except for Mavalya Mataji. She opened his legs and made him stand. But within twelve months, the legs returned to their previous condition and stayed that way, so we left off going there."[33] His explanation for the failure is that the goddess had decided "not to even glance at him."[34] This was despite all the father's efforts, which included funding a *sāvamanī* feast there.

The work of shrines is not focused on reincarnation. Gold is clear: "Pilgrimage to Rajasthani shrines, *jātrā*, indeed has little if anything to with *ātmā*, its accumulation of merit, or ultimate release. It is also largely unconcerned with future births. The work of the shrines is for this life and on this body."[35]

Nature is alive in this village. Deities are active in human lives. Those living there are fully aware of the option of Western medicine but find that the success rate is no different from the shrines. These shrines continue to thrive because they seem to work.

CRITICAL REFLECTION ON THE SPIRITUALLY INFUSED UNIVERSE

This leads to the work of Astuti and Bloch. In this work, anthropologists work closely with a community to stimulate a critical reflection on the significance of ancestor. The anthropologists force questions of coherence and evidence. In addition, they discover a much more self-critical disposition in the community.

The work is in the village Betania, which is a Vezo coastal village in Madagascar. Ancestors dominate the discourse. Astuti and Bloch muse:

> Whenever an illness occurs and is found not to respond to whatever medical treatment might be available, people will wonder whether the ancestors are causing it and will take appropriate steps to find out through expert divination or by raking their own memories. They might remember a dream in which one of the recently dead complained that her house, that is, the tomb, was dirty or that she was hungry or cold. An offering of food might be provided in order to buy time; after throwing small balls of rice to the four cardinal points and to the sky, an explanation will be provided for the delay—the money is short and has become expensive—and a promise made—that the long awaited "work for the dead," that is the construction or repairs of the ancestral tomb, will be performed as soon as possible. The ancestral presence is also manifest when people, as a matter of course, align themselves with their ancestors' wishes by respecting their many taboos, or when they anxiously decide to try their luck and breach one that has become too difficult to maintain. As life unfolds at its

own pace, the ancestors are called upon for a variety of reasons: to inform them that a new mattress has been bought, or that the construction of a new house is about to begin; to ask for their protection when a long journey is about to be undertaken or a new canoe is ready to be launched; and to bear witness to various key moments in the life cycle of their descendants—from the first time a newborn is taken outside the house, all the way to the time when she will enter the tomb. The ancestors are people who were once alive and are now dead.[36]

It is interesting to note how ancestors and science are both players in this worldview. As Astuti and Bloch note, the ancestors become significant after medical treatment has not been effective. This, however, is part of a larger worldview where ancestor veneration is widespread and all-pervasive. To questions about evidence for the ancestors, the primary response is the dream world. According to Astuti and Bloch, the community believes that the spirit of the dreamer and the spirit of the dead can meet up. Central to their explanation is that the visitation of the ancestor with their spirit (their *angatse*) is always forced on the dreamer.

Now this is where the work of Astuti and Bloch gets interesting. Building on the approach taken by Paul Harris and Marta Giménez, they offer the community a series of narratives that invite participants to think about the precise nature of ancestor existence. The questions asked include ones about the body (do the eyes and the heart still work?), as well as questions about the ancestors' knowledge (can they hear conversations, and does the ancestor know the name of the surviving spouse). On one level, the results were unsurprising. Astuti and Bloch explained:

> The results of the exercise show that all participants, irrespective of narrative context, drew a distinction between bodily and mental processes, as they were more likely to say that bodily processes (92 percent) rather than mental ones (62 percent) cease after death. In other words, in their reasoning participants by and large followed the distinction, which is often made, between the body that rots and the angatse that survives.[37]

However, there are some surprises. There was a significant minority of participants who believed in the extinction of both the physical and the mental. Yet, these participants still believed in the importance of observing the appropriate rituals and, crucially, getting them right.

Getting the ritual right is an important part of the process. One example captures the significance of ritual. When the elder of the family is seeking to communicate with the ancestors,

> he adopts a special seating position, a special tone of voice, a special demeanor. Everyone else does the same, as they all follow the appropriate fomba, the customary ways of doing things that were laid down by none other than the

ancestors themselves. But when the talking, the feeding, the working is over, the elder, as he eases himself out of his formal posture, clearing his voice and taking in a deep, liberating breath, always announces that "it's over and there is not going to be a reply"—from the ancestors, that is. As people get up, stretch their legs, and help themselves to the leftover rum, they laugh at the joke: the idea that they might actually sit around waiting for the ancestors to answer back is clearly very amusing. Even if people expect that the ancestors will answer back eventually (if they are displeased by what they have seen and heard, they will punish the living in their own time and in their own ways), there and then, as the interaction between the living and the dead comes to a close, it is a joke to think that the ancestors can act in this world as if they were hearing, seeing. . . .[38]

For Astuti and Bloch, their focus is on the village attitude to ritual that creates an environment where even the skeptics participate and take the ritual seriously. For Astuti and Bloch, deference and trust are deep bonds of community connection. However, there is more here. There is a sense of mystery grounded in the talk of ancestor, a toleration of some pluralism, and a humility embedded in their worldview. The mystery is revealed in the humor—there is no immediate expectation of a response from the ancestors. Pluralism is seen in the willingness to permit a significant group to dissent from the standard narrative. The humility is seen in the recognition that the details of these processes of ancestor survival are hard to determine.

Yet there is an agreed basic narrative around the mental being different from the physical and the significance of dreams. To dismiss this thoughtful worldview as simply superstitious and nonscientific is to ignore the rich complexity of the community.

IMPLICATIONS FOR A SPIRITUALLY INFUSED UNIVERSE

The combination of deism and superstition has made the concept of a spiritually infused universe difficult to defend. The argument in response has been that, first, deism is not good at persuading the modern person to faith. Second, the category of superstition has limited value. It is a word with different meanings at different times, many of which are very unhelpful.

At this point, I wish to add a third consideration. In the opening chapter, we considered, at some length, the remarkable achievement of Charles Taylor. A key theme embedded in that text is the sense of impoverishment that modernity brings. Our world is not enchanted; it is not infused. Therefore, Hollywood has sought to fill the void. Along with Harry Potter, we have *Season of a Witch, The Witches of Eastwick, Twitches Too, Arthur the King, Merlin, Superstition, Warlock, The Colour of Magic, Seventh Son, Into the Woods,* and so the list goes on. The world described by reductionist science is too limited for the human imagination. Now, of course, wishful thinking does not make an enchanted world true. However, it does point to a deep human dynamic that is at work. We want a universe full of magic and forces beyond the material.

There is more to this consideration. It is the secular philosopher Alain de Botton, who mused that the religious worldview has one major strength over the secular worldview. Religious people constantly say, "thank you." They say thank you for the new day; they say grace before meals; they say thank you for the gift of other people in their lives. As de Botton puts it:

> To feel grateful is to allow one's self to sense how much one is at the mercy of events. It is to accept that there may come a point when our extraordinary plans for ourselves have run aground, our horizons have narrowed and we have nothing more opulent to wonder at than the sight of a bluebell or a clear evening sky. To say thank you for a glass of wine or a piece of cheese is a kind of preparation for death, for the modesty that our dying days will demand . . . That's why, even in a secular life, we should make space for some "thank yous" to no one in particular. A person who remembers to be grateful is more aware of the role of gifts and luck—and so readier to meet with the tragedies that are awaiting us all down the road.[39]

Even in a complete secularized worldview, the language of superstition has some value. It is a reminder that there is a sense of "good luck" (the only language available is the language beyond the scientific) that one has not fallen victim to cancer when young or the random car accident or the misguided youthful extravagance that ends in tragedy. Living with a sense of gratitude—to no one in particular—is the key.

If deism is not justified, superstition is a weapon, and modernity is nostalgic and even needs the sense of a spiritual, then, perhaps, we need to approach the worldwide consensus, especially in Africa and Asia, that the world is indeed spiritually infused. The African worldview has a certain elegance. The lived experience is not completely unintelligible. And as we saw with ancestor veneration, there are ways in which these cultures do handle complex questions about the precise veracity of the ancestors. So, in one sense, the argument I am offering is a plea for some gentleness in assessing these ancient and deep-seated beliefs that persist even with the arrival of science.

However, it is important that I am not misunderstood. Superstition as a category does ask an important question about which practices have some potential validity and which are clearly false and damaging. I am not seeking to defend the Rajasthani Pilgrims tour of shrines in the quest for an effective deity to heal a child. I want to be sympathetic; I want to criticize an easy Western denial; but for reasons that will become apparent in the later chapters in the book, I do not think their worldview is true. We need clear reasons for exactly what spiritual causation is and on what occasions it happens.

The African theologian Charles Nyamiti has an interesting take on this matter. He defines superstition as "belief or practice for which there is no real basis in either science or true religion."[40] Nyamiti's illustrations include "amulets, the evil eye, divination, interpretation of dreams and omens, and at times even in idolatry and the cult of spirits."[41] The primary problem with this, Nyamiti explains, is the denial of human agency and responsibility. Often humans just see themselves as entities manipulated by unseen forces, which are beyond their control. This is not good.

However, Nyamiti offers an interesting parallel with the West. He writes:

> One of the types of "superstition" in the West is the belief that rational sciences can account for everything. Here, the scientist appears as the veritable pendant (or counterpart) of the African medicine-man; he is the one who can give the final answer to all human problems and the key to their solution. This rationalism has even penetrated into Western Christianity. To solve his spiritual problems the Christian is less and less inclined to seek the advice of a priest, but rather of the modern medicine-man: the scientist, the psychoanalyst. This has also led to a certain passivity: everything seems to depend on irrational fate, which is sometimes taken as an excuse to give up any personal commitment or intellectual effort.[42]

Let us agree that superstition (where human responsibility is entirely negated by the manipulation of spiritual forces) is problematic. But, let us also note how the role of reductionist science in our culture is problematic. Reductionist science is given a disproportionate status in terms of explanation, and it has the propensity also to deny human responsibility (criminals can cite genetic and environmental explanations for their behavior).

A spiritually infused reality is one where the spiritual realm is taken seriously as a part of causal explanations for events and where human agency continues to be affirmed. We are influenced by the spiritual realm, not determined by it. Both traditional African religion and modern science reductionism can deny the legitimate space for human agency, and when they do so, they become a superstition.

The time has come for the argument to shift. We have examined the triumph of these two concepts—deism and superstition—in the realm of contemporary apologetics. Now, we need to provide an account of the New Apologetics. The task now is to develop an account of spiritual causation that makes sense within a modern scientific framework.

NOTES

1. Dale B. Martin, *Inventing Superstition: From the Hippocratics to the Christians* (Cambridge, MA: Harvard University Press, 2009), ProQuest ebrary. Web. 26 July 2016.
2. Ibid. Martin takes the view that the concept of the supernatural actually emerges with Descartes in the sixteenth century.

3. Ibid. When exactly the word "superstition" is used in text is not clear. Perhaps it is in Acts 25:19, which, according to Martin, would place the first usage of the term in 80 CE. More likely it is the exchange between Pliny the Younger (Roman governor of Bithynia) and the emperor Trajan in 112 CE, where Christians are described as a "contagious superstition," which is undermining the effectiveness of the Roman Empire.

4. Ibid.

5. Fabrizio Conti, "Preachers and Confessors against 'Superstitions': Bernardino Busti and Sermon 16 of His *Rosarium Sermonum*," *Magic, Ritual, and Witchcraft*, 2011, Vol. 6 (1), pp. 62–91.

6. Ibid. For Aquinas, see Thomas Aquinas (*Summa Theologiae*, II, II, Q. 92, art 1). For di Chivasso, see *Summa Angelica*, published in 1486.

7. Keith Thomas, *Religion and the Decline of Magic: Studies in Popular Beliefs in Sixteenth- and Seventeenth-Century England* (London: The Folio Society, 2012–originally published in 1971), Volume 1, pp. 27–28. Thomas is working with a very modern definition of superstition. As he describes his project in the introduction, he writes: "Astrology, witchcraft, magical healing, divination, ancient prophecies, ghosts and fairies, are now all rightly disdained by intelligent persons" (p. xxi).

8. In my view, Thomas overstates the situation in the medieval church when he writes, "The medieval Church thus appeared as a vast reservoir of magical power, capable of being deployed for a variety of secular purposes. Indeed it is difficult to think of any human aspiration for which it could not cater." Ibid., p. 43.

9. Helen Parish and William G. Naphy (eds.), *Religion and Superstition in Reformation Europe* (Manchester, UK: Manchester University Press, 2002), p. 2.

10. Martin Luther, *Luthers Werke*, 7:596 as quoted in Bridget Heal, "The Virgin Mary in Protestant Nuremberg," in Parish and Naphy (eds), *Religion and Superstition in Reformation Europe*, p. 26. Luther was not the first to make this a major theme of his work. Back in 1395, the Lollards in their Twelve Conclusions also made items such as holy water their target.

11. Luc Racaut, "A Protestant or Catholic Superstition? Astrology and Eschatology during the French Wars of Religion," in Parish and Naphy (eds.), *Religion and Superstition in Reformation Europe*, p. 154.

12. Ibid., p. 155.

13. Sixtus V bull, *Coeli et Terrae* (1586), as quoted in Ibid., p. 155.

14. David Hume, *Of Superstition And Enthusiasm* [e-book]. Raleigh, NC: Generic NL Freebook Publisher; n.d. Available from: eBook Collection (EBSCOhost), Ipswich, MA. Accessed July 28, 2016., p. 1.

15. Ibid., p. 2.

16. Roger Scruton, *Spinoza* (London: Phoenix Paperback, 1998), p. 48.

17. Spinoza, *The Theological-Political Tractate*, in Michael L. Morgan (ed), *Spinoza: Complete Works* (trans. Samuel Shirley), p. 388 (Indianapolis, IN: Hackett Publishing Company, 2002).

18. Ibid., Letter 73, p. 942.

19. Ibid., Letter 76, p. 950.

20. Ibid., *The Theological-Political Tractate*, p. 389.

21. Ibid., *The Theological-Political Tractate*, p. 457.

22. Susan James, *Spinoza on Superstition: Coming to Terms with Fear* (Budel, Netherlands: Uitgeverij DAMON, 2014), p. 7.

23. Ibid., p. 8.

24. Ibid., p. 9.

25. Ibid., p. 9. James goes on in the essay to argue that Spinoza was overly hard on superstition and does not give sufficient credit to the comfort that superstition can bring.

26. Michael Della Rocca, *Spinoza* (New York: Routledge 2008), p. 5.

27. Steven B. Smith, "Spinoza's Paradox: Judaism and the Construction of Liberal Identity in the *Theologico-Political Treatise*", *Journal of Jewish Thought & philosophy* 2, Vol. 4 (1995): 209.

28. Keith Thomas, *Religion and the Decline of Magic: Studies in Popular Beliefs in Sixteenth- and Seventeenth-Century England* (London: The Folio Society, 2012, originally published in 1971), Volume 1. p. 43.

29. Jacob K. Olupona, *African Religions: A Very Short Introduction* (Oxford: Oxford University Press 2014), p. 4.

30. See John S. Mbiti, *Introduction to African Religion* (2nd edition) (Portsmouth, NH: Heinemann Educational Books 1994), pp. 70–79.

31. Ann Grodzins Gold, *Fruitful Journeys: The Ways of Rajasthani Pilgrims* (Prospects Heights, IL: Waveland Press 1988), p. 63.

32. Ibid., p. 134.

33. Ibid., p. 171.

34. Ibid., p. 171.

35. Ibid., p. 147.

36. Rita Astuti and Maurice Bloch, "Are Ancestors Dead?" in Janice Boddy and Michael Lambek (eds.), *Wiley Blackwell Companions to Anthropology: Companion to the Anthropology of Religion* (Somerset, NJ: Wiley-Blackwell, 2014), p. 104.

37. Ibid., p. 110.

38. Ibid., p. 108.

39. Alaine de Botton, "Ideas for Modern Living: Gratitude," in *The Guardian*, 14 March 2010, found at https://www.theguardian.com/lifeandstyle/2010/mar/14/alain-botton-ideas-modern-living-gratitude?CMP=share_btn_link (accessed August 5, 2016).

40. Charles Nyamiti, "The Doctrine of God," in John Parratt (ed.), *A Reader in African Christian Theology* (London: SPCK, 1987), p. 59.

41. Ibid., p. 59.

42. Ibid., p. 60.

Chapter Three

A Spiritually Infused Universe

The opening two chapters have set the scene. The first chapter made the argument that the shadow of deism has hovered over almost all attempts at apologetics. We have surrendered the natural world to science and only need God to start the entire process. The difficulty with this view is that God becomes a remote hypothesis about the origins of the world, not an active, saving entity in the world around us. deism ran parallel with superstition—the other tool to disenchant the world. As we saw, the concept of superstition is a slippery concept, but it has become a useful weapon to attack anyone who affirms a spiritually infused universe. It is an especially good word for Westerners to denigrate the beliefs of indigenous cultures.

Now the positive task of this book needs to be developed. The task is to defend the concept of a spiritually infused universe, which is animated by forces that are part of our lives. The steps in this argument are as follows: first, we outline an account of a spiritually infused universe that sees the spiritual as the dominant reality, in which the achievements and methodology of modern science can be placed. This is the task in this chapter. Second, we will think through an account of revelation and authority, which can be trusted to describe accurately the spiritual nature of the universe. The case will be made that we have good reason to trust the disclosure of the spiritual realm as described by the eternal Word—Jesus Christ—and taught in the Christian tradition. Third, we will then work through the account of the spiritual realm as so revealed and defend the coherence and plausibility of certain key doctrines.

The project begins with the crucial concept of the spiritually infused universe. This chapter starts with a historical narrative followed by a mapping exercise. There is considerable literature in the realm of science and religion; it has been a major preoccupation for decades, if not centuries. The historical narrative shows that the possibilities for a constructive relationship between science and religion are more hopeful today than they have been for decades. The mapping exercise shows that most accounts of the relationship between science and religion tend to see them as separate objects that, at best, occasionally intersect. Instead of this, an alternative needs to be found that sees the spiritual as the dominant reality, in which the natural sciences operate.

The next stage is to offer the holistic account of science and religion, where science is seen as a subset of the spiritual. To do this, there is a sustained discussion of the work of Keith Ward. The achievement of Ward is to frame the discussion of science and religion in a philosophical framing of idealism. In so doing, he provides the perfect philosophical scaffolding for a spiritually infused universe.

THE HISTORICAL NARRATIVE

"Contemporary science" presents a variety of different faces to the world. The noisiest is probably Richard Dawkins.[1] However, it is important to remember that Dawkins is a biologist. Biology is a relatively new discipline. It burst on the scene in its modern form with the remarkable achievement of Charles Darwin (1809–1882) and has made extraordinary strides with the arrival of genetics. So often, when a new discipline emerges, with a distinctive set of tools and insights, it goes through a rather conceited phase. This was certainly true of physics. Modern physics emerged with Sir Isaac Newton (1642–1727). Although Newton was a devout Christian, he provided the mixture of calculus and classical mechanics that enabled an entire discipline to plot nature using mathematical equations. It was a remarkable idea, and it provided the basis for a worldview with considerable explanatory power. However, within a hundred years of Newton writing *Principia Mathematica* (1687), the emerging discipline of modern physics believed that there was no need for God.

The image of the mechanical universe held sway in the late seventeenth century. John Hedley Brooke notes, "This mechanization of the natural world became such a feature of late seventeenth-century science that historians have sometimes spoken of the death of nature, as organic analogies were displaced by images of clockwork. The impact of mechanical analogies varied from science to science, often proving premature in the study of living systems. In the long run, however, there was scarcely any branch of science that was not affected."[2] The shift of metaphor from organic images for the universe to mechanistic ones is crucial in the demise of the spiritually infused universe.[3] When Aristotle was musing on planetary motions, he suggested that you need to think of planets as agents of life and initiative. Others talked of the Earth having a soul like a vegetable. The shift to a mechanical universe was crucial. Brooke writes, "Despite the lack of consensus among natural philosophers as to what was meant by the mechanical philosophy, they spoke of it as a new theory of matter, a new theory of causality, and a new theory of method. It could be presented as a new theory of matter in that the ultimate components of things were particles, stripped of qualities such as color, taste, or smell and divested of forms, seeds, spirits, and, in the philosophy of Descartes, of all inherent powers of activity."[4]

It was probably Pierre-Simon Laplace (1749–1827) who was the Richard Dawkins of physics. Laplace wanted to solve the problem that puzzled Newton: Why do the planets follow the same direction around the sun? In response, Laplace wrote two books: *Exposition du système du monde* (*The System of the World*) and the five-volume *Mécanique celeste* (*Celestial Mechanics*). These books did not simply seek to answer the Newtonian puzzle about the direction of the planets but also attempted a history that explains the genesis of planets. His book provoked considerable attention. And when Napoleon asked him why God is not mentioned in the first volume, Laplace famously replied, "Sire, I had no need of that hypothesis." However, what is less well-known is Laplace's overall worldview. He was an advocate for "causal determinism." So, Laplace, in *A Philosophical Essay on Probabilities*, writes:

> We ought then to regard the present state of the universe as the effect of its anterior state and as the cause of the one which is to follow. Given for one instant an intelligence which could comprehend all the forces by which nature is animated and the respective situation of the beings who compose it—an intelligence sufficiently vast to submit these data to analysis—it would embrace in the same formula the movements of the greatest bodies of the universe and those of the lightest atom; for it, nothing would be uncertain and the future, as the past, would be present to its eyes.[5]

This is known as Laplace's "demon." Laplace believed that if "an intelligence" knew the initial configuration of atoms at the start of the universe, then that intelligence would be able to see every subsequent event in the future. The idea here can be divided into two: first, everything is caused by the immediate, preceding state (or anterior state, as he puts it here); and second, in the end, atoms are the cause of everything that happens. The first is known as "causal determinism"; and the second is known as "reductionism."

It is odd how powerful this mechanist picture of the universe is on our culture. It is obviously contentious. Ward observes that there

> are at least seven highly dubious assumptions involved in this hypothesis. Is there nothing that really exists except elementary particles? Are all properties

even of the physical universe subject to precise quantitative measurement? Can one ever exhaustively describe every feature of the universe, much less know that one has done so? Is there a finite and closed set of physical laws? Are these laws completely universal in their application, so that nothing lies outside their scope? Is every event in the physical universe completely predictable, even in principle? And do causes necessarily determine their effects, in such a way that nothing could happen except what does happen?[6]

All of these assumptions can be contested. However, let us focus on the problem of originality in this universe. According to Laplace, Shakespeare's startling creativity and Beethoven's Fifth were all anticipated by the preceding configuration of atoms in the universe. Laplace is a materialist; he, like Dawkins, is assuming that ideas are identical with brain states. This is difficult to sustain in a coherent way. As Ward helpfully summarizes:

> In general, if there are ever any new thoughts, or any sorts of things which have never happened before in the universe, then these things are in principle unpredictable by natural science (except as a sort of guess about the future, based on how things have gone in the past). Even if we could predict Laplace's brain, we could never predict his thoughts.[7]

The vast majority of contemporary physicists reject entirely the causal determinism and reductionism of Laplace. Indeed, when John Polkinghorne lists the ten qualities of the scientific view of the world, it is a long way from the clarity and determinate qualities of Laplace's universe. Polkinghorne's ten qualities are: Elusive, Intelligible, Problematic, Surprising, Chance and Necessity, Big, Tightly-knit, Futile, Complete (within the terms it sets for itself), and Incomplete.[8]

Of course, the key difference is the emergence of quantum mechanics—the study of atomic and subatomic systems. A world of neat causation disappears. Instead, we have the paradox of Heisenberg's uncertainty principle, where one cannot simultaneously speak properly of both the location and motion of an electron; and this is a truth about electrons that is "irreducible, which is to say that quantum processes are in some sense genuinely spontaneous—without any specific causes."[9] The interesting truth about the quantum world is that mathematics still makes it intelligible (so it is still operating under a strange set of rules), but it is still worlds away from the crude models of mechanistic, reductionist science. Philip Clayton is right when he observes the following:

> The Copenhagen interpretation of quantum mechanics, long the dominant interpretation, holds that this indeterminacy reflects not just a limit on our current knowledge, but a *fundamental ontological openness in the world itself.* If physics is therefore blocked from a complete, deterministic account of even the physical world, many argue, the hope for a reduction of all knowledge to

fundamental physics must be dashed. The achievements of Laplace's imaginary demon, who (Laplace imagined) could predict all future objects and events in the universe given an exhaustive knowledge of its physical state in the present, are not possible even in principle.[10]

Now, why is this so significant? The truth is that faith is always in conversation with the cosmology of the day. We can expect no more. Walter Eichrodt explains that the biblical cosmology reflects the worldview of the day:

> Israelite cosmology exhibits, as is only to be expected, extensive agreement with the general ideas of the ancient world on the subject. . . . Resting on pillars, it [i.e., heaven] overarched the earth, hard as a molten mirror. Poetic hyperbole can compare it with a veil or tent which Yahweh has stretched over the earth.[11]

And so, the narrative goes on. This veil separates the waters of Earth from the waters of heaven, which are stored away and ready to be unleashed in the event of, say, a "flood." The cosmology assumed in Scripture is the cosmology commonly held by the elites of that age. The themes of Scripture are not refuted by changing models of the universe, in the same way as the insights of Shakespeare are not refuted by changing understandings of illness.[12] If Scripture had assumed the cosmology of Newtonian physics, then that too would have been falsified by the effects of Einstein's theory of relativity and quantum mechanics and the emergence of a new cosmology courtesy of the New Physics.

Some cosmologies are friendlier to faith than others. I think the case can be made that the cosmology of the New Physics is especially friendly to faith. Primarily, this is because we have rediscovered the mystery of the world; the spiritual realm is no longer absurd and, in some sense, is disproved. So, in the same way as modern science makes possible genuine human freewill (i.e., persons can be similar and have the same choice but make different decisions thanks to the intrinsic openness of the universe), it is possible to see a spiritual realm coexisting with the description of physical causation provided by science. Ward is, I think, right, when he writes the following:

> My own view is that the third millennium of Christian existence will bring a new integration of scientific and religious thought, the development of a more global spirituality, and a retrieval of some of the deepest spiritual insights of the Christian faith, which have been underemphasized or overlooked.[13]

The science that birthed deism has definitely gone away. We know empirically that this universe is not a machine, determined by prior causal states, and largely self-regulating. Instead, the physics of today suggests an openness, a complexity, and genuine space for agency and decision.

The narrative section of my argument is this: first, faith always works with different cosmologies. The biblical witness worked with the cosmological model in its day; we work with the cosmological model of our day (which will also be superseded). Faith is not disproved because the cosmological model has changed. Second, the science of Laplace underpins the theology of deism. But this science is now exposed as a hopelessly inadequate model of the universe. Therefore, deism as a response to science should be rejected. Third, the New Physics invites mystery, awe, and respect for greater complexity that opens afresh a richer discourse of the spiritual.

Much has been made in this chapter of the ways in which the assumptions underpinning a deistic worldview have been undermined by the emergence of a different worldview due to the New Physics. However, one cannot evade the question: what exactly is the relationship between the spiritual dimension and the causation that is scientifically measurable and discernible? We turn to the mapping question.

MAPPING THE OPTIONS

Maps are political. If you can frame the debate, then you can often triumph in the debate. If the choice is just capitalism or communism, then most Americans would prefer capitalism. If the choice has six options, where capitalism and communism are just at the end, then many Americans might prefer a compassionate conservatism or a progressive welfare support. The map can create the options. The map can limit the options.[14]

When it comes to map making the science and religion debate, Dawkins and his sympathizers are dominant. Their map is very simple. You have a choice of "opposition to science" (i.e., you are a creationist that denies evolution) or "surrender to science" (i.e., you concede that science explains everything of significance in the world). This map dominates the popular secular imagination. The challenge for theists is to create a credible alternative.

We turn now to an extended discussion of alternative maps in the science and religion debate. Although the reader may, without losing track of the argument, simply move towards the end of this chapter and pick up the total argument of the book, this section is intended to be significant. The sub-argument in this section is that most taxonomies in science and religion are "intersect" taxonomies. The concept of a spiritually infused universe is not truly considered. So now starts an extended discussion of different "science and religions" maps.

Clayton poses the problem very clearly when he writes, "How should theology conceive the God-world relation? Simply identifying God and the world is problem because theism requires that God serve as the source of the world. But if God's actions come from outside the natural world, they will conflict with natural laws and introduce new energies into closed physical systems, both of which set theology at loggerheads with the presuppositions, methods, and results of the natural sciences."[15] Now how precisely the divine interacts with the creation is at the heart of this project. The vision of a spiritually infused universe, where nature is alive and animated, is a distinctive quest in the literature. So, as already stated above, this part of the chapter will begin by looking at the different taxonomies that scholars have offered to make sense of the voluminous literature on science and religion.[16] We shall discover that none of the approaches are really in conversation with the concept of a spiritually infused universe.

Perhaps the most substantial taxonomy was offered by Ian G. Barbour in his *Religion in an Age of Science*. He identifies four basic approaches. The first is conflict. Under this heading, he places "scientific materialism" and "biblical literalism." The second is independence. Here he places those who see that science and religion have contrasting methods (here he places Langdon Gilkey) and differing languages (those using the famous Wittgensteinian analogy of "language games"). The third is dialogue—so, for example, the boundary question: Was Christianity a factor in the rise of science? Barbour also considers the lively advocates, for example, Michael Polanyi, who see many methodological similarities between scientists and theologians (for example, both use models). The fourth is integration. This approach subdivides into three. Natural theology deduces God from the physical world; some theologians try to create a theology of nature—this is where Barbour places Arthur Peacocke; and the systematic synthesis by using a philosophy that provides a mediating role between religion and science, for example, process philosophy.

Where now does a spiritually infused universe fit in? Most of these four approaches see science on one side of the divide and religion on the other. The image assumed seems to be that over in that corner is science and over in this one is religion. So, staying in the boxing ring metaphor, they can be fighting; ignoring each other; talking to each other; or have a mediator helping them get along.

Other taxonomies are equally unhelpful. Ted Peters, for example, identifies five different conceptions of the relationship between science and religion. These are:

- Scientism, which he defines as "There is but one reality, the finite reality of nature, and the natural sciences provide the only methods for giving us the truth."[17]
- Ecclesiastical Authoritarianism, which, as the name implies, is the view that revelation always trumps scientific discovery.
- Scientific Creationism, where the text of Scripture is treated as a scientific description of the origins of the universe.

- The Two-Languages theory, which was made famous by Langdon Gilkey, and has Wittgenstenian overtones. It is the view that "scientific theory and religious faith represent two separate and distinct ways of knowing."[18] For Peters, the difficulty with this view is that it denies connection between science and religion; it forbids "cross-disciplinary conversation."[19]

And finally, the view that Peters advocates for is: Theology and Science in Consonance. Peters explains: "It recognizes where we are at the outset: theology sings one song and science another. Nevertheless, it gives us something to listen for. We can listen for those measures where both make a sound at the same frequency, where we hear a momentary bar of harmony. Then we can at least ask if this might someday lead to a shared melody."[20]

Again, as with Barbour, with the exception of scientific creationism, we have science and religion operating as two distinct objects.[21] Scientism assumes science is right; ecclesiastical authoritarianism assumes the church is right; and the last two (two languages and theology and science in consonance) assume two separate disciplines that either go their own ways or occasionally might mutually illuminate.

Perhaps a word on scientific creationism is helpful here. It is important to note that creationists are trying to affirm divine or spiritual causation. The various versions (for example, intelligent design) tend to stress that at certain points in the creation of the world a divine action was essential—for example, the emergence of humans. The best-known version of creationism takes as historically and scientifically reliable the opening of Genesis. They lampoon the idea that out of a primeval soup, the amazing diversity of the universe emerged. They find it utterly implausible that giraffes and butterflies come from the same source. Design by God seems to make much more sense.

The difficulties with creationism are numerous. First, it is not justified by the biblical text. There are two creation narratives. The opening chapter of Genesis highlights the significance of the utterance of God in bringing about the world for the purposes of illuminating how the world reveals the nature of God. For the ancient mind, words reveal thoughts. So, in Genesis 1, the fact that word brings about creation invites us to see in creation something of the nature of God. As David Fergusson puts it, "Genesis 1–11 contains not history and science as we understand these terms but a theological account of the origins of life and the status of the world and human beings as created....It does not tell us *how* scientifically the world came to be as it is, but it does proclaim *that* God made the world and *why* God made it."[22] The second difficulty is that the evidence of the evolutionary narrative is overwhelming. Fergusson lists the four factors: the big bang theory; radiometric dating of rocks confirms the Earth is several billions years old; the fossil record shows the changes to more advanced forms of life; and the evidence for human evolution through natural selection and genetic mutation is extensive. Fergusson rightly concludes, "In these aforementioned respects, physics, geology, paleontology, and biology tend to confirm each other, and together provide a coherent view of the origin of the universe, and the history of our planet."[23] Creationism is not an option.

We need a taxonomy that brings the worlds of science and religion more closely together. And perhaps the options in the divine action debates may help. Divine action, by definition, involves some sort of divine causation. Clayton identifies eight positions in the literature:

1. Naturalist and physicalist theologies
2. Deism of various types
3. The view that all history represents a single divine act (Maurice Wiles)
4. "Double agency" views according to which both God and natural causes determine the outcome of every event (Austin Farrer and A. N. Whitehead)
5. "Top-down" accounts of divine action that leave the string of natural causes intact and inviolate (Peacocke)
6. Claims that divine interventions can be asserted only as salvation-historical or "transhistorical" or mystical truths, and hence do not conflict with science
7. Claims that God normally respects the integrity of the natural order, but at least once transformed it (the resurrection)
8. Robust assertions of interventions of God and miraculous outcomes on a regular basis (C. S. Lewis, C. John Collins)[24]

Let us pause with this debate and consider the issues in the light of Taylor's critique of secularism.[25] One and two are straight positions emerging from modernity. Here, God is not really "active." Position three is extremely popular and has considerable support in the academy. In his book, *God's Action in the World*, Wiles starts with a deep commitment to human freedom and agency, coupled with a sense of completeness of the scientific narrative. Therefore, Wiles sees providence as "the gradual emergence of our world as a single divine act. . . . [I]t is a purposeful occurrence, whose disparate features are held together by a unity of intention."[26] In effect, then, providence for Wiles is the creation and sustaining of the universe. Partly because of the theodicy problem, he is deeply suspicious of direct and particular interventions in creation—why cure one child with leukemia and not all children? Let us concede there is a power in this question. However, let us also locate Wiles as a classic illustration of the pre-shrunk religion of Taylor.

Double agency, the fourth position, has the difficulty that everything is an action of God. One finds this in many accounts of providence that assume the classical account of God. Paul Helm, for example, takes a "risk-free" view of providence. Working with the traditional, timeless God of the tradition, Helm's God is the primary cause of everything that happens in the universe. Although there are secondary causes (e.g., human agency or a plant being watered that leads to the plant growing), ultimately, God is the primary cause. Human freedom, for Helm, does not need some form of "self-causation or some version of indeterminism."[27] Now, for a spiritually infused universe, the classical account of God is problematic.[28] We need greater imminence in God. So, in addition with the countless issues of coherence (how do you reconcile timelessness with divine action?), a spiritually infused universe needs a greater connectivity between God and the world. So, some sort of temporality within the life of God is appropriate and necessary. Clayton's sixth and seventh positions are all from theologians who are trying to justify an aspect of the Christian tradition but respect the autonomy of science. Emil Brunner is a good representative of this position. Brunner shares the emphasis of Wiles on the role of God as creator and sustainer of the universe. And he is nervous about miracles. Brunner writes, "God has given the world its 'orders,' and it is precisely in these orders that He constantly reveals His Creator-Spirit, and His Power as Creator. Order and regularity are characteristics of His arrangements. The very order which can be mathematically conceived is the expression of a mathematical Creator Spirit."[29] However, he does want to recognize particular divine actions in respect to salvation history. So, for Brunner, a biblical understanding of miracles is this: "The difference between the biblical miracles and the miracle stories of paganism is this—that, apart from a few insignificant exceptions on the fringes of the Old Testament, they are all intended to serve this one end alone, the miracle of the revelation of the free God. They are all seen in the light of 'Saving History' (*Heilsgeschichte*); they are miracles of revelation and salvation, not miracles which draw attention to themselves."[30] For Brunner, the scientific order is complete and normally undisturbed (he thinks, for example, even the Incarnation can operate within the natural order).[31] However, there are spectacular exceptions that are revealing of God, of which the best illustration is the resurrection. In summary, Brunner sees providence as primarily the creating and sustaining of the universe, but concedes that occasionally for the purposes of salvation history disruptions of this normal order can be brought about by the sovereignty of God over the creation.

In all these options, we have not yet found an account that can affirm a spiritually infused universe. *The spiritually infused universe needs a holistic view of reality that accords the scientific account its due within a larger spiritual narrative.*

NEW TAXONOMY AND THE SPIRITUALLY INFUSED UNIVERSE

The task, then, is to develop a map of the science and religion literature that has a spiritually infused universe front and center. This cannot be exhaustive, but we find six representative positions, of which the last is the only one that is ultimately satisfactory. The first two options are found in all maps (including those already discussed of Barbour and Peters), but they are included here because I want to offer a critique from the perspective of the spiritually infused universe.

Option one: scientism and denial. This is our target for our New Apologetic. Despite the narrative outlined at the start of this chapter, naturalism abounds. Michael Ruse documents some of the many examples of shocking prejudice by distinguished scientists. Steven Weinberg said, "Religion is an insult to human dignity."[32] Francis Crick wrote, "If revealed religions have revealed anything it is that they are usually wrong."[33] Scientism and the denial of the spiritual realm are very much part of the contemporary scene. Peter Atkins is perhaps the clearest. He writes, "There is no reason to suppose that science cannot deal with every aspect of existence. Only the religious—among whom I include not merely the prejudiced but also the underinformed—hope that there is a dark corner of the physical Universe, or of the universe of experience, that science can never hope to illuminate."[34]

There is a triumphalism in this approach. Edward O. Wilson, a sociobiologist and entomologist, argued that science must try and become the new religion: It should incorporate the language of soteriology. Given religion is so much a part of the human genetic evolution, we do need a modern scientific substitute. Wilson writes, "The epic of evolution is probably the best myth we will ever have."[35] It is worth noting that such an approach birthed the work of Michael Dowd, an evolutionary evangelist, who tours the world encouraging people to see the meaning of life in the context of evolution.[36] He is trying to infuse this reductionist talk with a spiritual dimension. For Dowd, God is there, but everything else is demythologized. So, for example, he writes, "From a science-based, evolutionary perspective, there is no place for belief in a literal Satan." But he does go on to write, "nevertheless, personalizing or relationalizing the forces of evil—especially those within us—can be helpful, whether or not we choose to use the words Satan or the Devil."[37]

The problems with this position are considerable. Mikael Stenmark suggests it is incoherent. The implication that only science can give us knowledge about reality is a philosophical claim, which is not itself scientific. "Hence scientism is self-referentially incoherent."[38] However, from my vantage point, this is a position grounded in Western, post-Enlightenment prejudice, which ignores the widespread human experience in almost every culture that sees nature as animated and alive.

OPTION TWO: THEOLOGY CONTROLLING SCIENCE

One characteristic of evangelical and fundamentalist Christians (and these terms, as Mark Noll points us, are elastic)[39] is a commendable commitment to a spiritually infused universe. Noll notes that, in particular, those Christians who fell under the spell of John Nelson Darby's dispensationalism were "suspicious of exclusively natural explanations for the physical world."[40]

In this model, the worldview of the Bible is simply true. There are angels and demons, miracles and judgment, and God created the world in seven days and will wrap up history when our Lord comes back on a cloud.

Creationism has already been discussed earlier in this chapter. It is important to note, however, that there was a scientific methodology central to this program. James Barr noted this in his book *Fundamentalism*. He writes, "[I]t is the conservative evangelicals who are accepting truth from natural science their understanding of the nature of truth and insisting that the truth of the Bible must be this kind of truth."[41] This is the reason why the first chapter of Genesis must be treated as a scientific text. It is almost as if to treat the text as poetic or "mythological" (in the sense of conveying a deeper truth) is not sufficient. Real truth for a fundamentalist is scientific truth.

Therefore, while it is commendable that this strand of the church witnesses to the veracity of the biblical worldview (and, therefore, a spiritually infused universe), the underlying methodology is very problematic. It surrenders the spiritual and seeks to respond to modern science by asserting the supremacy of the biblical witness over scientific discoveries. It uses a scientific methodology, while trusting a religious authority. This inherent contradiction is the reason why it cannot be the basis of a spiritually infused universe.

OPTION THREE: SCIENCE AS THE DOMINANT NARRATIVE WITH SPIRITUALITY AS THE ADDENDUM

This position is best represented by Michael Ruse. In his book *Science and Spirituality*, he insists that the dominant narrative must be science. Ruse writes, "My approach to philosophy is that of the naturalist. My interest in limits does not belie my belief that the highest form of knowledge is scientific knowledge. I want to make my philosophy as much like science as possible."[42] Ruse then provides an historical narrative. He thinks the machine metaphor has triumphed while conceding there are some questions that science finds hard to answer, such as the primordial question: Why is there something rather than nothing?[43] And even on morality and minds, there is a recognition of the limitations of science.

The project of Ruse is interesting. It is an overture to people of robust faith: He wants to show that you can accept the scientific narrative and still have a view of divine providence. In the details of Ruse's argument, he is less generous than his introduction seems to promise. Miracles are possible through the order of grace; therefore, the resurrection of Jesus is possible. However, explains Ruse, "there is an important distinction here between the miracles of Christianity and the miracles of something like intelligent design theory. The latter is trying to do the work of science, arguing that unbroken law is not enough to furnish the living world with the complex organisms that it contains. The Christian miracles are not trying to do the work of science at all. They are about something entirely different, and they are simply laid across the world of science."[44] He suspects that water could be turned into wine, but really, the host was shamed by the presence of Jesus into bringing out the good wine for his guests. And he shares Hume's sense that arguments for faith from miracles because one can never know that a law of nature has been violated.

The irenic tone of Ruse is to be appreciated. But for my purposes, this assumes a metaphysics that makes spirituality an addendum to an otherwise physical world entirely understood by science. This is not the spiritually infused universe. It is one where faith is permitted a little space provided it recognizes the sovereignty of science.

OPTION FOUR: NATURAL SCIENCE, SOCIAL SCIENCE, AND SCIENTIFIC THEOLOGY – A STRATIFIED REALITY

Alister E. McGrath, in his three-volume *A Scientific Theology*, believes that the critical realism of Roy Bhaskar provides the best framework for thinking about the relationship between science and religion (or, in his case, Catholic, Orthodox, and evangelical Christianity). Bhaskar wrote *The Possibility of Naturalism: A Philosophical Critique of the Contemporary Human Sciences* in 1979. Bhaskar wanted to show that "the human sciences can be sciences in *exactly the same sense*, though *not in exactly the same way*, as the natural one."[45] This shared methodology is what Bhaskar means by naturalism (which is rather confusing given there is an entire philosophical tradition using the term to describe a person who is a scientific materialist). Anyway, McGrath likes the way Bhaskar weaves together the natural sciences with the social sciences. There is a recognition of the social location of the knowing process yet a resolute commitment to a reality to be studied that can be described in better or worse ways.

One achievement of Bhaskar is to provide a strong argument against all forms of reductionism (i.e., the view that ultimately everything is explicable in terms of the fundamental laws of physics). Bhaskar explains that the problem with this is that something can be rooted in and emerge from something else but that does not mean that the former is nothing but the latter. As McGrath explains, "Emergent strata possess features that are 'irreducible'—that is, which cannot be conceived solely in terms of lower levels. One cannot 'reduce' biology to chemistry or physics, precisely because the biological stratum possess characteristics which go beyond those in which it is rooted. If it were possible to explain the origins of biological life in chemical or physical terms, that would not amount to the reduction of biology to either of those disciplines."[46] This must be right. For Bhaskar, one should give some appropriate integrity to the insights emerging from each strata of the process.

Bhaskar has four strata in his schema: psychological sciences, social sciences, biological sciences, and molecular sciences. McGrath wants to add a scientific theology to the strata. From this vantage point, explains McGrath, "A scientific theology may legitimately be regarded as a response to an existing reality, whose existence is independent of the actuality or possibility of human observation."[47] So we arrive at the following picture: For McGrath, there really is a world that socially conditioned human beings have a responsibility to interpret and describe. There are different disciplines that do this work in the natural sciences, in the social sciences, and in the theological sciences (which McGrath calls a scientific theology). Each strata has insights that are not reducible to the lower levels; and each strata has its own distinctive methodology.

There is a systematic neatness here that is admirable. And, in principle, the spiritually infused universe might be compatible with this schema. However, Bhaskar is guilty of a similar assumption as Ruse. The model of knowing remains the natural sciences. This is the dominant methodology. We work hard to make theology work within that parameter.

OPTION FIVE: A MEDIATING PHILOSOPHY AND THE SPIRITUALLY INFUSED UNIVERSE

Some who want to stress the spiritual dimension try to redefine reality so that both science and religion can be affirmed. This is the quest for a mediating philosophy between religion and science. Perhaps the strongest contender in recent years has been process theology. Barbour has argued that process theology, with its rejection of an omnipotent God, who is outside the system, can be helpful in linking the worlds of science and religion.[48] Process theology is derived from the work of A. N. Whitehead and offers an elaborate metaphysic that grounds divine agency firmly in the natural system. David Ray Griffin takes a similar line as Barbour with his "theistic naturalism."[49]

McGrath is extremely critical of this approach. He considers process theology as "an implausible construction"[50] and mistaken in a very fundamental way. But furthermore, he does not want a mediating philosophy. So he writes, "Why should both natural scientists and Christian theologians be obligated to adopt any intermediate world-view—whether one as uncompelling as process theology, or the rather more resilient, plausible and interesting possibilities offered by Platonism—in entering into a productive dialogue?"[51]

McGrath's assessment of process theology is harsh. Granted, the version that denies "*creatio ex nihilo*" is problematic; but there are real insights in the way it links divine agency with change and recognizes the inevitable temporality that must be part of God's life. However, this is an opportunity to reflect on the role a mediating philosophy might play. McGrath takes the line that the "classic Christian formulations of the faith"[52] are the basis of his scientific theology. But of course, the creeds (presumably) are all couched in historically limited philosophical worldviews. As he notes, there are three great streams of Christianity—Catholicism, Orthodoxy, and evangelicalism.[53] Each stream has its own philosophical trajectory. It is an inevitable and legitimate question: Which stream of Christianity, with its distinctive philosophical trajectory, is in conversation with science?

As we saw earlier, McGrath does draw on a philosophical stream of thought for his project: His inspiration is the philosophy of critical realism as espoused by Bhaskar. McGrath has an appropriate sensitivity to the inevitable historical conditioning of our theological worldviews. Therefore, some engagement with philosophy is inevitable.

McGrath is right in that the quest for a philosophy to provide an Esperanto to serve the two separate disciplines is doomed to failure. This is the hope of some process philosophers; they do expect the Whiteheadian vocabulary of Concrescence and Actual entity to become the language of both science and religion. This is asking too much of a mediating philosophy. A spiritually infused universe cannot depend on a new language emerging that reconciles the worlds of science and religion.

OPTION SIX: HOLISTIC ENGAGEMENT OF SCIENCE AND RELIGION

There are aspects of earlier approaches that can be taken further into this account of a spiritually infused universe. McGrath's critically realist account of a stratified reality is helpful; the recognition that we are in conversation with the best philosophical options available is important. However, one difference is that I am seeking to place the scientific methodology in a framework that makes it a subset of the spiritual, rather than equal partners or even, more common, with theology as the servant of science.

There are a number of writers who are allies in this quest. Lisa L. Stenmark documents the growing number of feminist philosophers of science who emphasize the wider context that transcends the scientific simplicity of "x is the cause of y." There is an emphasis on "context, values, and social locations," which means that "we are no passive onlookers...who merely "discover" facts.[54] On this model, you treat engagement with the empirical world as analogous to the complex task of getting to know people. Stenmark writes, "Knowing others is never fixed or complete, in part because the 'who' we know is never fixed or complete."[55]

Getting to know people is a rich analogy for the vision of a spiritually infused universe. Stenmark uses the analogy to inculcate a certain humility in our interpretations of the world and recognition that the task is never complete. However, for my purposes, the analogy can go further. A person can be described in two different ways—one in terms of mental activity and the two in terms of physical activity. Now, it might be contentious to try and decide which description is primary, but I think most people would agree—to take two extremes—a description in terms of loves (e.g., "she loves music") is more helpful in understanding a person than a description in terms of the effectiveness of the digestion tract (e.g., "she is good at absorbing the nutrients out of food"). Therefore, a case can be made that mental activity—the thoughts, agency, decisions, hopes, fears, aspirations, humor, and loves of a person—are more helpful for understanding what a person is really like than the physical activity—the physical appearance and biology of a person. Now, of course, the mental and physical are intimately connected: There are complex relationships between our likes and our bodies. Agency, for example, depends on a body. But on this analogy, from the vantage point of really understanding a person, the mental is primary and the physical secondary. After all, once the mind has gone, the body might remain but the person is diminished.

Now, we are on the cusp of an analogy for a spiritually infused universe. The mental is the spiritual dimensions of the universe; the physical is the mechanics of the universe. In terms of what is really going on, the spiritual is a vitally important realm to understand. This analogy suggests that, on a proper understanding of the universe, the physical (i.e., the world of the natural sciences) is really a subset of the spiritual.

This analogy is instantly suggestive of several major movements in philosophy. Some will be reminded of personalism. Personalist thought has many different forms, but what they share is a sense that the person is the key to understanding reality. Others will recognize a platonic tendency. The suggested framework for the spiritually infused universe, with which I am going to work, is a version of idealism. It is to the work of Ward that we turn to next.

KEITH WARD — IDEALIST THEISM

I will be reading Ward from the right (i.e., the more conservative side) rather than the left. His schema for a spiritually infused universe is perfect. He is an advocate for idealism, which is very unfashionable. Almost everyone is a "Naturalist." Barry Stroud, when delivering the presidential address at the meeting of the American Philosophical Association in 1996, asserts, "'Naturalism' seems to me in this and other respects rather like 'World Peace.' Almost everyone swears allegiance to it, and is willing to march under its banner.'"[56] But what exactly is naturalism? Stroud explains, "naturalism says that there is nothing, or that nothing is so, except what holds in nature, in the natural world."[57] This means that naturalism is opposed to "supernaturalism," which is "the invocation of an agent or force which somehow stands outside the familiar natural world and so whose doings cannot be understood as part of it."[58] Among philosophers, naturalism has triumphed and with it the assumption of atheism.

Once, idealism was more popular; after all both Kant and Hegel were idealists. However, today, they are scarcer. The challenge of defending idealism is considerable. So how does Ward do this? There are many definitions of idealism. It is important to understand Ward's definition. He writes, "Philosophical idealism is the opposite of philosophical materialism, which claims that everything that exists is a form of matter. Idealism holds that matter cannot exist without mind, and depends on mind for its existence. Personal idealism holds that there is one supreme mind on which everything else depends, and which is personal—that knows, thinks, feels, and intends."[59] Although mind is the fundamental reality and that matter depends on mind for its existence, it is still important to note that it is not a denial of the reality of matter (hence kicking stones would prove nothing). It is true that George Berkeley took an immaterialist line, most idealists (in whose company Ward is found), such as Hegel, do believe that there is a material universe, but it is dependent on mind.

Ward concedes that there are several ways one could construct an account of God. However, personal idealism provides an attractive account of God. Although he avoids the term, there is a panentheistic feel. Ward writes, "God and the material universe thus form a unity, though one in which the mental or spiritual aspect has ontological and causal priority."[60]

Ward's argument has two elements. First, against naturalism, he explains that they are building an edifice on matter, yet they do not know what matter is. Ward is worth quoting at length:

> Scientists used to think that all material things were made up of indivisible atoms, which had a specific location in space and in time, which had mass, weight, or gravitational attraction, and which moved around with a specific velocity. But since the beginning of the twentieth century that view has been completely overturned. Within the atom there is a whole world of sub-atomic particles, and it seems that these are not really particles at all. They are more like fields of force, and Heisenberg's Principle of Indeterminacy asserts that particles like electrons do not have a specific location and momentum at the same time. They seem to be spread out, and only take on a specific location or velocity when they are subjected to experimental interference. Moreover, on virtually all theories in quantum physics, particles interact with each other non-locally, without immediate spatial contact. In relativity theory, space-time itself bends and contracts, and though space-time does not seem to be material, it is envisaged as a reality which governs the motions of material objects. Hard lumps of matter seem to have disappeared, and have been replaced in science by such strange entities as dark energy, dark matter, superposed particles, and multiple space-times.[61]

Naturalism, then, is undermined because the statement "everything is made of matter" makes very little sense if we do not know what matter is.

Ward is trying to undermine a prejudice. It takes various forms. One form is the assertion "all knowledge depends on experience." Again, modern science makes this harder to sustain because physicists are constantly talking about entities and forces, which we cannot experience. And there are a host of puzzles around perception, of which color is the most interesting. One can actually have an experience of red by simply stimulating the right part of the brain. The assumption that the source of experience is a publicly observing, stable world, occupied by many minds, is just that—an assumption. But Ward does agree that knowledge should start from experience, he just wants the experience to be understood broadly, to include thoughts and perceptions. This would mean consciousness must be part of the equation.

So, this is the second element to Ward's argument: the centrality of the human self. The mystery of consciousness requires a self. For Ward, the self is not simply a successive set of experiences: It is a potentially unified entity that psychologists work hard to integrate. In addition, he needs to push back on all forms of determinism. There needs to be genuine freedom. Ward makes much for the paradox of a reasoning person concluding that she does not have the capacity to reason as physically determined. He points out that one only ends up in this tormented place because of a crude materialism that is not justified by modern science. Again, the Copenhagen interpretation of quantum mechanics (which is the most careful description of the form of quantum mechanics we are talking about) is helpful here. Ward has plenty of allies. Clayton, for example, is careful when he writes, "[I]t does seem accurate to conclude that indeterminacy in the physical world is a necessary condition for human (or other) free will. For consider the converse: if all events are *determined* at the physical level, then the world does not exhibit the sort of causal openness that would leave room for conscious agents, when they evolve, to affect the outcome of events."[62] Ward is even more blunt: "We cannot, on grounds of a commitment to natural science, rule out the possibility of free and physically undetermined causes—the actions of personal subject-selves, which actions are determined by envisaged goals selected by the agents themselves out of a range of non-physically determined alternatives."[63]

While it is true that indeterminacy is a helpful condition for human free-will agency, there is still the mystery of exactly how does the agent freely cause an action. In an essay by T. J. Mawson, he advocates for top-down causation, where either the human agent creates quantum "measurement" events on the brain or perhaps the human agent is intervening in a "relatively large number of places more or less at once at the relatively macroscopic level in the brain, the relatively macroscopic effect . . ."[64] The picture here is that we are familiar with "bottom up causation," now we need to conceive of "top-down causation." Mawson defines this as "the complex physical constitution of human persons generates a new capacity of such conscious organisms to be real cause, in addition to all the physical causes within the system."[65]

To be compatible scientifically, a spiritually infused universe needs different causation possibilities. The concept of "top-down causation" is helpful. But what is even more helpful is the transformation in our understanding of scientific laws. The old picture of immutable laws, which are consistent in every part of the universe, is no longer an option. Instead, "the principles of order in nature are much more local, diverse, piecemeal, emergent and holistic than the old model of one absolute set of laws (which would be, basically, the laws of the 'master science,' physics) dictating the behaviour of fundamental particles in such a way that, in principle, the behaviour of all complex biological, personal and social entities can in principle be deduced from them."[66]

Nancy Cartwright is a key voice in this area. She argues for a "dappled world." She writes, "We live our everyday lives in a dappled world quite unlike the world of fundamental particles regimented into kinds, each just like the one beside it, mindlessly marching exactly as has forever been destined. The everyday world is one where the future is open, little is certain and the unexpected intrudes into the best laid plans, where everything is different from everything else, where things change and develop, where different systems built in different ways give rise to different patterns."[67]

Ward commends both the agent causation of Mawson and the dappled world of Cartwright. He then wants to combine it with an "open theology."[68] So, for Ward, we have a theistic mind, underpinning and shaping the universe, working with certain contours that create stability and predictability, which at the same time allow for human agency and divine agency. Ward's account has many intellectual debts—the agent of power and love that creates ex nihilo is the classical account from Augustine and Aquinas, and the dynamic agent with the universe and sustaining the universe is from Hegel and the process theologians.

For Ward, there is a sense that all theists (who believe that God is spirit) need to be idealist. After all, the ultimate reality is then spirit—(an immaterial Being)—which is the cause and sustainer of the material world around us. Moving from the self to God can create a powerful apologetic narrative. Alvin Plantinga notes, "Naturalism is the idea that there is no such person as God or anything like him; immaterial selves would be too much like God, who, after all, is himself an immaterial self."[69] If the idea of an immaterial self becomes a live option, then the following steps might create the theism option. So, human thoughts are not reducible to brain states. Therefore, spirit or mind is different from matter; and when it comes to agency, mind directs the matter. So by analogy this material world is dependent on Spirit (which, with the help of revelation—i.e., the witness of the world religions—is rightly affirmed as God). In the same way, minds can work in bodies; therefore, God (and other spiritual entities) can work in the world. An argument for theism has been established.

Ward's most sustained discussion of spiritual causation is found in his book *Divine Action*. Here, Ward argues that God functions in the world in the same way that the human mind functions in the human body. Ward writes, "We are subject to physical laws; and we do act freely. However difficult it may be to give an adequate theoretical account of these facts, it seems that if human reason can be integrated with natural causality, there is little reason why Divine action should not also be so integrated."[70] Ward believes that God is, if you like, the cosmic ecosystem who is constantly searching for space to maneuver within the universe. This is made possible through prayer; the loving God is always trying to maximize the opportunities for love to be realized. However, God does not override human freedom but enlarges and expands a loving vision in humans. God's action is beyond any scientific model because, by definition, the model does not take into account the spiritual realm.

The mysterious relationship between mind (or consciousness) and the brain is a helpful analogue. The thought—for example, say an elaborate opening in chess—cannot be reduced to the neurons transmitting electrochemical signals. The thought would not be identical to the scientific mapping of those neurons (the latter is just a mapping, while the thought is much more interesting). This distinction is important for the Christian faith for two reasons: first, we believe that God is spirit and yet has the capacity for agency and decision; therefore, we are reaffirming Ward's personal idealism—consciousness not dependent on anything physical. And second, for any account of life after death (even a bodily resurrection), we need the possibility of consciousness not dependent on a physical brain. Therefore, the mind is the best illustration of spirit and matter infused together.

We are now at a point where we can clarify the relationship between spirit and science in a spiritually infused universe. It starts with the basic insight that for any action there are many causes and many explanations. Imagine a moment when I am telling a joke at a dinner party; this joke involves throwing water over a host. Now the least interesting cause is the hand motion towards the glass and the throwing of the water over the host. One would have very little interest in the connection between neurons and the hand action. A better and more helpful explanation is that I was telling the John the Baptist knock-knock joke (i.e., "Knock, knock." "Who's there?" "John." "John Who?" "John the Baptist."—at which point you throw water over your victim). The primary explanation in this case is human agency around a joke, which results in an action.[71]

With most events, many of the causes are physical, which science describes helpfully. But other causes are also operating—spiritual causes. The physical causes are visible and measured by science. The spiritual causes are less visible and often subject to careful interpretation from within a religious tradition, but they are compatible with modern science. In the case of illness, the doctors are doing a remarkable task of providing antibiotics that help fight an infection, but the mental state of the patient—the disposition and determination to recover—are also factors in healing. The mental state is in the arena of the spiritual; and in cases where a congregation is praying, Christians would add the agency of God is also present in the system working with, through, and beyond the other factors.

THE CONCEPT OF SPIRITUAL CAUSATION

The rest of this book will assume that the concept of spiritual causation is appropriate, intelligible, and plausible. It is appropriate because mind is the ultimate reality. And mind underpins everything that is and is active in and through everything that is. Therefore, there is a sense in which physical causation has been made possible by spiritual causation. It is intelligible because we work from the analogy of human agency and physical causation to spiritual agency in a physical world. Mawson's picture of "top-down causation" where a person is making quantum measurement events to the brain (either in one place or several places simultaneously) is helpful. Now we need to imagine that if mind can be causal agent in the brain, then God or angels or other spiritual dynamics can be causal agents in the world.[72] Therefore, a divine action in the world could be quantum measurement events in a certain place or perhaps in many places.

So, in the Eucharist, as the priest says the Great Thanksgiving, an aspect of God—the revealing, redeeming aspect called the eternal Word—which was fully present in Jesus and comes by means of a "quantum measurement event" into the bread and wine. Perhaps in an ordination service, the combination of the community gathered and the bishop representing the apostolic succession can call on God to make a "quantum measurement event" in the brain of the person being ordained to create a priest, with a distinctive vocation. This does not mean that these actions are scientifically accessible, partly because science cannot access such measurements. It looks like the universe was designed to permit agency that is not open to regular scientific detection. This is, of course, part of the theistic claim.

Is this plausible? In my judgment, it is. Much depends on whether you trust the witness of the religious traditions that point to such agency. Naturally, we do need reasons to trust these traditions. As we saw in the last chapter, words such as superstition are unhelpful. We do have the worldwide witness that nonmaterial agency is real. The picture emerging from science does not exclude the possibility of nonmaterial agency. So, then, the question is: What types of agency are there?

This is a real question. On what grounds are angels affirmed and new age crystals denied? This takes us into the whole realm of authority and revelation. Who can we trust to tell us about the spiritual realm?

NOTES

1. For a fuller treatment of my views on Richard Dawkins, see *Against Atheism* (Oxford: Wiley Blackwell, 2010). The discussion of Laplace is taken from this book.
2. John Hedley Brooke, *Science and Religion: Some Historical Perspectives* (Cambridge, UK: Cambridge University Press, 1991), p. 117.
3. See John Hedley Brooke for an excellent description of this shift in Brooke, *Science and Religion: Some Historical Perspectives*, pp. 119–25.
4. Ibid., p. 124.
5. Pierre-Simon Laplace, *A Philosophical Essay on Probabilities*, Translated by Frederick Truscott and Frederick Emory (London: Chapman and Hall, 1902), p. 4.
6. Keith Ward, *Divine Action* (London: Collins Flame, 1990), p. 83.
7. Keith Ward, *The Battle for the Soul* (London: Hodder and Stoughton, 1985), pp. 47–8.
8. John Polkinghorne, *One World: The Interaction of Science and Theology* (London: SPCK, 1986), chapter 4.
9. Paul Davies, *Cosmic Jackpot: Why Our Universe Is Just Right for Life* (Boston and New York: Houghton Mifflin Company, 2007), pp. 63–4.
10. Philip Clayton, "Theology and the Physical Sciences," in David Ford with Rachel Muers (eds.), *The Modern Theologians: An Introduction to Christian Theology since 1918*, third edition, p. 349 (Oxford: Blackwell Publishing, 2005). His italics.
11. Walter Eichrodt, *Theology of the Old Testament* (London: SCM Press, 1967), p. 93.
12. For a good discussion of the ways in which illness is treated in Shakespeare's plays, see Amanda Mabillard, "Worst Diseases in Shakespeare's London," in *Shakespeare Online*. 20 Aug, 2000. http://www.shakespeare-online.com/biography/londondisease.html.
13. Keith Ward, *God, Faith & the New Millennium: Christian Belief in an Age of Science* (Oxford: Oneworld, 1998), p. 14.

14. One of the best illustrations of the power of map making is the entire Christian Theology of Other Religions debate. It was the book by Alan Race, *Christians and Religious Pluralism* (London: SCM Press, 1982), that set out the now famous "pluralism, inclusivism, and exclusivism" debate. Successors to the debate have tried to modify the range the options. See, for example, Paul Knitter, *Introducing Theologies of Religions* (Maryknoll, NY: Orbis, 2002). However, the traditional three options have all but triumphed in most textbooks.

15. Philip Clayton, "Theology and the Physical Sciences," in David Ford with Rachel Muers (eds.), *The Modern Theologians: An Introduction to Christian Theology since 1918* (third edition), p. 346 (Oxford: Blackwell Publishing, 2005).

16. Alister McGrath finds all attempts to organize the field unhelpful. He feels the groupings end up being too restrictive. While one can understand his concern, there is a need to get a sense of the different options. And for my purposes, the map that concentrates on making sense of a spiritually infused universe is not yet available. For McGrath, see Alister E. McGrath, *A Scientific Theology, Volume 1: Nature* (Edinburgh and New York: T&T Clark, 2001), p. 70.

17. Ted Peters (ed.), *Cosmos as Creation: Theology and Science in Consonance*, (Nashville, TN: Abingdon Press, 1989), p. 14.

18. Ibid., p. 16.

19. Ibid., p. 17.

20. Ibid., p. 17.

21. There are other taxonomies out there. Mikael Stenmark, "How to Relate Christian Faith and Science" offers his own taxonomy. He suggests three positions: the competition view (faith and science are trying to do the same job), the independent view (faith and science are doing completely different jobs) or contract view (faith and science are doing jobs that overlap to some extent). He opts for the contract view, but wants the different situations of religion and science to be recognized. Science has a methodological distance, while faith has an existential inescapability, which makes them operate in human lives in different ways. For my purposes, the worlds of science and religion are, once again, seen as separate objects. See Mikael Stenmark, "How to Relate Christian Faith and Science" in B.Stump and Alan G. Padgett (ed.), *The Blackwell Companion to Science and Christianity*, (Oxford: Wiley Blackwell 2012), p.63.

22. David A. S. Fergusson, *The Cosmos and the Creator: An Introduction to the Theology of Creation* (London: SPCK, 1998), p. 55. (His italics).

23. Ibid., p. 55.

24. Philip Clayton, "Theology and the Physical Sciences," in David Ford with Rachel Muers (eds.), *The Modern Theologians*, p. 346.

25. For further discussion of providence, see my Farmington Paper, "Modern Theology: 9. Providence," *Farmington Papers*, October 1997.

26. Maurice Wiles, *God's Action in the World* (London: SCM Press, 1986), p. 54.

27. Paul Helm, *The Providence of God* (London: IVP, 1993), p. 79.

28. This is a vast and complex area. What sort of God is compatible with a spiritually infused universe? It is worth noting that Aquinas and Augustine clearly believe the universe is spiritually infused yet believe in a timeless God. Let me, therefore, acknowledge the complexity of the debate. Suffice it to say, I am persuaded by certain feminist theologians that embrace of the universe must involve God absorbing the temporality of the universe. For the best contemporary statement of the classical account of God, see Katherine Sonderegger, *Systematic Theology: Volume 1, The Doctrine of God* (Minneapolis, MN: Fortress Press, 2015). For a feminist critique, see Grace Jantzen, *God's World, God's Body* (Louisville, KY: Westminister John Knox, 1984).

29. Emil Brunner, *The Christian Doctrine of the Creation and Redemptions: Dogmatics Vol. II*, Translated by Olive Wyon (Eugene, OR: Wipf and Stock Publishers, 1952), p. 152.

30. Ibid., p. 167.

31. Ibid., p. 168. He writes, "But, this miracle of the God-Man is achieved without eliminating the natural order.'

32. Michael Ruse, *Science and Spirituality: Making Room for Faith in the Age of Science* (Cambridge, UK: Cambridge University Press, 2010), p. 1.

33. Ibid., p. 2.

34. Peter Atkin, "The Limitless Power of Science," in John Cornwell (ed.), *Nature's Imagination* (Oxford: Oxford University Press, 1995) p. 125.

35. E. O. Wilson, *On Human Nature* (Cambridge, MA: Harvard University Press, 1978), p. 201.

36. See Michael Dowd, *Thank God for Evolution* (New York: Viking, 2008).

37. Ibid., p. 169.

38. Mikael Stenmark, "How to relate Christian Faith and Science," in J. B. Stump and Alan G. Padgett (ed.), *The Blackwell Companion to Science and Christianity*, p. 68 (Oxford: Wiley Blackwell, 2012).

39. Mark A. Noll, "Evangelicalism and Fundamentalism," in Gary B. Ferngren (ed.), *Science and Religion: A Historical Introduction*, p. 262f (Baltimore and London: The John Hopkins University Press, 2002).

40. Ibid., p. 264.

41. James Barr, *Fundamentalism*, Second edition (London: SCM Press, 1981), p. 93.

42. Michael Ruse, *Science and Spirituality: Making Room for Faith in the Age of Science* (Cambridge: Cambridge University Press, 2010), p. 9.

43. Ibid., p. 129. Ruse writes, "I conclude, therefore, that the primordial question is not answered by science and is not obviously a meaningless question or directed towards a pseudo-problem."

44. Ibid., p. 207.

45. Roy Bhaskar, *The Possibility of Naturalism: A Philosophical Critique of the Contemporary Human Sciences,* 3rd ed. (London: Routledge, 1998,) p. 174.

46. Alister E. McGrath, *A Scientific Theology: Reality*, volume 2 (London and New York: T&T Clark, 2002), p. 216.

47. Ibid., p. 225.

48. See Ian G. Barbour, *Religion in an Age of Science* (San Francisco: Harper San Francisco, 1990).

49. David Ray Griffin, *Religion and Scientific Naturalism: Overcoming the Conflicts* (Albany, NY: State University of New York, 2000).

50. Alister E. McGrath, *A Scientific Theology, Volume 1: Nature* (Edinburgh and New York: T&T Clark, 2001), p. 41.

51. Ibid., p. 41.

52. Ibid., p. 42.

53. Ibid., p. 35.

54. Lisa L. Stenmark, "Feminist Philosophies of Science," in J. B. Stump and Alan G. Padgett (ed.), *The Blackwell Companion to Science and Christianity*, p. 86 (Oxford: Wiley Blackwell, 2012). Stenmark is making use of the work of Lorraine Code here.

55. Ibid., p. 87.

56. Barry Stroud, "The Charm of Naturalism," in *Proceedings and Addresses of the American Philosophical Association*, 1996, Vol.70:2, p. 43. Later in the lecture, Stroud does admit the existence of Alvin Plantinga as a contemporary exception to this universal march. Perhaps in the notes I should concede that much of the progress of the natural sciences does depend on methodological atheism. One should not move to spiritual causation too quickly. But the temptation is to let a methodological naturalism (namely that you are searching for causation in nature) to slip into a situation where naturalism becomes a prejudice. It is assumed that nature is all there is.

57. Ibid., p. 44.

58. Ibid., p. 44.

59. Keith Ward, *The Christian Idea of God: A Philosophical Foundation for Faith* (Cambridge: Cambridge University Press, 2018), forthcoming. Quotations taken from the manuscript submitted for publication. I am grateful to Ward for giving me this access for this project.

60. Ibid., p. 6 (of manuscript).

61. Ibid., p. 7 (of manuscript).

62. Philip Clayton, "Theology and the Physical Sciences," in David Ford with Rachel Muers (eds.), *The Modern Theologians*, p. 349 (Malden, MA: Blackwell Publishing, 2005).

63. Keith Ward, *The Christian Idea of God* (Cambridge and New York: Cambridge University Press, 2017), p. 18–19 (of manuscript).

64. T. J. Mawson, "Freedom and the Causal Order," in Nancy Cartwright and Keith Ward (eds.), *Rethinking Order After the Laws of Nature*, p. 154 (London: Bloomsbury, 2016).

65. Ibid., p. 143.

66. Keith Ward, "Introduction," in Nancy Cartwright and Keith Ward (eds.), *Rethinking Order After the Laws of Nature*, p. 2 (London: Bloomsbury, 2016).

67. Nancy Cartwright, "The Dethronement of Laws in Science," in Nancy Cartwright and Keith Ward (eds.), *Rethinking Order After the Laws of Nature*, p. 26 (London: Bloomsbury Academic, 2016).

68. Keith Ward, "Concepts of God and the Order of Nature," in Ibid., p. 217.

69. Alvin Plantinga, "The Evolutionary Argument Against Naturalism," in B. Stump and Alan G. Padgett (ed.), *The Blackwell Companion to Science and Christianity*, p. 106 (Oxford: Wiley Blackwell, 2012).

70. Keith Ward, *Divine Action* (London: Collins Flame, 1990), p. 76.

71. I am grateful to Nancy C. Murphy and her essay "Does Prayer Make a Difference?" in Ted Peters (ed.), *Cosmos as Creation: Theology and Science in Consonance* (Nashville, TN: Abingdon Press, 1989). Her discussion of causation is very helpful, see pp. 240ff.

72. One should note that one of Mawson's goals is to avoid any form of immaterial entity called a self. Much depends on what is meant by immaterial entity. If one is thinking simply of thoughts, then thoughts are clearly immaterial. If one means a soul, then one can understand Mawson's hesitation. I tend to treat spirit and mind as synonyms; and perhaps, when it comes to life after death, I use the word "soul," but they are all the mind or spirit of a person.

Chapter Four

The Necessary Prologomenon

The Legitimacy of Trust

The challenge now is for the "West" (by which I mean European and American cultures) to defend a "spiritually infused reality" within the catholic (in the literal sense and, therefore, not restricted to the Roman Catholic Church) tradition of Christianity. The argument in this chapter is that it is possible to be a rational and scientifically sensitive person and persuaded that the catholic faith has revealed the ways in which reality is spiritually infused. This chapter is a defense of revelation, disclosed in the eternal Word, and transmitted through the community of the church.

So, the journey thus far: In the first chapter, I argued that the reaction against religion is less to do with good arguments and more to do with a mood shift. A part of this mood shift was the emergence of deism—a view that surrendered the world of all enchantment and confined the spiritual to one entity that was called God. This pre-shrunk religion conceded so much to reductionist science that it is not surprising it provoked these two responses: First, if the spiritual is only found well beyond the empirical, then what difference does the spiritual make to me? And second, if science explains the empirical world, then is it not only a matter of time until science explains the origins of the world? Religion was on the back foot (to use a metaphor from cricket).

In the second chapter, we examined the sibling of deism, namely superstition. We looked at the way it is an unhelpful term, with numerous different meanings, which ironically continues to haunt modernity. In the third chapter, we engaged with the issue of science. The basis for this mood shift was a reductionist science that is now completely rejected in the light of the transformation of worldview due to Albert Einstein and quantum mechanics. The relationship between aspects of reality described by the empirical sciences and those properly captured under the term "spiritual" is best captured with the mind/brain analogy. In the same way that consciousness is linked with the brain but not reducible to it, so the spiritual realm is linked with the material world but not reducible to it.

Building on the account of spiritual causation offered at the end of the last chapter, we now have a difficult task, which has two elements. First and foremost, what follows is a defense of an enchanted Christian narrative as objectively true. We focus on four doctrines—the sacraments, apostolic succession, the existence of angels (as agents created by God who are connectors with the spiritual realm), and the existence of saints who can intercede for humanity. The reason why angels and saints play such a significant role is that they personalize our experience of the world. Our spiritually infused universe is not simply a sense of generalized spirituality with no particular agency or awareness but is full of invisible companions such as angelic entities and saints.[1] This experience of the world is widespread in the folk religion of many Roman Catholic countries. The second element to this task is to provide an account of Christian theological reasoning that explains why Christians should affirm the reality of angels and saints and not affirm the idea of new age crystals or reincarnation.

To defend the enchanted Christian narrative, the following strategy is needed. The narrative needs a defense of revelation. The only way the existence of angels and saints can be affirmed is to believe that somewhere somehow God has revealed these entities as part of the metaphysical reality. This is now my task.

THE PROBLEM

The problem with revelation is easy to state: There are many books and persons claiming to be revelations of God. For traditional Muslims, the Qur'an is the very utterance of God. For orthodox Jews, the Torah preexists creation and is the blueprint for creation. For Mormons, the gold tablets given by the angel Moroni permitted Joseph Smith to translate the golden plates, producing the Book of Mormon, which is the Word of God. The Bhagavad-Gita is literally translated as the Song (*Gita*) of God (*Bhagavad*), which captures the eternal declaration of wisdom and spirituality. And alongside these options, we have the Bible. How do we decide which one is the real Word of God?

Traditions of Enquiry

Human knowing is hard work. There is nothing easy in the process at all. Different cultures look at the world and see entirely different realities—from the drab reductionism of "just atoms" to the rich animist traditions of Africa. Subcultures in modern America make completely contrasting claims about reality, from the 9-11 Truthers who "know" that President George W. Bush organized the destruction of World Trade Center[2] to those who insist Area 51 in Nevada is the home to crashed alien crafts.[3] The factors that make a belief plausible appear to be heavily shaped by the cultural context.

The sense that all-knowing is partly shaped by the participation a person has in a community is widely recognized. Even in the sciences, it is recognized that there are "traditions of enquiry." Alan G. Padgett writes:

> The notion of value-free science has largely been replaced by a greater appreciation for the fact that all the academic disciplines or sciences are in fact *human practices* which take place with *established traditions of inquiry*. . . . To learn a natural or human science is not simply to be trained in pure *a priori* reasoning or in universal axiomatic systems of deductive truth, but is closer to being apprenticed into a valuable skill which requires mentoring into a community of experts, a way of thinking, an angle of vision, and a specific labor. A student of any specialized science is thus inducted into a community of truth-seeking fellow scientists, whose reasoning is shaped by that tradition of inquiry.[4]

Even in the sciences, one learns certain practices within a community that sets certain interpretative rules. Complete certainty is impossible: One is always working within a tradition.

This is a key theme of Alasdair MacIntyre's work. He has helpfully delineated the "tradition-constituted" nature of knowing.[5] MacIntyre's achievement combines a historical sensitivity with a commitment to the possibility of truth. He describes how a tradition of enquiry develops: It always starts within a community. A tradition begins when particular beliefs, institutions, and practices are articulated by certain people and/or in certain texts. It is inevitable that in such a community, procedures for enquiry will be established, and authority will be conferred on these texts and voices. A rationality develops. For MacIntyre, this is true for all forms of knowledge. From accountancy to art history, communities form and develop a rationality that shapes the processes of evaluating and knowing.

MacIntyre does think it is possible for changes to occur in a tradition and for shifts from one tradition to another one. His illustration is the shift from Aristotelian to Galilean-Newtonian mechanics. The shift was justified by the explanatory power of the Galilean-Newtonian model: The Aristotelians had a range of anomalies that disappeared when you made the shift in traditions. Charles Taylor has called this the "supersession" argument. Taylor writes, "You move from A to B via the overcoming of some error-inducing factor, such as a confusion, an elision, a too-simple palette or possibilities, and the like. It is clear from the standpoint of B that outlook A was conditioned by this error. The way of A to B was in fact mediated by the recognition of this error, as one is confident that now we are waking and before we were dreaming, because getting from there to here involved waking up. There is an asymmetry here."[6] Taylor goes on to identify four features of the logic of supersession arguments. These are: first, "these arguments establish not a single proposition as being true and incorrigible, but rather a comparative: Whatever else is right, moving from A to B involves an epistemic gain."[7] The shift is an improvement on the initial position. Second, "our ordinary understanding of an argument showing B to be superior to A operates through some third feature, a 'criterion.'"[8] Now, this criterion, explains Taylor, is "some error-reducing move."[9] This might be a confusion in position A of two distinct ideas or the overlooking of certain relevant ideas or other factors. Third, "the appeal to a criterion frequently makes sense when we can hope that the proponents of both A and B can accept it as decisive."[10] The vision underpinning the transition is that in the conversation between these two traditions, A is introduced to criterion C; A is then persuaded to compare tradition A with tradition B; and A then moves to B. Fourth, the fact that everything makes sense from the standpoint of B creates the problem for "people formed in the culture of mediational epistemology."[11] Now Taylor's summary of the four features of the supersession argument is helpful. However, it is important to note that MacIntyre does admit that, in some sense, "reality" is making a difference. In an extended discussion, MacIntyre explains that when members of the community have accepted the belief tradition of a rival community, they are able to compare their new beliefs with their own beliefs. MacIntyre writes:

> Between those older beliefs and the world as they now understand it there is a radical discrepancy to be perceived. It is this lack of correspondence, between what the mind then judged and believed and reality as now perceived, classified, and understood, which is ascribed when those earlier judgments and beliefs are called *false*. The original and most elementary version of the correspondence theory of truth is one in which it is applied retrospectively in the form of a correspondence theory of falsity.[12]

MacIntyre goes on to admit that the precise nature of this correspondence is complicated. It is not between propositions and facts. "Facts," writes MacIntyre, "like telescopes and wigs for gentlemen, were a seventeenth-century invention."[13] It is more complicated because the mind is more complicated. It is, explains MacIntyre, a dynamic entity, which is constantly creating pictures and then reworking those pictures as the mind discovers that the picture is insufficient to the experience of the world. MacIntyre writes, "So the most primitive conception of truth is of the manifestness of the objects which present themselves to mind; and it is when mind fails to re-present that manifestness that falsity, the inadequacy of mind to its objects, appears."[14]

The strength of this position is that there is an account of truth that links mind and reality. It is also one that takes very seriously the power of traditions in community to shape our way of looking at the world. Let us now apply MacIntyre's (and Taylor's) methodology to our spiritually infused universe. What MacIntyre helps us understand is that what looks strange from outside a tradition might indeed be intelligible within a tradition. For a person standing outside the Christian tradition (and for many in the Christian tradition), angels and saints look bizarre. But for the person standing inside the tradition, this might be entirely appropriate deductions within the tradition. What is important to note is that this principle of "bizarre from the outside intelligible from within" is true of all traditions. To go back to the New Physics for a moment, one explanation for the mysteries of quantum mechanics, especially in relationship to Schrödinger's famous cat in a radioactive box, is to postulate that action brings about two parallel universes simultaneously. Paul Davies explains: "When the universe splits, our minds split with it, one copy going off to populate each world. Every copy thinks it is unique. . . . The splitting is repeated again and again as every atom, and all the subatomic particles, cavort about. Countless times each second, the universe is replicated."[15] This would include every decision we make. For example, when deciding between coffee or tea in the morning, what actually happens is that both options are realized in two universes that spring forth: In one universe, coffee is consumed, and in the other, tea is consumed. Now, from the outside, this seems preposterous. To understand this conversation, you need to be within the tradition of enquiry of contemporary quantum mechanics. Only after you have studied the key texts, learned to reason like a physicist, and understood the contemporary debates are you in a position to understand this possibility and then, and only then, comment on its potential validity. What is true of the New Physics is equally true of theology. This "tradition-constituted" way of knowing provokes a certain reflection. It looks like living in traditions is the only way that humans can form worldviews. This truth about the human condition is revealing. We can legitimately deduce that such a significant fact about human knowing is theologically significant. It looks as if God does not want any human to claim an Archimedean vantage point, where all objective truth can be discerned. Instead, we "see through a glass darkly" (1 Corinthians 13:12); we are forced to live in conversation with each other; we are invited to learn from each other; and we must always hold our understanding of the truth with some humility. This is not to suggest that there is no truth. For MacIntyre, there are better and worse ways of looking at the world. The supersessionist account of traditions asserts that one tradition can be more accurate than another. But we are always grounded in a tradition; we are always working with a vantage point; and we are always trusting that our understanding is appropriate and likely to be true. Later in this chapter, more will be said about the deposition underpinning our holding of the truth.

For now, this provokes two questions. The external question is this: Is it possible that the Christian "tradition of enquiry" is accurately describing the way the world really is? The internal question is: Can the existence of angels and saints be legitimately deduced from the authorities and key texts that shape the Christian tradition?

Authority in Religion

We start with the first of those two questions. Is it possible that the Christian "tradition of enquiry" is accurately describing the way the world really is? This is one of the oldest and hardest questions to answer. It concerns the complex question of the relationship of doctrine to truth. To make this discussion manageable, this chapter will focus on eight options before proceeding to sketch out the alternative that will become the basis for the argument that is developed in the rest of this book. These are the options, with the representative advocate indicated:

1. Truth in a realist sense is unavailable (Don Cupitt).
2. Metaphysical truth about particular traditions is unavailable (John Hick).
3. Values of justice determine the validity of any religious tradition (Grace Jantzen).
4. Christianity is a decision—a leap of faith—which is beyond reason (William James).
5. Christianity is an act of trust in the Christian tradition as embodied in the Church (George Lindbeck).
6. Christianity is the truth that requires a complete conversion (Alan Torrance).
7. Christianity "out narratives" all other options (John Milbank).
8. Christianity can be defended as rational and is the most likely tradition to be true (Richard Swinburne).

Truth in a Realist Sense Is Unavailable

Don Cupitt is probably the theologian of Taylor's "immanent frame." In a series of books that started with *Taking Leave of God* (1980) to most the recent *Creative Faith: Religion as a Way of Worldmaking* (2015), Cupitt sketches out a non-realist theology that turns God into a symbol and makes the ethical central.[16] A non-realist theology is, of course, reacting to "realism," which in this context has a distinctive meaning. Michael Dummett defined realism as, "the belief that statements of the disputed class possess an objective truth value, independently of our means of knowing it: they are true or false in virtue of a reality existing independently of us. The anti-realist opposes to this the view that statements of the disputed class are to be understood only by reference to the sort of thing which we count as evidence for a statement of that class."[17] In short, realists believe there is a real world out there beyond language; non-realists (or anti-realists) consider such talk unhelpful because it is inaccessible and, therefore, irrelevant. Cupitt keeps company with such philosophers as Richard Rorty. Rorty makes his philosophical assumptions clear when he writes the following:

> To say that truth is not out there is simply to say that where there are no sentences there is no truth, that sentences are elements of human languages, and that human languages are human creations. Truth cannot be out there—cannot exist independently of the human mind—because sentences cannot so exist, or be out there. The world is out there, but descriptions of the world are not. Only descriptions of the world can be true or false. The world on its own—unaided by the describing activities of human beings—cannot. The suggestion that truth, as well as the world, is out there is a legacy of an age in which the world was seen as the creation of a being who had a language of his own.[18]

Rorty believes that a person who recognizes this reality is not a nihilist but an ironist. It is a person who sees the irony that a "final vocabulary" is needed, but this worldview cannot and is not justified by any correspondence between language and reality.

Cupitt likes Rorty. Cupitt writes, "I agree with Rorty that we ... now find ourselves having to live without old-style metaphysical or theological underpinning for our final vocabulary. Yes: for me too everything is contingent, a product of history and open to reassessment, including all my own ideas about God and metaphysics. There are no guarantees and no certainties. Nothing is entrenched and everything is negotiable. Like Rorty, I do not want even to try to go back to a time when there were 'absolutes.'"[19] For Cupitt, we are all in the business of painting a verbal picture. Some of these verbal pictures are destructive of life and living; others are life-enhancing. Working on this foundation, Cupitt sets out his vision of God. Cupitt writes, "God personifies religious values. ... A god simply is the imagined actuality of the religious ideal which we experience as summoning and commanding us. 'Be holy as I am holy,' it says."[20] So God is a symbol of our values—values that are calling us to be holy and ethical. Such a God cannot actually exist. Cupitt explains, "The only religiously adequate God cannot exist. The world being what it is, he has to *be* ideal to function *as* the religious ideal."[21] For Cupitt, an actually existing God is too confusing. On worship, for example, worshipping an ethical ideal is perfectly proper—we should acknowledge the ultimate worth of justice. To worship a big invisible God in the sky is morally problematic. Why should this invisible ego want so much affirmation from humanity? This non-existent God is the perfect object of veneration. This brief summary is sufficient for our purposes. Problems abound at every level. Philosophically, to cut the link between language and the real world completely is very problematic. Granted, so-called naïve realism (i.e., the view that words are simply describing reality) lacks the sophistication to make sense of the layers of interpretation that different traditions place on reality. We do need to recognize that the quest for a true interpretation of the world is hard work. But as MacIntyre shows, there are clear moments when we improve on our current understanding of the world and move to an alternative interpretation for good reasons. In so doing, we get closer to the "truth." Some sort of correspondence of language to the world (the old correspondence theory of truth) is important to retain.[22] The consequences of cutting that link results in the absurdity that the world might be flat, new age crystals might work, and science is no truer than any alternative worldview. A version of extreme cultural relativism is inescapable. If, philosophically, it is inadequate, then theologically, it is woeful. As a motivator for the survival of religion, it is pathetic. People are being invited to struggle out of bed on a Sunday morning and sit in a church to meditate on a symbol of their values. The mystery of church attendance is not why it is declining but why it is so persistent when church is so bad. Women and men go to church because they believe that the language points to a reality beyond. Prayer is not the articulation of our ethical expectations to an ideal symbol of those expectations; instead, prayer is the deepest communing with the source of everything that is.

The Cupitt account is assuming an atheism.[23] Now, technically, Cupitt evades this charge on the grounds that atheism is also a claim about reality that is unobtainable and beyond all language. Cupitt concedes that atheism is a metaphysical claim, which is, therefore, as absurd as all other metaphysical claims. However, strangely (in the sense that there is no reason in his philosophy for this), the practice of Cupitt's religion assumes the complete absence of any transcendent entity. It is a triumph of atheism in practice. For a defense of a spiritually infused universe, this position will not work. It is the immanent frame of Taylor; it is empty of any spiritual realities. It is completely inadequate.

Metaphysical Truth about Particular Traditions Is Unavailable

John Hick made an appearance in the opening chapter. There, he was treated as an example of a "deistic" response to the challenges of modernity. The God underpinning the Hick approach is one that creates but does nothing more. And his pluralist theology of religion means that any description of that God is impossible.

Now in this section, we are looking at Hick's approach to doctrine and truth. In his Gifford Lectures, *An Interpretation of Religion*, Hick sets out the parameters of his position. There seem to be three features. First, he does believe that religious language has a cognitive intent. He is an advocate of critical realism, where "the element of interpretation plays an even larger part than it does in sense perception—thereby preserving our cognitive freedom in relation to the much greater and more demanding value of the reality in question."[24] For Hick, the very challenge of interpreting the transcendent safeguards our human freedom with respect to the divine. It is precisely because God is not obvious that we are able to exercise our freedom in ways that are antagonistic to God. Given he is a critical realist, he opposes the work of Cupitt because it does not recognize that the "core of religious language has normally been understood and is today normally understood by believers and disbelievers alike as basically cognitive."[25] Second, Hick believes that religious language will be subject to eschatological verification. Hick distinguishes between direct verification (to use his example, "There is a clock on the mantelpiece in that room"[26]) and indirect verification (for example, where John is an honest person). Religious verification is indirect. It is indirect in two ways. One way will be in tracking "features of the universe, as it changes through time, which trace the difference that the existence of God makes."[27] The other way is the idea of heaven—"the conscious communion with God," which "would confirm the reality of God beyond the possibility of rational doubt."[28] The third feature is that some historical disagreements about religion are, in principle, resolvable using the methods of modern historiography. So, did Jesus die on the cross (as claimed by Christians) or not (as claimed by Muslims)? This question should be settled "by unbiased assessment of the historical evidence."[29] He concedes that, in practice, the assessment of the evidence is subject to such disagreement that decisive resolution is "elusive."[30] However, the fourth feature is that there are many trans-historical truth claims (e.g., What happens after we die? Is the universe eternal?), which, in principle, might be resolvable but in practice are unresolvable—the unanswered questions of the Buddha. (According to the Pali texts, the Buddha listed ten "unrevealed, the undetermined or unresolved questions."[31] These propositions include "the world is eternal," "the world is not eternal," "the soul is identical with the body," "the soul is not identical with the body," and so on.) Now Hick explains that religious traditions have a range of myths; some of which are in response to the questions posed by the Buddha. It is at this point that the key to understanding Hick's approach to religious language becomes clear. He writes:

> I have suggested that such topics [the kind of question identified by the Buddha] can appropriately be called mysteries. On the hypothesis present in this book the Real *an sich* is the ultimate mystery. For the relationship between the

> Real and its *personae* and *impersonae* is, epistemologically, the relationship between a noumenal reality and the range of its appearances to a plurality of perceivers.... [Hick, then, explains that talk of the ways in which the Real intersects with the world can be both literal—e.g., the Lord brought the children of Israel out of Egypt—and analogical—e.g., God is wise or God is good.] But nevertheless such literal and analogical language about the objects of religious worship or meditation always intends to be about the Real itself. And as such it functions mythologically: we speak mythologically about the noumenal Real by speaking literally or analogically about its phenomenal manifestations.[32]

For Hick, religious discourse is in a realm of its own. Even when the language appears to be direct such as "God healed me," once the word God is invoked, then it becomes mythologically. It is all grounded in his Kantian epistemological assumptions. The noumenal is inaccessible: We can never know what God is like in Godself; all we are handling are the appearance of that Real. Given the appearances are described in contradictory ways (Buddhism does not believe in a personal God, while Christianity does), then we have to resign ourselves to the corollary that we can never know what is true about God.

Hick likes to think he is keeping company with the mystics. However, this is not the case. Although it is true that some mystics insisted that God is unknowable, the word God still had content. It was the God revealed in Scripture: It was the God shown to us by Jesus Christ. So—to use a metaphor—the unknowable God was in a certain ballpark. If one asserted that God is evil, the mystic could still say that is mistaken because the unknowable God has revealed to humanity a truth about Godself, and that is that God is loving.

David Cheetham seeks to defend Hick by celebrating the fact that within each particular religion, you can live as if it is true while recognizing that when thinking about religious diversity, a different perspective is needed. Cheetham writes, "Hick's pluralistic hypothesis is intended as a second-order philosophical exercise rather than a first order discourse."[33] This sounds like Cheetham is commending a hypocrisy: the prayers are said in church as if they true, but upon rational reflection on the discourse, one knows that the truth is unobtainable. Hick is overstating the epistemological distinctiveness of religious language. Is the truth about black holes—as they are in themselves—ever really possible? If one starts with that question in cosmology, then one will end up deciding any attempt to distinguish between better and worse descriptions of black holes is futile. Instead of this in principle rejection of any possible analysis from the perspective of truth of different accounts of God, we need an alternative that is willing to work a little harder to see how different accounts of God can be evaluated.

Values of Justice Determine the Validity of Any Religious Tradition

The idea that some ethical criterion should be the determinate of truth is found in a number of writers. Hick, for example, works with an ethical criterion. However, I take as representative of this position the much more radical work of the feminist philosopher of religion Grace Jantzen.

Jantzen always wanted to think differently about traditional topics. *God's World, God's Body* is a resolute defense of a Christian version of pantheism.[34] But although she wanted to think differently, her methodology was recognizable as firmly in the Anglo-American traditions of philosophy of religion. The departure from that came in her *Becoming Divine: Towards a Feminist Philosophy of Religion*.Inspired by Luce Irigaray, the French psychoanalyst and philosopher, Jantzen makes a compelling argument. The focus is on the embodied person—not a mental abstracted from reality— where personhood is achieved through struggle. She attacks Anglo-American philosophy because it is preoccupied with rational argument and the justification of beliefs. She explains that "the assumption throughout is that religion is essentially about beliefs."[35] And she asserts that Anglo-American philosophy of religion is working "on ground [that] is in fact necrophilic."[36] What does she mean by this? Her targets are Richard Swinburne, Ward, and Vincent Brümmer. In all cases, God is seen as a cosmic mind, and the best analog for this mind is the human mind. "Ward is wholly oblivious of the irony that although his book is overtly devoted to exploring the material basis and structure of the universe, the embodiment of the self is never discussed, gender never gets a mention, birth, death, and the material conditions of selfhood are hardly noticed: it is rational consciousness that counts."[37] The problem is not simply philosophy of religion but also moral philosophy. So, in ethics, Jantzen complains that the focus is on the agent—has "x" done the right thing—a generic male. There is very little interest in "the other, the object or recipient of the agent's action."[38] This is necrophilic because of the preoccupation with death. Jantzen writes:

> Western civilization, dominated by masculinist structures, has had both a fascination with and a dread of death. Perhaps the most vivid illustration of this is its continuous involvement with war: waging wars, planning wars, building ever more sophisticated equipment for war, writing history as though wars were the most important of events, even conducting philosophical arguments on the model of attack and defense, as we have seen.... And our language is saturated with military metaphors. From the "fight" against cancer, crime, poor housing, or whatever is the current "enemy" to the "battle" of the football pitch, the language of war is ubiquitous and taken for granted. If speech-patterns both reflect and structure our subjectivities, this fact alone should give us pause. The preoccupation with death is matched by a fascination with other worlds, some other form of reality beyond the uncertainties of this present life, bound up as it is with the material body.[39]

This analysis of the "western symbolic"[40] is a key theme of her trilogy *Death and the Displacement of Beauty*. Partly inspired by Michel Foucault, Jantzen aspires to provide a narrative that demonstrates how embedded the death preoccupation is in Western and Christian thought. In volume one, *Foundations of Violence*, she works through Homer, Socrates, Plato, Seneca, and Plotinus and shows that their preoccupation with an eternal, immortal soul makes "death, violence and mastery . . . the story of western culture."[41] In volumes two and three (edited by Jeremy Carrette and Morny Joy after her untimely death), she develops this narrative by exploring the explicitly religious roots of violence and death in Judaism and Christianity. Religious constructions of violence, Jantzen argued, were grounded in the male fear of women.So, how should we respond? Throughout her work, she argues that there is, running parallel with this narrative of death, an alternative. Grounded in the experience of women, seen in the account of some mystics, there is also a world of natality—these "voices of dissent."[42] This is the world where new life can be affirmed and beauty and creativity can flourish. In *Becoming Divine,* the solution is to challenge the assumption. We need a destabilizing double reading, which is "a sort of reading which on the one hand pays close attention to a text, but which, in that very attention, discloses a rupture in that text which requires a radically different reading of it, thus destabilizing it and in the undecidability thereby created opens the possibility of thinking otherwise."[43] The result is a "new religious symbolic focused on natality and flourishing rather than on death, a symbolic which will lovingly enable natals, women and men, to become subjects, and the earth on which we live to bloom, to be 'faithful up to the process of the divine which passes through' us and through the earth itself."[44] In volume three of the trilogy, *A Place of Springs*, she invokes the seventeenth-century Quakers. Jantzen writes, "Whereas society was mired ever more deeply in an obsession with death and violence which became the symbolic of later modernity, Quaker women were much more concerned with choosing life, developing life and peace."[45] She argues that the key difference was the location of the divine. "Whereas the rest of society—for all their religious differences—held to a concept of God sharply other than the world (a concept which in its extreme forms came to be known as deism), Quakers believed that the divine was *within* human persons, a life and light and seed and fountain—they mixed their metaphors happily—in everyone."[46] The question about the truth of Christianity is much less important for Jantzen. Elaine Graham is very helpful when she summarizes the Jantzen project with respect to truth in this way:

> This is about who has the power to define the nature of authentic and authoritative religious experience; but this is contingent upon implicit understandings of the nature of God, knowledge and meaning. To refuse to uphold truth as correspondence with propositional belief also entails a break with "good old

God" and a break with an onto-theological tradition, into an alternative concept of the divine as yet to be the actualised horizon of becoming. "Divinity in the face of natals is a horizon of becoming, a process of divinity ever new, just as natality is the possibility of new beginnings." It is also, essentially, a break with realism, since Grace is more interested in the creative possibilities for and the pursuit of transformation towards an ethic of flourishing and natality. Talk about God must by necessity open up new rules of discourse, new models of subjectivity—but to remain locked in the paradigm of propositional truth would be to limit such possibilities. This resonates with her contention that the search for a new moral imaginary is informed by its efficacy in serving "the practice of justice."[47]

The value of justice as a criterion for the appropriateness of a metaphysical framework is explicit in Jantzen's work. However, as Graham makes clear, this is no exhortation for orthopraxis over orthodoxy. Jantzen's is representative of this position because her entire project is an attempt to live in the symbolic world of an ultimate account and think through an account that is focused on life and birth-giving rather than death and dying. This is her project.

Once inside the Jantzen project, one cannot help but be impressed. She creates a powerful narrative that is a challenge to the fundamental assumptions of so much contemporary discourse. However, I do have some difficulties.

Jantzen has a real difficulty with "reason" and "rationality" being the ultimate arbiters of truth in religion.

> [N]o topic in the philosophy of religion, traditional or feminist, remains unaffected once we recognize that we are not straightforward, rational, autonomous Cartesian egos, but are embodied, sexuate persons in a web of life, caught up in unconscious desires and fears. Becoming divine must be possible for such complex subjects, or it is not possible at all. What is obvious is that the ideal of the rational passionless man, becoming god-like in mastery and knowledge and exerting his dominance over all (m)others is a fantasy that tells us more about male psychosexual development than about godliness. Yet it is a dangerous and destructive fantasy, played out in masculinist symbolic structures—religion, law, science, economics—on the bodies of women, Blacks, lesbians and gay men, whoever threatens the fragile and fractured self.[48]

At the very basic level of arguments in favor or arguments against "the existence of God," Jantzen believes patriarchal assumptions are operating. The lack of location, embodiment, and crucial desire is exposed. She attacks the philosophy seminar with the inevitable binaries—for and against God—which forces students to turn thinking into a game that has very little to do with life.

However, there is an irony here. Jantzen is, herself, constructing arguments. These are arguments against the Western symbolic, which is preoccupied with death. She provides reasons, which paradoxically are against the primacy of reasons. One can legitimately attack the limited range of reasons offered and allowed: One can legitimately question the "battle" metaphor with winners and losers in debates. But I do not think you can deny that "reason" embodied in valid arguments is the tool that Jantzen is using. It is incoherent to use rational arguments to undermine the validity of rational argumentation.

Perhaps more importantly, Jantzen is right to argue that the gender and justice implications of any theological construction must be taken seriously. Feminist theology is a valuable tool. The emphasis on becoming and temporality in the life of God is an insight that can and should be part of our theological understanding of God. But these insights need to be explained; they need to be subject to scrutiny. In short, the God-given tool of reason, in the framework of good arguments, needs to be used. Jantzen would like to evade the following question: Which account of the transcendent makes most sense? In my judgment, this is not possible.

Christianity Is a Decision—a Leap of Faith—Which Is beyond Reason

William James gave expression to a popular way of handling the complexities of truth and religion. He has been widely interpreted as a philosopher who invites others to affirm as true their trust that God is there. As a skillful lecturer and writer, his lecture "The Will to Believe" has been reproduced extensively and has been widely read.[49] The argument in this essay involves three steps. First, he makes a set of distinctions. James explains: "Let us call the decision between two hypotheses an option. Options may be of several kinds. They may be—1, living or dead; 2, forced or avoidable; 3, momentous or trivial and for our purposes we may call an option a genuine option when it is of the forced, living, and momentous kind."[50] So, a "live" option is one that is genuinely available to you; I am unlikely to become an occultist for a multitude of sociological factors. A "forced" option is where you have no choice but to decide. "Momentous" captures the life-changing nature of the decision. Then, second, he sets out his thesis. James writes:

> The thesis I defend is, briefly stated, this: Our passional nature not only lawfully may, but must, decide an option between propositions, whenever it is a genuine option that cannot by its nature be decided on intellectual grounds; for to say, under such circumstances, "Do not decide, but leave the question open," is itself a passional decision,—just like deciding yes or no,—and is attended with the same risk of losing the truth.[51]

James is inviting us to recognize the risks involved in leaving the "question open." The illusion is that agnosticism creates space for possibility. But the truth is that "not deciding" often closes down options. Very few people would get married if they had to be confident rationally that this marriage is going to succeed. The very nature of the promise is momentous. We are promising, regardless of what happens, to stick with this person. Rational confidence in this situation is hard. But leaving the "question open" is actually a major decision. The other person is not going to wait indefinitely for the other person to be sure rationally. The joys of marriage are being irretrievably lost as one waits.

Hick did considerable damage to James' argument. He interpreted the argument as an extension of Pascal's Wager. The Wager is, of course, the famous calculation of the benefits of belief over unbelief. And Blaise Pascal argues that, given belief offers eternal life and unbelief might result in hell, one should opt to believe. Hick is harsh on this argument, considering it "essentially non-religious."[52] Hick goes on to write that "William James has used the same basic idea"[53] in his argument for faith. Robert J. O'Connell has pushed back on Hick's reading of James. O'Connell retorts that Hick "has failed to bring into play the profound ambivalence James manifests towards both the Wager and Pascal's *Pensèes* more generally. James's summary of Wager's substance is surprisingly parallel to Hick's."[54] And on this point, O'Connell is right. The critique that James offers of the Wager is this:

> We feel that a faith in masses and holy water adopted wilfully after such a mechanical calculation would lack the inner soul of faith's reality; and if we were ourselves in the place of the Deity, we should probably take particular pleasure in cutting off believers of this pattern from their infinite reward. It is evident that unless there be some pre-existing tendency to believe in masses and holy water, the option offered to the will by Pascal is not a living option.[55]

James is clear. He is not a twentieth-century version of Pascal. Hick goes on to complain that James is close to the schoolboy who said, "Faith is when you believe, 'cos you want to, something which you know ain't true."[56] He goes on to argue that James has a view of faith as a prudent gamble, far removed from the biblical or believer's view of faith. With O'Connell, I share a sense that James is dismissed too quickly. The underlying ideas are much more complex and much more interesting. James is right to see that some decisions are "forced." Any decision about practice is forced. I will either say the Morning Office or not say the Morning Office. If I decide not to decide, then I end up not saying the Morning Office. I will either attend church or not attend church. If I decide not to decide, then I end up not attending church. The truth about all agnostics is that they live like atheists. We do not find the phenomenon of an agnostic who attends church every other Sunday and prays every other day. Agnostics make a decision. They live like atheists.

In a very striking passage, James writes:

> Believe truth! Shun error!—these, we see, are two materially different laws; and by choosing between them we may end by coloring differently our whole intellectual life. We may regard the chase for truth as paramount, and the avoidance of error as secondary; or we may, on the other hand, treat the avoidance of error as more imperative, and let truth take its chance. Clifford, in the instructive passage which I have quoted, exhorts us to the latter course. Believe nothing, he tells us, keep your mind in suspense forever, rather than by closing it on insufficient evidence incur the awful risk of believing lies. You, on the other hand, may think that the risk of being in error is a very small matter when compared with the blessings of real knowledge, and be ready to be duped many times in your investigation rather than postpone indefinitely the chance of guessing true.[57]

James gives two options here: first, make the chase for truth as paramount, or second, let truth take its chance. Those who insist on waiting until evidence has determined the truth are guilty of letting truth take a chance. Those who opt to start living the practices are chasing the truth and making that the priority.

James is on to something important here. His argument takes the following form:

1. Reason cannot resolve the question of God's existence.
2. If you opt to leave the question open, then you opt for atheism and do not participate in any religious practices.
3. Yet, God might exist. And as one participates in religious practices, one might discover that there is an authenticity to these practices.
4. Therefore, pursue the truth and exercise your right to decide to pursue those practices in the quest for the discovery that God is underpinning those practices.

The key idea is that knowing can come through the practices. Presumably, one could participate in religious practices and decide that there is no authentic depth pointing to the transcendent. At that point, one would stop exercising one's will to believe. But stepping into the circle, without the confident affirmation of good arguments that persuade the seeking, is legitimate.

As I develop my own position, James is part of the structure. But before concluding this section, there is one further difficulty that needs discussion. As Hick complains, it does sound like geography will determine which tradition one opts for. Live options in Saudi Arabia are different from the live options in Kentucky, United States. But this is where we return to the start of the chapter. When we recognize the tradition-constituted nature of knowing, we accept that geography and culture are inevitable parts of the process of knowing. We do opt into the live options in our culture. This does mean that the type of religious belief that one tries will depend on where you are. But, as we already noted, this is also true of the type of economic assumptions or scientific narrative. Options are culturally shaped. This is part of our social reality.

Christianity Is an Act of Trust in the Christian Tradition as Embodied in the Church

This is the classic postliberal position. Identified with George Lindbeck (among others), it has become the position of many mainline theologians.[58] Hans Frei is the pioneer. His reflections on biblical hermeneutics created an important challenge to the limitations of the historical critical method. Frei wanted us to read Scripture as if it were the "real world." Instead of constantly denying its historical veracity and, therefore, searching for some cosmic moral, Frei wanted us to take the biblical worldview seriously. However, for philosophical clarity, we had to wait for Lindbeck's book, *The Nature of Doctrine*. Lindbeck begins by identifying three different approaches to the study of religion and doctrine. He writes:

> One of these emphasizes the cognitive aspects of religion and stresses the ways in which church doctrines function as informative propositions or truth claims about objective realities. . . . A second approach focuses on . . . the "experiential-expressive" dimension of religion, and it interprets doctrines as noninformative and nondiscursive symbols of inner feelings, attitudes, or existential orientations. . . . A third approach, favored especially by ecumenically inclined Roman Catholics, attempts to combine these two emphases. But the cognitively propositional and expressively symbolic dimensions and functions of religion and doctrine are viewed, at least in the case of Christianity, as religiously significantly and valid.[59]

The first, then, treats religion as propositions, which are either true or false. The second treats religion as symbols that express feelings. And the third is a Roman Catholic combination of the two. Against these three, Lindbeck argues for a "cultural-linguistic" approach. The analogy operating here is the concept of language and grammar. Religion is the language; doctrine is the grammar.

In the Lindbeck model, one lives in the church and learns a language, which seeks to capture how a human relates to the divine. Doctrine helps us understand how the language should be used appropriately. Now, what is the relationship to truth? John Allen Knight notes that "Lindbeck uses 'truth' in three ways: 'ontological' truth concerns whether a claim corresponds to reality; 'intrasystematic' truth concerns the internal coherence of a set of claims; and 'categorial' truth concerns the adequacy of the categories of a cultural-linguistic system."[60] Now, Lindbeck does want to affirm that in some sense the assertion "Jesus is Lord" is true. He expresses sympathy with the propositional view of religious language at this point. He concludes his discussion on truth by explaining:

> In conclusion, a religion can be interpreted as possibly containing ontologically true affirmation, not only in cognitivist theories but also in cultural-linguistic ones. There is nothing in the cultural-linguistic approach that requires the rejection (or the acceptance) of the epistemological realism and correspondence theory of truth, which, according to most of the theological tradition, is implicit in the conviction of believers that when they rightly use a sentence such as "Christ is Lord" they are uttering a true first-order proposition.

Lindbeck seems to be holding together a cluster of affirmations. He does not believe that there is a way around language. Language is central in our relating to the world. He wants his framework to help with ecumenical and even interreligious conversations—so his system cannot affirm that every assertion inside a cultural-linguistic system is true in a correspondence sense. However, he wants also to affirm that it is possible that the claim "Jesus is Lord" is indeed ontologically true.

Knight is helpful here. He exposes this ambiguity at the heart of the postliberal project. He argues that the entire postliberal project is heavily shaped by Wittgenstein. He explains that "postliberal theological method is closely related to a Wittgensteinian understanding of meaning-as-use and more generally to Wittgenstein's antitheoretical orientation to philosophy. . . ."[61] This opens up the postliberal project to the criticism that it is fideistic. It does seem as if there are no external connections: The language and grammar of Christianity cannot be justified to those outside the church. Knight then writes, "the postliberal project stands in need of a theory of truth."[62] To offer these linguistic and cultural bubbles that one is gently socialized into is an insufficient framework for doctrine. We need some connection. Earlier in this chapter, I argued that MacIntyre's account of the "tradition-constituted" nature of knowing is insightful. In this respect, postliberalism is a sibling of this approach. There is no easy way out of traditions. But, as Knight has explained, postliberals do not have a good answer to the question—"Why Christianity?" Why do we step into that particular tradition?

Christianity Is the Truth That Requires a Complete Conversion

This position is a sibling of the postliberal position described above. The criteria of knowing are intrinsic and internal to the Christian tradition. Alan Torrance develops an approach that argues that knowing depends on a complete conversion or repentance. Early in his essay, his target is what he calls "critical immanentism" that infects so much modern theological method. In brief, David Strauss is a key figure. He is the one who accepts a distinction, supplied by Gottfried Wilhelm Leibniz, between necessary truths supplied by reason and contingent truths grounded in sense perception. Once you have this distinction, Scripture becomes tricky. Gotthold Lessing talked about the ugly broad ditch that divides eternal truths from the mess and complexity of history. How can eternal truth be revealed in the complexity of history? Instead, we need to use "reason," with all its conceptual clarity and independence from history.

Torrance explains why this is mistaken by using Søren Kierkegaard. Kierkegaard sees the prejudice of those seeking to use judicious reason to judge the biblical narrative. Instead, explains Torrance, "the conditions for the recognition and affirmation of Christian truth are intrinsic to the event of revelation."[63] The idea here is this: The drama of Scripture explains how the truth of Christianity is appreciated. It is a complete conversion. Torrance explains that "the recognition and perception of God's presence in Christ is the consequence of an event of paradigmatic *metanoia*, of transformation (metamorphosis), and of reconciliation of mind. . . ."[64] Christianity itself explains why some see and others do not. Some cannot see because their eyes have not been opened by the agency of the Holy Spirit that brings about a transformation of the mind and, in particular, of reason. For Torrance, Alvin Plantinga's concept of certain beliefs being "properly basic" is helpful. Plantinga argued that certain beliefs cannot be justified. His famous illustration is the existence of other minds. One cannot establish an argument that satisfactorily establishes the existence of other minds, but it is still rational to believe in other minds. Plantinga concludes his book, *God and Other Minds*, with the assertion: "Hence my tentative conclusion: if my belief in other minds is rational, so is my belief in God. But obviously the former is rational; so, therefore, is the latter."[65] Torrance likes this idea and develops it thus:

> The implication of Kierkegaard's, Bonhoeffer's, and Barth's arguments is that the event of God's self-communication in the Word perceived by the Spirit conditions and establishes "properly basic" beliefs, to borrow Alvin Plantinga's terminology. These are beliefs that do not need to be justified or accounted for with reference to other more basic beliefs or suppositions. That is because they are basic and warranted—warrant that neither is nor must be demonstrable by making recourse to universally accessible evidence.[66]

Torrance goes on to quote approval from Bonhoeffer: "Jesus' testimony to himself stands by itself as self-authenticating. . . . The fact of the revelation of God in Christ cannot be either established or disputed scientifically."[67] Early in Torrance's essay, he suggests that his argument could "be supported by biblical exegesis and by analysis of patristic debate about the meaning of *metanoia* in the New Testament."[68] In an extended footnote, Torrance explains:

> One could consider the account of Peter's recognition of Jesus that "flesh and blood" could not deliver and the fact that the recognition involved the reconstitution of Simon as Peter. One could consider the extensive eye/sight and ear/hearing metaphors in the Synoptic, Johannine, and Pauline corpora implying that the conditions of acknowledgement require to be given and are not innate. There is the Pauline emphasis on the fact that the discernment of truth requires a transformation of minds, which cannot be "schematized" by the secular order (Rom 12:2). Finally, there is the extensive utilization of the regeneration or "born from above" metaphors in the Johannine corpus. In sum, central to and, indeed, held in common by the New Testament writings is the fundamental emphasis that revelation involves and includes the provision by God ("from above") of the conditions for the recognition of God through God's free and creative presence. They are not innate or immanent in our flesh and blood but the result of the creative reconciliation of our minds and paradigms.[69]

Now, this is important. The difficulty with Torrance is the same difficulty identified with postliberalism. How exactly does the Christian discourse link and relate to other discourses? Torrance's insight is that the Christian tradition does want to claim that knowing depends on the gift of faith: God is an agent at work in the moment. Some cannot see because they have not been granted the gift of faith. Now, at this point, it is easy to object that this sounds unreasonable: Any tradition could claim that knowledge of the truth depends on a nonrational conversion to that tradition. One cannot convert to every tradition, so this cannot be a reasonable requirement for knowledge of the truth.

The objection has some force, but Torrance can legitimately make a response. The various themes identified by Torrance from the New Testament stress that it is not so much that we—as agents—convert to Christianity but that God is the agent. In this sense, Torrance is following Barth. The idea that knowing is dependent on the agency of God is both likely and plausible. If we are going to know what God is like (given God is the creator and quite unlike anything else we know or experience), then assuming that knowledge depends on God's agency in our minds makes sense. Part of the position I will be developing is that this idea of God being an active agent in helping us see the truth of Christianity is an intrinsic aspect of trusting that God has spoken in Christ.

Christianity "Out-Narratives" All Other Options

A theme is emerging within many of these accounts of knowledge. The theme is this: How do we reconcile truth with historicism (i.e., the social, cultural, and historical location of all-knowing)? John Milbank in *Theology and Social Theory* sets out an option that radically affirms the tradition-constituted basis of knowing, yet he also believes that Christianity is the truth. Against MacIntyre, Milbank writes:

MacIntyre, of course, wants to argue against this stoic-liberal-nihilist tendency, which is "secular reason." But my case is rather that it is only a mythos, and therefore cannot be refuted, but only out-narrated, if we persuade people—for reasons of "literary taste"—that Christianity offers a much better story.[70]

Now, Milbank is an advocate of what he calls "a true Christian meta-narrative realism."[71] So, Milbank has the following picture. There are countless communities and many traditions. Some traditions are deeply destructive. And in *Theology and Social Theory*, he outlines the destructive narrative of modernity, which is grounded in an "ontology of violence." In contrast to this, he claims that the Christian narrative is grounded on an "ontology of peace." Now, although there is no way of identifying "tradition-transcendent" reasons why the Christian narrative is better, it is still logically possible that Christianity is true. This is what Milbank believes is the case. The Christian narrative is a meta-discourse that embraces all human life and activity. The task of evangelism is to "narrate" the Christian story in a compelling and attractive way that people opt for this story rather than the destructive alternative. For Milbank, rationality is always "tradition-constituted." Truth is a term always relative to particular traditions. One opts into the Christian story because one is persuaded of its narrative power. The implications of Milbank's extreme historicism are dramatic. Unlike MacIntyre, there is no dialogue between traditions. There are no good reasons for one to decide to move from this picture of the world and then, because of an encounter with another tradition, to another picture of the world. Unlike MacIntyre, there is no sense that reality can be described in better or worse ways. His traditions are insulated; they are not connected; they have nothing to do with each other.

Yet his historical narratives in his work admit the complex interplay of traditions. Augustine was shaped by his Platonism; Aquinas engaged with Islamic thinkers and learned about Aristotle. There is a fluidity in traditions that Milbank seems to be unable to accommodate.

Christianity Can Be Defended as Rational and Is the Most Likely Tradition to Be True

We conclude this selective list of options by considering the position of Richard Swinburne. Swinburne has defended theism and, in later books, Christianity as the most likely religion to be true. He defended theism in his trilogy on God. In *The Coherence of Theism*, he explains his account of religious language and defends the coherence of the idea of God. In *The Existence of God*, he argues that there are good inductive arguments for the existence of God. In *Faith and Reason,* he argues that belief in the creed of Christianity, which he sees as being more probable than alternatives, is sufficient for the practice of religion. Right at the outset, it is interesting to note that he is dealing in probabilities. These are inductive arguments that demonstrate that it is more probable than not that God exists. When it comes to his discussion of revelation, a similar approach can be seen.

In *Revelation: From Metaphor to Analogy*, Swinburne explains why the Christian revelation is more likely to be true than the alternatives. It is vintage Swinburne. It takes us through certain steps. He explains that we need to expect that it is likely that the Creator would want to provide a revelation. God would want to provide humanity with certain information. This information would include "general moral truths," certain "factual information which will enable them to apply those moral truths," "information of how, if at all, God became incarnate and provided any atonement for their sins," and finally, information about heaven and hell.[72] The next stage is to explain how limited the revelation options are. God could have provided a "culture-relative revelation"[73] (i.e., one that works with the knowledge of a particular culture) that would be easily understood by the initial recipients but not by those who came later. Nevertheless, Swinburne, opines, some sort of cultural connection is essential. The alternative, a "culturally independent"[74] revelation, would produce very general propositions that would be difficult to translate into other languages for other cultures. Swinburne summarizes:

> So far I have been arguing that if there is a God there is a good a priori reason for expecting a propositional revelation, in connection with an atoning incarnation; and for expecting some means to be provided for preserving and rightly interpreting that revelation for new centuries and cultures.[75]

One can sense that Swinburne is "stacking the deck" here (to use another metaphor, this time from cards). The result, unsurprisingly, is that Swinburne defends Scripture, justified by the resurrection of Jesus, grounded in the church, which is the guide for the community.

Although Swinburne does touch on other religious traditions, the treatment is limited and not at all empathetic. His location as a Christian is heavily influencing his assessment of the arguments and, therefore, the likely probabilities. Yet any account of authority in religion should take the following elements into account: his appeal to the principle that there are good and bad arguments, his recognition that reason has a role to play, and his insistence that incoherent positions cannot be right.

Theological Traditioned Truth

This section was provoked by the following question: How can one know that the Christian narrative is true? This question has provided the necessary examination of a different account of truth and authority. It is now necessary to bring together the threads emerging from our survey. Those positions that reject any possibility of truth (non-realism) or insist on metaphysical truth being so much more problematic than truth in other realms (Hick's position) are, in my view, too problematic to be helpful. We need an account of authority and truth that recognizes the complexity yet does not make such judgments impossible.

As the survey illustrates, this book is not taking any single position. It is not postliberal or an advocate of Swinburnian rationality. Instead, the approach sees a range of insights in different positions. Hopefully, the option I shall now develop can coherently weave together these insights into a position which I am calling "Theological Traditioned Truth."

There are seven features of Theological Traditioned Truth. These are:

1. Tradition-constituted approach to knowing   It is now recognized as axiomatic that there is no Archimedean vantage point from which all the different communities and traditions in the world can be judged. We are all located. We are all engaging the world through a particular language that creates linguistic options for interpretation. We all weigh arguments that are heavily influenced by the history of our community. Knowing is a constant conversation with our past interpretations, present experiences (including the worldviews of other communities), and likely future adjustments. MacIntyre (and Taylor) create a framework that helps us understand how judgments and changes in traditions occur.

2. Certain rational principles are universal   Although there are difficulties with Swinburne's sanguine analysis of the revelation options, on one key issue, he is right. Built into the structure of language are rational fundamentals that make communication possible: These include the basics of logic (e.g., law of non-contradiction) and the appropriate recognition of validity in arguments. Ward, in *Religion and Revelation*, explains that:

> There are some very basic rational criteria which can be brought to bear upon all claims to truth, in religion as elsewhere. Rationality involves the use of intelligent capacities, including the capacity to register information correctly, to compare similar pieces of information, to deduce and infer in accordance with the rules of logic and relate means to ends effectively. A rational person can act on a consciously formulated principle in order to attain an intended goal. . . . Such simple forms of reasoning are necessary to any form of intelligently ordered social life. They are not, and cannot be, culturally relative.[76]

Theological Traditioned Truth wants to recognize these rational fundamentals, but is there a conflict with the emphasis on the "tradition-constituted" nature of knowing? Ward thinks not. When considering which tradition these basic criteria belong to, Ward responds, "that they belong to the tradition of being human, as such . . . [T]hey are principles of rationality which are built into the necessary structure of human social life, and thus function as desirable ideals for any community that wishes to survive for any length of time."[77] There is a complexity here. The truth is that logic itself has a history; it is part of a tradition. Discoveries are made in logic. There is a long journey from Aristotle to deontic logic (a logic focused on obligation and permission). Logic, in all its complexity, is not tradition transcendent. However, as we saw in our discussion of Jantzen, she constructs arguments (which have a logical form) for, ironically, her anti-rationality position. There is something inescapable about the fundamentals of logic. In addition, instead of locating the fundamentals of logic in the reality of being human, as Ward does, it might be more helpful to locate these fundamentals in the structure of language. It is as we seek to describe the world and be understood by others that logic becomes an indispensable tool.[78]

3. Discourse similarities   We must resist the temptation to bracket theological discourse out from the rest of life discourse. This is a temptation both religious and secular. The religious person wants to stress that God is completely different from the rest of creation; therefore, discourse about God will end up being completely different from any other discipline. The secularist wants to affirm the intelligibility of all other forms of discourse and how peculiar, and, therefore, strange, religious discourse is. While the religious emphasis has some merit, the best account of religious language has worked hard to keep some connection with the rest of linguistic description of the world. Aquinas, for example, formulated his doctrine of analogy very carefully both to respect the difference that God makes, while also making some sort of human discourse possible.

In addition, many of the problems that surround religious language are found in other discourses. Compare the discourse of economics to the discourse of theology; there are striking similarities. There is clearly an economic realm, but understanding and interpreting it are very difficult. There are different schools that interpret the data in very different ways; and there are different measurements for the data. Although there clearly is an economy, knowledge in this realm is very difficult. The reason why knowledge is so difficult is because the economy is complicated. A multitude of factors is constantly operating: The precise reasons for economic growth are difficult to determine, and predicting outcomes of increasing interest rates are difficult. When it comes to knowledge, truth, and authority, economics and theology are very similar.

Economics is an illustration. The principle of "discourse similarities" extends right across all disciplines. Knowing is hard in physics ("What exactly is a black hole?"), accountancy ("Is this a legitimate legal option?)," architecture ("Will this building withstand an earthquake?"), and soccer ("Why can a team do so well one week and so badly the next?"). It is important to see the similarities in terms of knowing across almost all disciplines.

These first three are true of all forms of knowing. The next four are focused on knowing in the Christian tradition.

4. Virtue epistemology as a natural theology Theological Traditioned Truth is theologically informed. This needs unpacking. A key question is: Why is knowing so complicated? Why are the answers to theological or metaphysical questions not clearer? At this point, I want to suggest we are in the business of natural theology. We are seeking to look at an aspect of the world and seek to understand what we can learn from God from that aspect.

Knowing clearly is difficult. This is true of every significant area of human discourse (see point four above). So, why is this? The processes of knowing forces us to live in a tradition. Traditions emerge in communities. Knowing must be a communal effort: Knowing builds both on those who have gone before and those who are fellow travelers in the knowing process. We are forced to live in community; we are required to learn from the past; and we need the voices of those around us. We have a natural theology that recognizes that knowing is a divinely intended way of forcing us to dialogue with the past and with others. But, more, the demands of knowing force us to hold our convictions with some humility. It is true that if we were born into a different community with a different tradition, then we would look at the world in a different way. Conceit and certainty are prohibited. The fruits of the Spirit, which are described in Galatians, are an inevitable outcome of the knowing process. Now, it is true that some people do manage to be certain and conceited, but it is also clear that such certainty and conceit are not justified, given what we know about the challenges of knowing.

One helpful resource at this point is "virtue epistemology." Virtue epistemology is a version of reliabilism—the view that a justified belief arises from a reliable faculty or process. It was Ernest Sosa, in 1980, who suggested that the category "intellectual virtue" is helpful: It is the type of person seeking the truth that matters.[79] With Linda Zagzebski, there was a shift. She suggested that "virtue epistemology" should be modeled on virtue ethics. She writes:

> I think of intellectual virtues as traits such as intellectual autonomy and courage, intellectual carefulness and fairness, and open-mindedness, but . . . I regard reliability as a component of virtue. An intellectual virtue, like a moral virtue, has a motivational component as well as a component of reliable success in reaching the end (if any) of the motivational component. What makes intellectual virtues intellectual is that they (or most of them) include motive dispositions connected with the motive to get truth, and reliability is entailed by the success component of the virtue. This strategy shows how the internalist feature of responsibility and the externalist feature of epistemic success can be combined in a unified concept—indeed, a concept that has a long history in ethics. In my view, justification is not the most important concept in epistemic evaluation; a justified belief ought to be analyzed as the parallel of a right act

in pure virtue ethics. The issue of whether a rational cognitive structure is foundationalist or coherentist is also a derivative matter, determined by what intellectually virtuous persons do. The evaluative component of knowledge is not justification, but what I call an "act of intellectual virtue." The theory is normative, but it can be interpreted as naturalistic in the sense in which Aristotle's ethics is naturalistic. That is, it does not reduce epistemic evaluative properties to natural properties, but what counts as a virtue, whether moral or epistemic, is intimately connected with the way human beings are constructed by nature.[80]

This is the way forward. Knowing is not simply arriving at truth about the world; instead, how we arrive at that truth is as important. The intellectual virtues of courage, open-mindedness, and fairness are vehicles that assist us in knowing that we have arrived at the truth. Theological Traditioned Truth wants to affirm this basic insight. The Christian can, and should, claim that part of the reason why knowing is so complicated is because God is interested in the virtuous life of the mind of the agent doing the knowing. Virtue epistemology is right to capture that a justified belief is linked, in part, to the intellectual depth and rigor of the person holding the belief.

Virtue epistemology is helpful on another level. Staying with the analogy with virtue ethics, doing the right action is good, but being a good person is better. When we take seriously our agency in the knowing process, this opens up possibilities that can link knowing and justice. Accounts of the world need to recognize a fundamental obligation to describe the world in such a way that it supports justice. This is where Jantzen is right: views of the world have significant consequences. Now, it may be objected that the truth might be unjust—a version of Satanism might be true. So, this is also a theological claim: Given we believe that at the heart of the universe is love and justice, it follows that any account of the universe must ultimately have loving and just consequences.

5. Centrality of practices can be a way of knowing Of the many factors that help us discover the truth (e.g., coherence, weighing of arguments, implications in terms of justice, etc.), practices are especially important. Strictly rational reflection can only get us so far: true knowledge depends on experience. This principle has a wide application. One does not know what it is like to be a parent unless one has a child. Imaginative reflection is always insufficient. Knowledge of parenting arises as the life is born, the connection between the parent and child is made, and the endless hours of worrying about that dependent life. What is true of parenting (and love and playing a musical instrument and knowing how to score a goal in soccer and countless other forms of knowledge) is also true in theology. In this respect, William James is right. Knowledge comes through practices. Christians claim that if time is created in a day for prayer, then the experience of prayer can make you aware of the presence of God. It is as one embarks on the practices that the truth of Christianity is discovered.

6. *A revealed theology: God seeks to be an agent helping us to see*
Torrance makes the argument that Scripture teaches that knowledge of God in Christ is itself dependent on repentance and recognition that God is the agent that helps us see the truth of the revelation. At this point, we have a revealed theology. There is a circular dimension to this position: If one believes Scripture is the revelation of God to humanity, then one will see that Scripture is the revelation of God to humanity. However, one cannot escape that part of the biblical witness that does involve this circle. The predicament is this. The human capacity to understand the truth of the revelation of God has been distorted by sin. Therefore, repentance is essential because it enables God to provide the grace to see the truth of the revelation.

This argument can be framed in both a strong form and a weak form. The strong form would be that all forms of natural theology are impossible and that other religions are misguided. This position has its roots in Martin Luther and John Calvin. As already indicated, I have sympathies with natural theology and would like to see other religious traditions as partners in the theological quest, with insights that we—as Christians—need to accommodate. The weaker form is that the act of opening ourselves to God (with appropriate authenticity and sincerity) creates the space for God to open our eyes (to use a popular biblical metaphor) to see part of the truth. In other words, we embark on certain practices (see point five) and, in so doing, God becomes an agent in the knowing process and helps us see the truth of the revelation.

7. *The invitation to trust* The picture of knowing that is being suggested here culminates in an invitation to trust. Now, trust is a disposition that goes beyond the evidence. One trusts an authority—the car mechanic, the accountant, and so on—when there are reputable credentials (e.g., a degree); previous positive experience (e.g., in the past, they gave good, informed advice); and no contrary evidence (e.g., there are no reports of malfeasance). When these conditions are met, trust is appropriate.

So, why does one trust the disclosure of God in Jesus Christ? It is important to note that it is the Incarnation that is the locus of revelation (more will be said about this in the next chapter). With Theological Traditioned Truth, we have an answer. We recognize the limitations of all processes of knowing. We are not invited to be certain completely. Instead, we step out and pray, we sense that the world is intended and ultimately loving. We apply our rational faculties and have good reasons to affirm the reality of God and the promise of God's disclosure. We recognize that the disclosure of God has taken a different form in different places: we celebrate areas of agreement and recognize also areas of disagreement. Given our location in the Christian tradition, we give appropriate scrutiny to the claims of the Incarnation. We work diligently to provide a coherent account. We examine the evidence. Although never completely sure, we find ourselves trusting the witness of the disciples (almost all of whom were martyred for their witness) that in Jesus they saw God. We then step into the circle trusting that the witness of Jesus to the transcendent is true. It is to our Christology that we need to turn to next.

NOTES

1. Naturally, it is an important question as to whether there are other spiritual entities. Islam, for example, talks of Jinn. As I will argue in this chapter, we need grounds to trust a description of the spiritual realm. And this is a central claim that Christians want to make for Jesus Christ.

2. 9-11 Truthers claim that the neoconservatives in the Bush administration needed a pretext for their military adventure in Iraq. This pretext was to organize the destruction of the World Trade Center. The best statement of this very unlikely argument comes from the distinguished philosopher David Ray Griffin. See David Ray Griffin, *Christian Faith and the Truth Behind 9/11: A Call to Reflection and Action* (Louisville, KY: Westminster John Knox Press, 2006). For my own attack on Griffin's position, see Ian S. Markham, *Go Into All the World: Faith and Engagement*, edited by Shireen R. Baker (Alexandria, VA: VTS Press, 2011).

3. Area 51 in Nevada has led to a proliferation of alien abduction stories. For a good study, see Bridget Brown, *They Know Us Better Than We Know Ourselves: The History and Politics of Alien Abduction* (New York: NYU Press, 2007). She writes, "Some of the hottest spots on this fantastic dystopian map of the United States include Groom Lake/Area 51 near Nellis Air Force Base in Nevada and Hangar 19 in Wright Patterson Air Force Base in Ohio, where alien technology and bodies are believed to be stored" (p. 127).

4. Alan G. Padgett, "Practical Objectivity: Keeping Natural Science Natural," in B. Stump and Alan G. Padgett (ed.), *The Blackwell Companion to Science and Christianity* (Oxford: Wiley Blackwell, 2012).

5. See Alasdair MacIntyre, *Whose Justice? Which Rationality?* (London: Duckworth, 1988). The full name for his approach is actually "tradition-constituted and tradition-constitutive enquiry" (p. 389).

6. Ibid. For Aquinas see Thomas Aquinas (*Summa Theologiae*, II, II, Q. 92, art 1). For Angelo da Chivasso see Summa Angelica, published in 1486.

7. Ibid., p. 341.
8. Ibid., p. 341.
9. Ibid., p. 341.
10. Ibid., p. 341.
11. Ibid., p. 341.
12. MacIntyre, *Whose Justice? Which Rationality?*, p. 356.
13. Ibid., p. 357.
14. Ibid., p. 357.
15. Paul Davies, *God and the New Physics* (New York: Touchstone, 1983), p. 116.
16. Don Cupitt has a vast and complex corpus. In the summary that follows, two texts are primary—*Taking Leave of God* and *Creation Out of Nothing*. Cupitt has also generated a significant secondary literature. One of the best studies is Gavin Hyman, *The Predicament of Postmodern Theology: Radical Orthodoxy or Nihilist Textualism?* (Louisville, KY: Westminster John Knox Press, 2001).

17. Michael Dummett, "Realism," in *Truth and Other Enigmas* (London: Duckworth 1978), p. 146.

18. Richard Rorty, *Contingency, Irony, and Solidarity* (Cambridge, UK: Cambridge University Press, 1989), p. 5.

19. Don Cupitt, *Creation Out of Nothing* (London: SCM Press, 1990), pp. 15–16.

20. Don Cupitt, *Taking Leave of God* (London: SCM Press, 1980), p. 108.
21. Ibid., p. 113.
22. I make this argument in *Truth and Reality of God* (Edinburgh: T&T Clark, 1998).
23. For a good discussion, see Scott Cowdell, *Atheist Priest?: Don Cupitt and Christianity* (London: SCM Press, 1988).
24. John Hick, *An Interpretation of Religion: Human Responses to the Transcendent* (New Haven, CT: Yale University Press, 1989), p. 175.
25. Ibid., p. 177.
26. Ibid., p. 177.
27. Ibid., p. 178.
28. Ibid., p. 179.
29. Ibid., p. 364.
30. Ibid., p. 364.
31. Ibid., p. 343. This is Hick's description.
32. Ibid., pp. 249–351.
33. David Cheetham, *John Hick: A Critical Introduction and Reflection* (Aldershot, UK: Ashgate, 2003), p. 144.
34. Grace Jantzen, *God's World, God's Body* (Louisville, KY: Westminster John Knox, 1984).
35. Grace Jantzen, *Becoming Divine* (Bloomington, IN and Indianapolis, IN: Indiana University Press, 1999), p. 20.
36. Ibid., p. 25.
37. Ibid., p. 29.
38. Ibid., p. 230.
39. Ibid., p. 130.
40. Grace Jantzen, *Death and the Displacement of Beauty: Foundations of Violence* (London and New York: Routledge, 2004). The phrase "western symbolic" is used on page 5.
41. Ibid, p. 91.
42. Ibid., p. 298.
43. Jantzen, *Becoming Divine*, p. 61.
44. Ibid., p 254.
45. Grace Jantzen, *Death and Displacement of Beauty: A Place of Springs*, edited by Jeremy Carrette and Morny Joy (London and New York: Routledge, 2010), p. 87.
46. Ibid., pp. 87–88.
47. Elaine Graham, "Redeeming the Present," in Elaine Graham, *Grace Jantzen : Redeeming the Present*, pp. 13–14 (Farnham, UK: Ashgate, 2013). The first quotation from Graham is from Jantzen, *Becoming Divine*, p. 254. The second quotation is from Jantzen, "Flourishing: Towards an Ethics of Natality," *Feminist Theory* 2/2 (2001): 219.
48. Jantzen, *Becoming Divine*, pp. 42–43.
49. Paul Stob, in his excellent study documents with some care, shows precisely how William James developed his extraordinary public profile. It was very much by design. See Paul Stob, *Rhetoric & Public Affairs: William James and the Art of Popular Statement* (East Lansing, MI: Michigan State University Press, 2013).
50. William James, *Will to Believe: And Other Essays in Popular Philosophy* (Auckland, NZ: The Floating Press, 1912), p. 15.
51. Ibid., p. 24.
52. John Hick, *Faith and Knowledge* (Ithaca, NY: Cornell University Press, 1957), p. 48.
53. Ibid., p. 48.
54. Robert J. O'Connell, S. J., *William James on the Courage to Believe* (New York: Fordham University Press, 1984), p. 47.
55. James, *Will to Believe*, p. 18.
56. Hick, *Faith and Knowledge*, p. 48.
57. James, *Will to Believe*, p. 31. The reference to Clifford is to William Clifford, *The Ethics of Belief and Other Essays*, introduction, by Timothy J. Madigan (Amherst, NY: Prometheus Books, 1999).

58. The list is long. However, the following would express sympathy with a postliberal approach: William C. Placher, Lewis Ayres, L. Gregory Jones, Stanley Hauerwas, Paul J. Griffiths, Bruce Marshall, and Reinhard Huetter.

59. George A. Lindbeck, *The Nature of Doctrine: Religion and Theology in a Postliberal Age* (London: SPCK, 1984), p. 16.

60. John Allen Knight, *Liberalism versus Post liberalism: The Great Divide in Twentieth-Century Theology* (New York: Oxford University Press, 2013), p. 203, footnote 17.

61. Ibid., p. 243.

62. Ibid., p. 263.

63. Alan J. Torrance, "Auditus Fidei: Where and How Does God Speak? Faith, Reason, and the Question of Criteria," in Paul J. Griffiths and Reinhard Hütter (eds.), *Reason and the Reasons of Faith* (New York and London: T&T Clark, 2005), p 28.

64. Ibid., p. 29.

65. Alvin Plantinga, *God and Other Minds: A Study of the Rational Justification of Belief in God* (Ithaca, NY and London: Cornell University Press, 1967), p. 271. He does not use the language of "properly basic" in this book. This came later. Plantinga is known as the leading light in the school of Reformed epistemology—so called because John Calvin is given the credit for emphasizing how belief in God is a legitimate assumption of life rather than a deduction from other data.

66. Torrance, "Auditus Fidei," p. 44.

67. Ibid., p. 44. Torrance is quoting Bonhoeffer, *Christology*, translated by John Bowden (London: Collins, 1966), pp. 32–33.

68. Ibid., p. 30.

69. Ibid., p. 29, footnote 7.

70. John Milbank, *Theology and Social Theory* (Oxford: Basil Blackwell, 1990), p. 330.

71. Ibid., p. 389.

72. Richard Swinburne, *Revelation: From Metaphor to Analogy* (Oxford: Clarendon Press 1992), pp.71–72.

73. Ibid., p. 76.

74. Ibid., p. 78.

75. Ibid., p. 83.

76. Keith Ward, *Religion and Revelation: A Theology of Revelation in the World Religions* (Oxford: Clarendon Press, 1994), p. 319.

77. Ibid., p. 320.

78. For an extended discussion of the nature of logic, see my book *Truth and the Reality of God* (Edinburgh: T&T Clark, 1998).

79. For Ernest Sosa, see his Ernest Sosa, *Knowledge in Perspective* (Cambridge: Cambridge University Press, 1991).

80. Linda Zagzebski, *Virtue Epistemology: Essays on Epistemic Virtue and Responsibility* (Cary, NC: Oxford University Press (US), 2001), p. 5.

Chapter Five

The Incarnation and the Trinity

Theological Reasoning in the Christian Tradition

In the last chapter, what I am calling Theological Traditioned Truth was explained. Grounded in "critical realism"—the view that the task of language is to construct accounts of our experience of the world that makes sense and explains the complexity as best as the account can—this approach acknowledges the traditioned nature of all-knowing and recognizes that God is at work in the task of revelation through the knowing process. Using this approach, the task now is to explicate the spiritually infused universe.

Now, an abstract sense that the universe is spiritually infused is of limited value. That we should experience the world as textured is not the same as knowing in what ways the universe is spiritually infused. At this point, the concept of revelation needs to be developed and defended. Some account of some authority that can tell us what the spiritual realm is like is needed. Two key Christian doctrines clarify both the authority and the appropriate way to reason to truth in the Christian doctrine. Those doctrines are (a) the Incarnation and (b) the Trinity. The Incarnation is the supreme witness of the disclosure of God made flesh—the very Wisdom of God in our midst. The Trinity is the way in which that disclosure is made compatible with our understanding that God is One and, therefore, models "theological reasoning" in the Christian tradition.

These two doctrines will be explored together. As a matter of history, Christian thought about these two ideas has meshed together. But, as we justify the "trust" that we are placing in the revelation of God in Christ, we can also understand how we "think" as Christians. We will see how patterns of thought emerged that help us reason to the truth that Christians want to affirm.

THE NEW TESTAMENT, THE INCARNATION, AND THE TRINITY

The model of theological reasoning in the Christian tradition is the doctrine of the Trinity. It is the defining and central claim Christians make about God. The doctrine of the Trinity is interesting. One does not find the doctrine directly explicated in Scripture. There is no proof text. Instead, it is a reflection on Christian experience, or, as John Macquarrie puts it, "it is language rooted in existence, in the community's experience of God."[1]

The origins of the doctrine of the Trinity are subject to lively debate. Matthew Bates, in his helpful book *The Birth of the Trinity*, identifies four approaches to the doctrine among theologians.[2] The first, he calls "Trinitarianism by Encounter with the Historical Jesus." This is the position Jules Lebreton[3] and, in a more popular version, C. S. Lewis.[4] It can be simply stated: The encounter with Jesus (and perhaps the Holy Spirit) forced the disciples to think in new categories, which became trinitarian. This position sees the doctrine of the Trinity fairly explicitly in the New Testament. It was a short step from the New Testament to Nicaea. The second position, Bates calls "Trinitarianism by Hellenistic Philosophical Imposition." This is the position of Adolf von Harnack.[5] On this view, there was a conflict between the Jewish church and the Hellenistic church. The latter brought concepts and language from Greek philosophy and imposed such language on the Christian story. The result, centuries later, was a doctrine that Jesus probably would not have recognized. The third position is "Trinitarianism as the Outgrowth of Mediated Jewish Monotheism." This approach stresses that there were plenty of quasi-divine figures found within monotheistic Second Temple Judaism. Larry Hurtado is an advocate of this position.[6] Hurtado marvels at the way Jesus was worshipped within the world of first-century Judaism and argues that it should be linked to a developing sense of divine agency. The fourth approach is the one advocated by Bates himself (although he has sympathies with the third). It is the "Trinitarianism by Continuity in Prosopological Exegesis." *Prosopopoeia* (which literally means character making) is a rhetorical strategy where the voice of another is used to impart a message. So, all those moments when Paul in the New Testaments puts words from the Old Testament into the mouth of Jesus our Lord can be seen as a sibling method of *prosopopoeia*.

An alternative map starts with Jewish monotheism. James F. McGrath, in his *The Only True God: Early Christian Monotheism in Its Jewish Context*, sets out a range of options. First, there are development theories. This subdivides into two types: the first sees the doctrine of the Trinity as a development of Christian experience—this is where he places Hurtado; the second sees the doctrine as a development from outside Christianity, which leads Christianity away from its Jewish roots (this is the position of Maurice Casey).[7]

In contrast to development theories, there are static theories. The representative advocate for a static theory is Richard Bauckham.[8] Here, Judaism was always dynamic: so the doctrine of the Trinity is not really a development but part of the internal dynamism of the Trinity. So Jewish monotheism was always flexible. Bauckham sees Jewish monotheism involving a "divine identity" that includes function, liturgy, and ontology.

Now, for McGrath, he takes the view that the position "that seems most promising emphasizes that the early Christian view of Jesus represented an adaptation within Judeo-Christian monotheism rather than a departure from it."[9] Although McGrath is not entirely happy with any of the options, his sympathies are more with Hurtado and Bauckham than Casey.

One cannot help but read Hurtado's impressive study and recognize that first-century Jews did have the apparatus to recognize in Jesus the eternal Word. Hurtado summarizes his position thus: "The high place of Jesus in the beliefs and religious practice of Judean Christianity that comes across in this evidence confirms how astonishingly early and quickly an impressive devotion to Jesus appeared. This, in turn, helps explain why and how it all seems to have been so conventionalized and uncontroversial already by the time of the Pauline mission to the Gentiles in the 50s."[10] Jesus, Hurtado shows, is granted a devotion that normally is kept for God alone. Hurtado makes the argument by identifying six features of Christian worship: the hymns that both celebrate Christ and are sung to him; prayers, some in liturgies, that are addressed to Christ; the use of the name of Jesus; the act of baptizing in the name of Jesus; the significance of the Lord's Supper; the confessions of faith in Jesus; and the words of the risen Christ having a prophetic dimension. Hurtado's overall argument, developed both in *Lord Jesus Christ* and, perhaps, for my purposes, his more recent study *How on Earth Did Jesus Become a God? Historical Questions about Earliest Devotion to Jesus*, has the following steps. Second-Temple devout Jews provided the group in which followers of Jesus developed a devotion to Jesus firmly rooted in a commitment to the one God of the Old Testament. A key text for this devotion within Jewish monotheism is Philippians 2: 5–11. There, explains Hurtado, we find "an astonishing 'binitarian' view, in which Jesus is linked with God and with divine purposes in an unprecedented way."[11] This did indeed generate major opposition, both within Judaism and among the Roman authorities. Persecution became the norm. Now, what exactly made the resurrected Jesus God? Here, Hurtado explains:

> Within the early Christian circles of the first few years (perhaps even the first few weeks), individuals had powerful revelatory experiences that they understood to be encounters with the glorified Jesus. Some also had experiences that they took to be visions of the exalted Jesus in heavenly glory, being reverenced in cultic actions by the transcendent being traditionally identified as charged

with fulfilling the heavenly liturgy (e.g., angels, the "living creatures," and so on). Some received prophetic inspirations to announce the exaltation of Jesus to God's right hand and to summon the elect in God's name to register in cultic actions their acceptance of God's will that Jesus be reverenced. Through such revelatory experiences, Christological convictions and corresponding cultic practices were born that amounted to a unique "mutation" in what was acceptable Jewish monotheistic devotional practice of the Greco-Roman period.[12]

Hurtado is right: the evidence does suggest that a conceptually lively Judaism did allow categories to emerge that made sense of the encounter with the Jesus. At the heart of devotion to Jesus is an experience—an experience of the resurrected Jesus. As Christians worked to make sense of this, the Church determined that in Jesus we see the Eternal Wisdom, the very Word of God, embodied in that life.

THE INCARNATION

Chalcedon, in 451 CE, largely got it right.[13] "We all with one voice confess our Lord Jesus Christ . . . truly God and truly human, the same consisting of a reasonable soul and a body, of one substance with the Father as touching the Godhead, of one substance with us as touching the humanity . . . to be acknowledged in two natures, without confusion, without change, without division, without separation."[14] To protect the experience of God disclosed in Christ, Christians need to believe that Jesus is completely human and yet, simultaneously, completely divine. We need to exclude any discourse that implies that Jesus is less than fully human and less than fully divine. As a theodicy, revelation, and a mechanism of salvation, we must be able to say that Jesus was really a person—as we are. But we also must be able to say that Jesus was really God—the creator of the universe.

William C. Placher notes how the Council of Chalcedon was following three principles. These are: first, the Council deliberately avoids the question of "how" exactly we can affirm this view of Christ. Placher writes, "Notice that the crucial section consists of four negatives: the two natures are without confusion, change, division, or separation. Those negatives draw the line against potential errors. They do not claim to penetrate the mystery of God far enough to understand how the relevant mechanisms work."[15] Second, the Council wanted to clarify that there were "two whats and one who."[16] So, what was Jesus? Jesus was both God and human. Who was Jesus? The one historical person who did a variety of things on Earth. And the third, explains Placher, is:

> In the relation of human and divine in Christ, however, there is always a kind of asymmetry. He acts both humanly and divinely, but the human in him is always obedient to the divine. The divine takes priority. That's what Chalce-

don kept from the Alexandrian tradition, where the divine Word was always the agent in Christ. In the incarnation of the divine Word, however, humanity is transformed—not just for Jesus but for all of us. It has become a different thing to be a human being.[17]

The political implications of the Incarnation are significant. And this, crucially, is a key part of the divine revelation. God is demonstrating the infinite value of human lives by becoming incarnate. God is teaching us that God really cares, showing us God's real nature.

A key part of the Christian response to *anafühl* is the conviction that God has indicated the importance of people by the Incarnation. *Anafühl* is the mood that finds the idea that the Creator of this 13.7-billion-year-old universe can take an interest in this fortuitous product of the evolutionary tale. Christians should understand this reaction: It is amazing. But the Christian claim is that it is both amazing and true. This was a crucial implication of the Council of Chalcedon.

But, is it true? The conceptual problems with the Incarnation are best handled by the recognition that we need a dynamic model of identity with a kenotic emphasis. In my judgment, many difficulties with the Incarnation are caused by an insufficiently dynamic model of identity. What does it mean for Jesus to be identical with God? If one operates with Leibniz's Law of Identity, then we rapidly run into problems. In what is called the "indiscernibility of identicals" by philosophers, the view emerged that for two things to be identical, they must have all properties in common. With God and Jesus, the problems are obvious: God is transcendent and omnipotent; Jesus is finite and limited. It is clear that they cannot be identical.

However, if we work with a more dynamic model of identical, then it might be possible to see how God and Jesus can be identical. One can arrive at a more dynamic model of identity if one thinks of the way in which a five-year-old child grows into a forty-year-old adult. There is a unique connection between the child and the subsequent adult. They are identical, despite the numerous differences, because there is a unique continuity that connects the youth with the adult.

This chapter is deliberately weaving the doctrine of the Incarnation with the doctrine of the Trinity. And at this point, the Trinity can help us with the challenge of making sense of the Incarnation. It is not necessary for Christians to believe that all of God is incarnate in Christ. Although Jesus is "all God," it is not true that all of God is in Jesus. If we did believe that all of God is in Jesus, then we would have no one sustaining the universe when Jesus was dying on the cross. It is the second person of the Trinity who is present in Jesus. The second person of the Trinity is, of course, inseparable from the other members of the Godhead, but that does not preclude the possibility of talking about a distinctive aspect of God's being in Jesus. The doctrine of the

Incarnation involves the eternal Word (i.e., the revealing, disclosing aspect of God) being completely and uniquely present in the life, death, and resurrection of Jesus. Jesus, then, is identical with God in this way: the eternal Word completely permeates the humanity of Jesus. This is done not in a way that eradicates the humanity but uses the humanity to disclose and reveal God.

Using Theological Traditioned Truth as our approach to the process of knowing, it does seem reasonable for a person who is engaging with the New Testament to determine that an Incarnational interpretation of that life and experience is legitimate. As we read the New Testament, we have sufficient clues to know that it took some time for Jesus to realize that, in his mind, there were two poles—a human pole and a divine pole. It is clear from the Gospels that Jesus was human: He wept, was hungry, tired, and exhausted by the crowds. It is also clear from the Gospels that Jesus knew he had a close relationship with God: He was intimate with his heavenly Father. The doctrine of the Incarnation does not require that Jesus know who he was. Brian Hebblethwaite makes the point well when he writes:

> As a human being, he shared a first-century Jewish, Palestinian, perspective. In all probability, he was unaware of who, ultimately speaking, he really was. As a human being, he was probably conscious only of a closeness to God, his heavenly Father, of the powerful and compelling inspiration of the Spirit, and of an unquestionable authority to speak and act for God among his fellow Jews. He shared many of the demonological categories of the day, regarding what we call epilepsy or schizophrenia as possession. And he shared much of the apocalyptic framework of first-century Judaism, even to the extent of expecting the "end" within the lifetime of his disciples.[18]

Hebblethwaite is advocating a "kenotic" Christology. Such a Christology admits that the second person of the Trinity—the eternal Word—"sets aside" or "empties" or "limits" the divine attributes to enable the Son to become human. However, the eternal Word is speaking when Jesus teaches us about the love and demands of God. And the eternal Word is at work when, out of love for humanity, Jesus is willing to go to the cross and die.

God was in Christ. This is the distinctive claim that Christians want to make. Although easy to misunderstand, we can provide an account of the Incarnation, which is true to the evidence of the New Testament and, at the same time, is coherent and plausible.

REASONING TO THE TRINITY

Having arrived at the Incarnation, we now return to the Trinity. Trinitarian discussion over the last twenty years has focused on the Social Trinity. Grounded in the work of Jürgen Moltmann, it sets forth a distinctive understanding of God. For Moltmann, it is wrong to start with the unity of God and talk about different aspects (or whatever) as the Trinity. He thinks this ignores the biblical witness, which sees dynamic relationality at the heart of God. God really is three centers of consciousness, all in perfect harmony, each involved in the work of the other, and modeling together a non-hierarchal way of being. In *The Crucified God*, he develops the implications of the Social Trinity in a very vivid way.

In an extended discussion of protest atheism (i.e., the view that one cannot believe in God because morally a good God cannot create such a painful and suffering-filled world), Moltmann argues that

> the only way past protest atheism is through a theology of the cross which understands God as the suffering God in the suffering of Christ and which cries out with the godforsaken God, "My God, why have you forsaken me?" For this theology, God and suffering are no longer contradictions, as in theism and atheism, but God's being is in suffering and the suffering is in God's being itself, because God is love. It takes the "metaphysical rebellion" up into itself because it recognizes in the cross of Christ a rebellion in metaphysics or better, a rebellion in God himself: God himself loves and suffers the death of Christ in his love.[19]

A key text for Moltmann is the cry of despair uttered by Jesus on the cross—"My God, my God, why have you forsaken me?" (Mark 15:34). For Moltmann, this is true. The Father has indeed deserted the Son. Suffering is now known right at the heart of the experience of God. Moltmann explains, "The Son suffers dying, the Father suffers the death of the Son. The grief of the Father here is just as important as the death of the Son. The Fatherlessness of the Son is matched by the Sonlessness of the Father...."[20]

Moltmann claims as his inspiration the work of Orthodox theologians who start with the differences between the persons of the Trinity and work back to a unity. For Moltmann, there are three persons who unite to form one God. And in the mystery of the Incarnation and the Crucifixion, God feels both pain and hurt as the Father lets the Son die.

Building on this idea, Moltmann's fullest account of the Trinity is found in *The Trinity and the Kingdom: The Doctrine of God*. Moltmann starts by complaining that too much theology has been written assuming a certain inflexible account of God's unity. Instead, we need to start with the Biblical witness and then think through an account of God's unity. So explains Moltmann, his intent is "to start with the special Christian tradition of the history of Jesus the Son, and from that to develop a historical doctrine of the Trinity."[21] His point is that when one reads the New Testament text closely, one can see a dynamic interplay between the Father and the Son (in particular) but also with the Spirit. This dynamic interplay needs to be taken much more seriously.

When it comes to his interpretation of the Trinity, Moltmann stresses the inter-relationships within the Trinity. So, the Father should not be understood as a remote, austere entity that rules the world but instead as that which eternally begets the Son. So Moltmann writes:

> [I]n the Christian understanding of God the Father, what is meant is not "the Father of the Universe," but simply and exclusively "the Father of the Son" Jesus Christ. It is solely the Father of Jesus Christ whom we believe and acknowledge created the world. . . . If God is the Father of this Son Jesus Christ, and if he is only "our Father" for his Son's sake, then we can also only call him "Abba," beloved Father, in the spirit of free sonship.[22]

So, the Trinity is not defined in terms of role but in terms of relationships. And as we understand the relationships within the Trinity, so we understand how we should relate to God.

Moltmann's treatment of the Son is similar: the emphasis on the relationship with the Father. Given it is the eternal Son who becomes human and dies, Moltmann emphasizes the difference in relation. Moltmann explains:

> The love of the Father for the Son, and the love of the Son for the Father are not the same—are not even congruent—simply because they are differently constituted. They do not stand in an equal reciprocal relationship to one another. The Father loves the Son with an engendering, fatherly love. The Son loves the Father with a responsive, self-giving love. . . . [T]he Son's sacrifice of boundless love on Golgotha is from eternity already included in the exchange of the essential, the consubstantial love which constitutes the divine life of the Trinity. The fact that the Son dies on the cross, delivering himself up to that death, is part of the eternal obedience which he renders to the Father in his whole being through the Spirit, whom he receives from the Father.[23]

For Moltmann, the answer to the question—why was it the Son who came and died and not some other member of the Trinity?—is embedded in the nature of the relationship between the Father and the Son.

Traditionally, the Spirit has always been associated with breath. In the resurrection appearance in John 20, Jesus "breathed" on the apostles and said to them, "Receive the Holy Spirit" (John 20:22). Moltmann develops this when he links the Spirit with the Son. He writes:

> [T]he inner coherence immediately becomes perceptible when we understand the Son as *the Word* (Logos). The Father utters his eternal Word in the eternal breathing out of his Spirit. There is no Word without the Spirit, and no Spirit without the Word.[24]

The point is that in the same way humans cannot have words without breath, so we cannot have the Word of God (the Son) without the breath (of the

Spirit). Both proceed from the Father (so, on this point, Moltmann agrees with the Eastern Church).

Moltmann believes that a very different politics will emerge from this understanding of God. The logic of monotheism, argues Moltmann, is monarchism.[25] The purpose of this social account of the Trinity is to challenge this monarchism. Moltmann writes:

> The doctrine of the Trinity which evolves out of the surmounting of monotheism for Christ's sake, must therefore also overcome this monarchism, which legitimates dependency, helplessness and servitude. This doctrine of the Trinity must be developed as the true theological doctrine of freedom.[26]

This extended discussion of Moltmann's views is intended to establish an important principle. One can "reason" appropriately in the Christian tradition and arrive at options that Christians can consider, which may not be true. Theological Traditioned Truth does permit a pluralism of metaphysical options to emerge. However, the account that I shall now offer is at the other end of the spectrum from this emphasis on three centers of consciousness in the mind of God.

Katherine Sonderegger makes the oneness of God central. Therefore, she writes on Moltmann:

> The theology undertaken here, a doctrine of God stubbornly taking its bearings from the Divine Oneness, must simply quietly, but firmly, say no; no, to such radical cruciformity in the doctrine of God, such radical rejection of monotheism and its exposition of Divine Perfections. Once again we must quietly state that Christology cannot be the sole measure, ground, and matter of the doctrine of God; there is more, infinitely more to the One, Eternal God.[27]

Sonderegger writes with a sensitivity to Judaism and the sense that Christians are worshipping the God of the Shema. Moltmann has a plurality at the heart of the God that manifestly conflicts with the monotheism that Christians share with Jews. Keith Ward concedes that the Biblical witness is suggestive of a Social Trinity but then shares the concern of Sonderegger that ultimately the Social Trinity is too problematic. He writes, "I concluded that the idea of the social Trinity not only threatens belief in one supreme God, but cannot be supported by argument and undermines the strongest reason for creation— namely that the perfection of the divine being is expressed uniquely and graciously in the relationship and responsiveness to created beings that only a communion of love can provide."[28] Ward's point about the social Trinity undermining the doctrine of creation is helpful. The emphasis in Moltmann that a loving God must have loving relations within the Godhead overlooks the idea that a key reason for creation was that God aspired to create more loving relationships with creatures capable of giving and receiving love.

Ward advocates for a "one-consciousness" account of the Trinity. He makes much of the doctrine of *perichoresis*—the co-indwelling of the three persons. Unlike those who want to argue that the Son has experiences that the Father does not have, Ward suggests that we need to talk about "one experience-stream in God, but that stream is complex."[29] The different persons bring different experiences to the one experience stream. So, we have a picture emerging of one God, with three different aspects. Ward writes:

> God as Father remains transcendent to all creation. God as Son manifests in creation. God as Spirit unites creation to the divine. It is one God, one omniscient and omnipotent being, who has these three aspects or modes of being. It is the threefold God who is omnipotent in the uniquely strong sense that God is the source of everything other than God and can intend and create without reference to any other being. The Father, the Word, and the Spirit have no independent wills, since they necessarily will all things in common. They have no private knowledge, since each person knows all that the others think and do. But they have different sources of knowledge (as transcendent, incarnate, and immanent in created things), and they do different things (support all things, suffer, and strive within human hearts). Word and Spirit implement the Father's will in particular ways, unique to them. Moreover, they necessarily cooperate in every divine action, contributing a particular element to every divine action (sustaining, manifesting, and cooperatively inspiring), which is the case is the action of all of them together. A "divine person" in this sense is not an individual substance of a rational nature—or at least that is an inadequate and misleading way of putting it. A divine person is a necessarily inseparable, complementary, and interconnected co-agent in every divine action, having no independent knowledge or will but implementing the will of God in a distinctive form of action and experience proper to it. Each person is a co-consciousness and co-agency, and inseparably together they constitute the one ungenerated and unrestrictedly omnipotent source of all.[30]

At this point, the specter of modalism looms. The problem with modalism is that the three modes of God do not describe the reality of God. This is especially true of chronological modalism; where the Father creates, the Son incarnates, and the Spirit comes to usher in the age of the church. Which of these three modes really captures God? Ward describes this objection and then responds:

> The three "persons" are like masks which God may put on or take off for specific purposes—a position which the words *persona* or *prosopon* readily suggest. This position would be denied if it was held that God really is threefold essentially and originally, permanently, indissolubly, and irreducibly. It is not an *option* for God to be threefold—that is what God essentially is. And God is not sometimes one person and sometimes another—God is always threefold. The position I hold is not modalist, in the meaning of the word, because God is essentially threefold.[31]

This is right, but Ward does need to go further. The question can still be asked: How do we know that this essential threefold is really showing us the reality of God? And the answer is that each aspect is part of the "one-experience stream." The three aspects of God cannot ever show us the complete, infinite nature of God; but the aspects of God we experience are all truly God, and the aspects are all feeding into this one-experience stream.

SOME TRINITARIAN COMPLEXITIES

There is a certain conceptual lack of clarity in many discussions of the Trinity. There are two areas that need attention. The first is the connection with the historical Jesus and the preexistent Christ, the Word, the Wisdom of God. The second is a cluster of issues around gender and the Trinity.

Dealing with the first, Stephen Webb flirts with the idea that historical Jesus, himself, somehow preexisted: the very flesh being part of God. His description of the Trinity is as follows: "God the Father is material (in a way we cannot completely imagine or understand) without being full corporeal, God the Son is anthropomorphically corporeal (and thus material in a way that is different from the Father), and God the Holy Spirit is the love they share—and it is this love that dynamically directs matter towards corporeal form."[32] Webb gently teases Robert Jenson and insists that the creedal claim, "We believe in one Lord, Jesus Christ. . . . For us and for our salvation he came down from heaven," means that we must have a pre-existent Jesus in heaven.[33] Webb's overall position seems to be a social Trinity with a Mormon materiality. Placher is more careful when he writes the following: "*Whenever* God is revealed, it is the Word, the second person of the Trinity, the one who became incarnate in Jesus, who is God's self-revelation."[34] Here, there seems to be clear differentiation between the eternal Word—the Son—in the life of God and the historical Jesus, in whom the Word dwelt. On this view, it sounds like the eternal Word is bigger than the historical Jesus. At the Virgin Birth, on this account, we get the flesh of the Incarnate Word. Placher goes on to quote Calvin, "The God who of old appeared to the patriarchs was no other than Christ," and Irenaeus, "For he is it who sailed along with Noah, and who guided Abraham; who was bound along with Isaac, and was a Wanderer with Jacob...God of God, Son of the Father, Jesus Christ."[35] For Placher's earlier emphasis on the Word being incarnate but not synonymous with the historical Jesus to work, one would need to interpret in Calvin and Irenaeus as "Christ" being differentiated in some sense from the historical Jesus.

The account of the Trinity outlined above sees the eternal Word is made manifest in the historical Jesus of Nazareth. So technically, it is not Jesus that pre-existed, but the eternal Word that pre-existed. And it is the eternal Wisdom of God that is then made manifest in the life of Jesus of Nazareth. Ward is illuminating here: "The Word of God is the eternal ideal in the mind of God which Jesus will actualize on earth."[36] Granted, certain Biblical texts seem to suggest that, in some sense, Jesus pre-existed,[37] but these can properly be interpreted as referring to the eternal Word that preexisted, which is now completely and utterly identified with the historical Jesus of Nazareth. This would mean that the Creed should be read in the following way. The identity of Jesus Christ is for us the fusion of the eternal Word with human flesh. Given Jesus is the eternal Word, then we can say that Jesus Christ, the eternal Word, came down from heaven. However, that moment of incarnation entailed a flesh made visible that is not part of the life of the Son—the eternal Word—in eternity. So, as we understand the language, we should recognize that there is a difference between the historical Jesus of Nazareth and the eternal Word in eternity past: the former was not there, but the latter was.

The second area is the question of gender and the Trinity. One criterion for the Theologically Traditioned Truth is the centrality of justice as a control on our theology. And it is true that there are two areas, pertaining to justice, where gender and the Trinity are central.

It is increasingly commonplace among evangelicals opposed to the ordination of women to ground the justification of their position in the eternal subordination of the Son to the Father. It was Wayne Grudem's *Systematic Theology: An Introduction to Biblical Doctrine* that made the argument that both the Father and Son are divine but the Son is eternally subordinated to the Father. This is the opening chapter. In a later chapter, he explains women are permanently subordinate to men because of the Son's subordination to the Father.

This is a fascinating case study in how a gender politics of sexism is shaping a theological debate. There is no doubt that the tradition very explicitly teaches that the Son is not subordinate to the Father. As Kevin Giles, in his rebuttal of this position, explains that to hold the eternal subordination of the Son "demands the rejection of the Athanasian Creed, which unambiguously affirms the eternal coequality of the eternally differentiated divine persons."[38] Giles brings out the political understanding of the doctrine of the Trinity (as taught by the overwhelming majority of Christian theologians), when he writes:

> This understanding of God analogically reflects the ideal for all human relationships. It suggests that permanently subordinating a race, socioeconomic group, or sex is not pleasing to God. The subordinating of any person is a reflection of the realities of a fallen world, not God's ideal.[39]

Giles is right: The doctrine of the Trinity supports right relations in the world. It does not undermine them.

The second issue we must address is the problem that many feminist theologians have with "Father" and "Son." This remains a sensitive issue: For many feminist theologians, the image of Father feeds patriarchy and sexism. Against this, we have the animated reaction of Donald Boesch, who writes:

> Radical feminists have no hesitation in referring to God as Mother, but this in effect transmutes God into a goddess. At the Presbytery conference on this subject at which I was speaking, I was asked by a laywoman, "What is wrong with the idea of a goddess?" The answer is that such a metaphor imputes sexuality to a God who is beyond sexuality. It also denies the transcendence of God, since goddess invariably refers to the Immanent Mother, the creative force within nature.[40]

There are a variety of difficulties embedded in this response. An incarnational faith like Christianity should not be feeding the binary of holy and God on one side and materiality and sexuality on the other. To link God and the world in some sense is appropriate and should not be feared. So Boesch is not convincing.

Ward takes the opposite line. Given there is a likelihood that there is intelligent life on other planets in other galaxies, we should not link our description of the Trinity to contingent human language.[41] Such words are contingent on the models for relationship that exist in our world. Therefore, Ward argues for a flexibility around images. Ward is sensitive to a potential difficulty here. If the image Father is not capturing an aspect of God that is truly part of God, then is not this lapsing into the problematic modalism (where our experience of God is not truly God). It is not sufficient to say that the divine "threeness" is sufficient. The actual experience of a father or mother needs to be captured by the term. So, on this view, if we take Ward's thought exercise seriously of extraterrestrial intelligence and God-talk, then Christians do need to argue that the analogous role of a birthing parent should be the image in this distant planet (presumably conceptually there must be some origin to a species that exists). The Father (or Mother) image cannot be unrelated to this true experience of God to humanity.

For this reason, following Placher and others, it is unhelpful to distance oneself from the language of father completely. This is the language of Scripture. It captures the important insight that God, the creator, is personal and has a love for us that is comparable to a parent's love for a child. Placher is right to suggest that adding to the personal images is both in Scripture (e.g., the mother hen image of Matthew 23:37) and in our tradition (e.g., Mother Julian of Norwich's description of Jesus as "our Mother, brother and savior"). Placher goes on to write:

Such examples from Scripture and the tradition encourage us to adopt a wider range of images for God. I also see no insurmountable objections to the formula: "Father, Son, and Holy Spirit, One God, Mother of us all."[42]

THE TRINITY AS A MODEL OF CHRISTIAN THEOLOGICAL REASONING

In summary, the argument thus far is this: The doctrine of the Trinity arises to make sense of the definitive Christian foundation that in a human life, God was made visible. If it is true that in Jesus of Nazareth the eternal Word was present, then God was present, is present, and still sustains the universe. And this means that Christians are forced to talk of at least two aspects of God—the Creator aspect and the Son aspect (revealing and redeeming). Given the witness of Scripture regularly addresses the interconnectedness of the Creator aspect and the revealing aspect through the agency of the Spirit (the Spirit hovers over the waters in Genesis[43] and the Spirit descends on Jesus at Baptism[44]), the church could not avoid talking about the mystery of the triune nature of God in God's oneness.

As we have seen, the doctrine is deduced from the Christians' distinctive experience of the eternal Word recognized in Jesus of Nazareth. The tradition then evolves through the hard and careful work of exegesis of the written text. All of this analysis is part of the shared reflection of the community, in this case, the church. Naturally, the precise understanding of the relationship between the persons and the oneness of God provokes lively debate; therefore, a pluralism, within some constraints, develops.

Let us, then, develop the five principles of Christian theological reasoning as modeled in the Doctrine of the Trinity but also anywhere the church seeks to be true to the tradition in formulating an insight about God and how God relates to the world. The first principle develops an appropriate distinction between the eternal Word and the written Word. Karl Barth is helpful here. He distinguishes between three Words of revelation. The first is the preached or proclaimed Word.[45] This is the prophet of the Old Testament or any act of proclamation, which discloses the nature of God to humanity. The second is the written Word, which is Scripture.[46] Naturally, there is a close link between Scripture and the proclaimed Word because "for it itself is the deposit of proclamation made in the past by the mouth of man."[47] And the third is the eternal Word made flesh—the Immanuel, God with us—the disclosure of God in the essence, words, and deeds of Christ.[48] Now, for Barth, there is an inevitable interconnectedness between these three Words—prophets and apostles had to proclaim, the written Word contains their proclamation, and all things point to the definitive disclosure, which is the Son—the eternal Word. Barth explains that "literally" in Christ, "We are, therefore, concerned with the singular Word spoken, and this time really directly, by God Himself."[49] Barth goes on: "But in the Bible we are invariably concerned with human attempts to repeat and reproduce, in human thoughts and expressions, this Word of God in definite human situations, e.g., in respect of the complications of Israel's political position midway between Egypt and Babylon or of the errors and confusions in the Christian Church at Corinth between AD 50–60."[50]

Barth's insight that Scripture is best understood as a meditation about what we learn of God in Christ is reinforced by the work of Richard Burridge. Burridge's work on the genre of the Gospels establishes convincingly that the intent of the authors of the Gospel was to produce a Greco-Roman biography of Jesus of Nazareth. It was intended to inspire but, more importantly, invite imitation.[51] And the New Testament is best understood as an exercise of unpacking the implications of the church imitating what we learn of God in Jesus.

Let me state this more strongly: The primary disclosure of God to humanity is the eternal Word made flesh. This is the control of all our theology. We interpret Scripture in light of what we learn through the primary Word, which is Christ. So, the genocidal tendencies of certain passages of Scripture or the affirmation of slavery or the propensity in parts of Scripture to affirm patriarchy or denigrate homosexuals need to be interpreted in light of the eternal Word that affirms the dignity of all whom Jesus meets.

Nevertheless, Barth is right. There is no access to the life of Jesus apart from Scripture. Therefore, properly, we talk of Scripture as the Word of God. And we must struggle with the text of Scripture to make sense of the revelation of God disclosed in Christ. This is the second principle: the need for exegesis. The church rapidly accepted this work of exegesis and the imperative of reading Scripture in the light of contemporary philosophical resources. Lewis Ayres explains:

> Beginning in the late second century...Christian theologians came to insist that the text of Scripture could best be read by means of a close analysis of words, sentences and other textual units, a close analysis that would employ such techniques of analysis as etymology, attention to an author's customary patterns of speech, the paralleling passages from different places in the canon, and a host of other techniques that were adapted from traditions of ancient literary criticism. These practices were applied within a common emphasis on the unity of the canon and the fulfillment of Israel's history and prophecy in Christ. . . . One important reading practice that would have significant implications for the future was a willingness to utilize contemporary philosophical resources to explore and fill out hints and ambiguities in the text.[52]

These reading practices of the church invite us to read in appropriately critical ways. We take into account the best "science" (or, perhaps, better philosophy) of our day; we search for appropriate unity across the witness of Scripture; and we take seriously the patterns of language and worldview embedded in an individual book or author.

This leads, naturally, to the third principle: We reason within the church both present and past. The community of the church today and the traditions of the church are recognized as an appropriate stage for our reflections on what God teaches us through revelation. Christianity is always a self-supporting circle. In the same way, the written Word is judged by the eternal Word, but all knowledge of the eternal Word is found in the written Word. We find a comparable circle here. The tradition creates the present and the present in the light of its own reflection on the eternal Word found in the written Word. A key part of this discernment includes bringing contemporary philosophy and science to issues the church faces. Including these other ways of knowing is why in the history of Christian thought we find both continuity and innovation. We build on the past, but as we engage with insights within contemporary culture, we innovate appropriately.

The fourth principle is the importance of internal consistency. We expect our account of God and God's relation with the world (i.e., the heart of the theological task) to be coherent and compatible with other truths.

This leads to the final principle: the inevitably of pluralism within limits. In the same way that every tradition of inquiry produces insights that are more certain than others, so theology is the same. It is fundamental for Christian theology to understand that we must properly talk of God as triune but accept that individuals can emphasize the unity and diversity of the Persons differently.

Now, these five principals are very Anglican. One will recognize Macquarrie's six factors that shape the character of Christian thinking—Scripture, Tradition, Reason, Experience, Culture, and Revelation.[53] This approach is compatible with the insights learned from Theologically Traditioned Truth. One theme of this book is that a "liberal" theological methodology (liberal in the sense that it is not committed to an infallible magisterium or Bible) can and should arrive at a rich understanding of the universe that sees it as spiritually infused.

This section of the chapter is now coming to an end. It is worth pausing and summarizing where we are. Grounded in our Theological Traditioned Truth, using the principles of theological reasoning modeled in the Trinity, we now have a procedure to critique exactly what the spiritually infused universe. Central to the process is the Incarnation. The first principle is the eternal Word. It is what we learn about the spiritually infused universe from the One who made God manifest. Jesus is our authority on metaphysics.

JESUS AS THE AUTHORITY ON METAPHYSICS

At this point, we arrive at the foundation of the argument for a spiritually infused universe. This is not simply an abstract sense of the spiritual: it is a spiritual universe that has life, energy, and spiritual realities all around us. Christians want to claim that the authority, which discloses to us what God is like *and what the spiritual universe is like*, is the Incarnation of God—the eternal Word made flesh. At the heart of the earliest Gospel about Jesus is the claim that Jesus is an authority of the spiritual realm. For this, we need to study the encounter of Jesus with demons in the Gospel of Mark.

Turning to Mark

Mark was for centuries the neglected Gospel. St. Augustine was probably responsible when he dismissed Mark as the "follower and abbreviator" of Matthew.[54] Stylistically, the Greek is clumsy—in places, it is almost inelegant; it is, as Rowan Williams puts it, "the Greek of the big cosmopolitan trading towns, not the Greek of the study or of the literary classes."[55] It lacks the teaching substance of Matthew or the poetic soaring theology of John. It is the plodding, almost pedestrian, Gospel.

Yet, this picture of Mark has changed dramatically over the last fifty years. This has happened in several ways. First, there is a fairly settled consensus that Mark is the earliest Gospel. To expand on the narratives of Mark makes more sense than Mark ruthlessly editing down Matthew and Luke. The "Two Document" hypothesis of the Synoptic Relationship (namely that Mark and an anonymous sayings source called "Q" were primary texts used by Matthew and Luke) means that Mark is the earliest text. This means that Mark is closer to the historical Jesus. As Placher observes, "Whoever the author was, he probably knew people who knew Jesus. In the face of contemporary skepticism, this may be worth emphasizing. Jesus died thirty-five to forty-five years before Mark wrote."[56] Placher is also right to express his distrust of the Jesus Seminar and other projects that read the New Testament focused on dissimilarities between the Gospels and the early church on the assumption that only that which is different from the teaching of the early church can be authentic. As Placher notes, "[I]ts bias is quite unfairly against the ways in which Jesus was a Jew of his time or in which the church followed his teachings."[57] Today, when we read Mark, we read a text that really connects us with the historical Jesus.

Now William Wrede's famous "messianic secret" looms large at this point.[58] Wrede draws our attention to the "mysterious" way in which Jesus forbids any of his followers to correctly identify him. He suggested the hypothesis that perhaps the "messianic secret" was the device that Mark used to explain why Jesus did not publicly identify himself as the Messiah when he was alive.

In response to this, other scholars have persuasively argued that issues for the historical Jesus were the expectations that his contemporaries would have about any claim to be the Messiah. This controlled disclosure by the historical Jesus becomes a literary theme in the Gospel of Mark. John Donahue and Daniel Harrington explain thus:

> A better and more widely accepted explanation is that Mark sought to redefine the term "Messiah" and other Christological titles in the light of Jesus' death and resurrection, and so he puts off revealing Jesus" true identity until his death (see Mark 15:39) and his resurrection (see Mark 9:9). . . . Ultimately the term "messianic secret" is a misnomer . . . "[M]ystery is a term with apocalyptic overtones connoting the disclosure by God of a truth hidden until a certain decisive point in the divine plan is reached. . . . From the opening of the gospel, readers know that Jesus is the "Messiah." What awaits full disclosure is the kind of Messiah Jesus is. The mystery is that of a suffering Messiah who is also God's chosen Son.[59]

Both historically and in the Gospel of Mark, there was appropriate nervousness about the public identification of Jesus as the Jewish Messiah because Jesus dies on a cross. Williams takes us a step further. For Mark, argues Williams, the secret is the relationship with God. So, Williams writes:

> The secret is that the event which will change everything, which will bring in the regime of God, which will forgive sins and release people from guilt and fear, is not an event brought about by naked power. The God is who is going to change everything, change forever the conditions in which human beings live, is a God who is "beyond" power as we understand it; a God who does not coerce belief or clinch arguments, but who repeatedly demands relation and trust.[60]

Jesus cannot explain that this is the way things are. Instead, Jesus invites us to see that this is the way things are. Explicit description that he is the Messiah is not the way to help people see the nature of God and how God seeks to work with humanity.

The second way is that we are increasingly aware of the literary achievement of Mark. There are distinct theological themes that are woven into the text. The use of the phrase *kai euthus*, which means "immediately" or "straightaway," occurs eleven times in the opening chapter of the Gospel. There is an urgency to the Jesus of Mark's Gospel. The disciples are depicted as confused and muddled, in ways that both Matthew and Luke feel obliged to clean up. The passion narrative is striking in its simplicity with the one cry from the cross of despair. The end of the Gospel has provoked endless speculation: Was it always intended for the Gospel to conclude on a preposition? Leslie Houlden, in his *Backwards into Light*, writes approvingly of the ragged edges of Mark's narrative that captures the confusion and doubt of many a contemporary believer.

However, the third is perhaps the most significant. The work of Burridge has made a compelling case that the Gospels are, as a genre, classic examples of Graeco-Roman biography.[61] This act of identifying the genre accurately helped modern scholarship to recognize a creative Gospel writer at work who is also connecting us with the real Jesus. The appellation that the Gospels were "sui generis" created the expectation in the reader that the Gospels were really all about the early church (hence the analysis of the Jesus Seminar). The appellation that the Gospels were ancient biographies of Jesus, which are appropriately and distinctively ordered to create a portrait that captures the essence of Jesus, reconnected us with the historical Jesus.

As a result of this changed picture, we now have a widespread consensus that admires the achievement of Mark. It is a literary Gospel; there are certain key themes around suffering and Christology that are distinctive; and it is connected, using the Graeco-Roman devices, with the historical Jesus. Probably the majority of New Testament scholars place the authorship of the Gospel in Rome. Looking closely at the eschatology of Mark 13, it seems likely that the author[62] had some knowledge of the First Jewish War with Rome, which occurred between 66–74 CE. This places the writing perhaps just before the partial destruction of the Temple (say 69 CE).

Teaching Authority in Mark

The theme of the teaching authority of Jesus is introduced early in the Gospel. Here, in Mark 1, the theme is introduced:

> They went to Capernaum; and when the sabbath came, he entered the synagogue and taught. They were astounded at his teaching, for he taught them as one having authority, and not as the scribes. Just then there was in their synagogue a man with an unclean spirit, and he cried out, "What have you to do with us, Jesus of Nazareth? Have you come to destroy us? I know who you are, the Holy One of God." But Jesus rebuked him, saying, "Be silent, and come out of him!" And the unclean spirit, convulsing him and crying with a loud voice, came out of him. They were all amazed, and they kept on asking one another, "What is this? A new teaching—with authority! He commands even the unclean spirits, and they obey him." At once his fame began to spread throughout the surrounding region of Galilee. (Mark 1:21–28)

The story of this exorcism is set in Capernaum, which is on the northwest shore of the Sea of Galilee. Presumably, Jesus was invited by the synagogue ruler to contribute an exposition of the text. His capacity to interpret the text made his hearers "astounded." For the hearers of Jesus to be astounded is a significant Markian theme; the response is found thirty-four times in the Gospel. They were astounded presumably because the teaching of Jesus was comparing well with the scribes (i.e., those who were expert in Torah). A person with an unclean spirit, which for Mark seems to be a synonym for a demon (he uses both terms interchangeably), cries out (which, in the Greek, is literally "shrieked out"—a cry of "deep emotion"[63]). When the demon says, "What have you to do with us?," it is a plural that is used. This probably refers to the demon's recognition that Jesus is a challenge to the entire "demonic power structure."[64] Then we have Jesus correctly described by the unclean spirit as the "Holy One of God." Jesus instructs the spirit to be silent (a term "used in the ancient world in magic spells for binding people and demons"[65]), and then the spirit is ordered to come out from the person.

Various interpretations have been offered of this passage. The first sees Mark has demonstrated a source link between teaching and the ability to do an exorcism. Adela Yarbro Collins, for example, writes, "Both the authority to teach and the power to exorcise have a divine source."[66] What Jesus says, argues Collins, comes from God; and what Jesus can do, also comes from God. The second sees this as capturing Mark's Christology. So Donahue and Harrington write:

> The narrative has a clear Christological function. Jesus' identity, which was announced earlier by a voice from heaven, is now shouted out by a spirit. Transcendent forces recognize him for who he really is. However human Jesus appears throughout the subsequent narrative, he is also a figure of mystery and power. Through this initial conflict with evil, Mark also stresses that Jesus is the stronger one who has withstood Satan's attacks (Mark 1:7,13) and despoiled his household (see 3:23–27). This in turn underscores the authority of Jesus as teacher. Jesus" word is so powerful that people abandon their occupations and follow him; it is more powerful than that of the scribes, and even the demonic powers cower before it. It is a word that is to be spread far and wide.[67]

For Donahue and Harrington, this narrative is all about correctly identifying Jesus as an agent that has power over the demons.

The third sees an authority that spellbinds a congregation, heals, and challenges demons. This is the line taken by James Edwards. He sees the start of this passage establishing the contrast with the scribes. Jesus is more effective as a teacher because Jesus "appeals to an immediate and superior authority resident in himself that he received as his baptism."[68] The scribes have authority courtesy of the "tradition of the elders" (see Mark 7:8–13), but Jesus has authority coming directly from God. The healing stories immediately follow this one; and this is, of course, the exorcism. So, Edwards concludes, "Not only are unclean spirits expelled, but broken people are restored to health and wholeness and to the possibility of restoration with their Creator, in whose image they are made. The exousia of Jesus is astonishing not as a display of Jesus" grandeur but as a power of redemption for captives."[69]

The fourth is a teaching seen both in word and deed that includes the power to control the demons. Francis J. Moloney makes much of the fact that the demon correctly names Jesus of Nazareth as the Holy One of God. Moloney explains: "In the ancient world, to call a person by name gave one the summoning a certain authority over the one summoned. . . . In the culture and religious world of the time, the evil spirit should have won the day. However, such cultural and religious absolutes do not apply to Jesus."[70] People, therefore, marveled at an authority so strong. And the teaching, they admired, was not simply the rhetoric of Jesus but also the power of Jesus in handling the demon.

There is much truth in all these interpretations. They are not mutually conflicting. However, I shall now suggest that another aspect operating in both the Gospel and in this passage is the epistemological focus. Mark wants to demonstrate that Jesus has authority of the spiritual realm because he has knowledge of that realm. And the knowledge goes both ways. It is William L. Lane who notes that when sick individuals name Jesus, they use terms such as "Lord" (Mark 7:8) or "Teacher" (Mark 9:17) or "Master" (Mark 10:51). However, when the demons name Jesus, they use terms such as "Holy One of God" (in this passage) or "the Son of God" (Mark 3:11) or "the Son of the Most High God" (Mark 5:7). Lane then writes, "The contrast in address is an important characteristic distinguishing ordinary sickness from demonic possession, and reflects the superior knowledge of the demons."[71] For Mark, Jesus both recognizes and is recognized by the spiritual realm. Jesus has authority over that realm because he has knowledge of that realm.

As Lane suggests, the Gospel is interesting because it is only the divine and demonic voices who correctly identify Jesus—the divine is at the baptism (Mark 1:11) and at the transfiguration (Mark 9:7). The disciples spend most of their time confused and puzzled. The sole exceptions are the confession of Peter, where he correctly affirms that Jesus is the Messiah (Mark 8:29), and the centurion, who says, having watched Jesus die, "Truly this man was God's Son!" (Mark 15:39). Mark is making an important point here. Jesus is the disclosure of God to humanity because Jesus is known and recognized as such by those who are in the spiritual realm.

The teaching authority of Jesus continues in the Gospel. The term authority "exousia" occurs nine times in Mark, with six referring to Jesus. Two are in this passage. The next one occurs when Jesus heals the paralytic man and explains to those watching: "But so that you may know that the Son of Man has authority on earth to forgive sins" (Mark 2:10), he then instructs the paralytic to take his mat and go home. The last three uses of the word are found in Mark 11, when Jesus is in Jerusalem. The opposition is beginning to form against Jesus.

As he was walking in the temple, the chief priests, the scribes, and the elders came to him and said, "By what authority are you doing these things? Who gave you this authority to do them?" Jesus said to them, "I will ask you one question; answer me, and I will tell you by what authority I do these things. Did the baptism of John come from heaven, or was it of human origin? Answer me." They argued with one another, "If we say, 'From heaven,' he will say, 'why then did you not believe him?' But shall we say, 'Of human origin'?" They were afraid of the crowd, for all regarded John as truly a prophet. So, they answered Jesus, "We do not know." And Jesus said to them, "Neither will I tell you by what authority I am doing these things" (Mark 11:27–33).

For the reader, the comparison with John the Baptist is clear. If John the Baptist has a divine origin, then how much more does Jesus have a divine origin.

There are three further references to exousia. The authority that Jesus has can be passed on to the followers of Jesus. So, in the first, Jesus appoints the twelve and gave them "authority to cast out demons" (Mark 3:15). The second is the sending out of the twelve, two by two, with "authority over unclean spirits" (Mark 6:7). And the third is less relevant for our purposes. It arises when Jesus is telling the story of a man "going on a journey, when he leaves home and puts his slaves in charge"—the word charge here is "authority" (Mark 13:34).

The invitation of the Gospel of Mark is to trust the teaching of Jesus because he has knowledge of the spiritual realm. It was Charles Williams who said of the first chapter of Mark that "Witness is born out of heaven and on earth and from hell."[72] Jesus is the pivotal point. Jesus is a gateway between the spiritual realm and the earthly realm. You can trust Jesus because Jesus knows. In the same way as the Gospel of John explicitly describes Jesus as the Word of God (the eternal utterance of God—the very Wisdom of God embodied), so Mark is here implicitly making a similar claim. The image of Word is one of communication. Words are an insight into our minds, into our thoughts. Jesus is the vehicle of communication for Mark. Jesus knows the spiritual realm; Jesus can control the spiritual realm; and Jesus can describe the spiritual realm.

Having arrived at the plausibility of the spiritually infused universe, Christology, for the Christian, is the next step. We trust that we can have knowledge of that realm by learning, listening, and being shaped by what Jesus did and said.

NOTES

1. John Macquarrie, *Principles of Christian Theology*, revised edition, (London: SCM Press, 1977), p. 191. Macquarrie uses the phrase "existential-ontological"; so, it is grounded in Christian community yet does capture some objective truth about God.
2. See Matthew W. Bates, *The Birth of the Trinity: Jesus, God, and Spirit in the New Testaments & Early Christian Interpretations of the Old Testament* (Oxford: Oxford University Press, 2015), pp. 13–28.
3. See Jules Lebreton, *History of the Dogma of the Trinity: From Its Origins to the Council of Nicaea, i. The Origins,* translated by Algar Thorold (London: Burns Oates and Washbourne, 1939).
4. See C. S. Lewis, *Mere Christianity*, revised edition (New York: Touchstone, 1996).
5. See Adolf von Harnack, *History of Dogma*, translated by Neil Buchanan (Boston: Little, Brown and Company, 1896–1905).
6. See Larry W. Hurtado, *Lord Jesus Christ: Devotion to Jesus in Earliest Christianity* (Grand Rapids, MI: Eerdmans, 2003).
7. See P. M. Casey, *From Jewish Prophet to Gentile God: The Origins and Development of New Testament Christology* (Louisville, KY: Westminster John Knox, 1991).
8. See Richard Bauckham, *God Crucified: Monotheism and Christology in the New Testament*, (Carlisle: Paternoster 1998).
9. James F. McGrath, *The One True God: Early Christian Monotheism in Its Jewish Context* (Urbana, IL: University of Illinois Press, 2009), p. 15.
10. Hurtado, *Lord Jesus Christ* p. 215. Hurtado is alluding to the biblical categories of Judean Christianity—i.e., Roman Judea/Palestine in the initial decades—where Jesus is seen as David's rightful heir, the royal-messianic redeemer sent from God (see Hurtado, p. 214).
11. Larry W. Hurtado, *How on Earth Did Jesus Become God? Historical Questions about Earliest Devotion to Jesus* (Grand Rapids, MI: Eerdmans, 2005), p. 106.
12. Ibid, p. 203.
13. Some of the material that follows is taken from my Ian S. Markham, *Understanding Christian Doctrine,* 2nd edition (Oxford: Wiley Blackwell, 2017).
14. John H. Leith, *Creeds of the Churches*, 3rd edition (Atlanta, GA: John Knox Press, 1982), pp. 35–36.
15. William C. Placher, *Jesus the Savior: The Meaning of Jesus Christ for Christian Faith* (Louisville, KY: Westminster John Knox Press, 2001), p. 49.
16. Ibid., p. 49.
17. Ibid., p. 50.
18. Brian Hebblethwaite, *The Essence of Christianity* (London: SPCK, 1996), p. 91.
19. Jürgen Moltmann, *The Crucified God* (London: SCM Press, 1974), p. 227.
20. Ibid., p. 243.
21. Jürgen Moltmann, *The Trinity and the Kingdom: The Doctrine of God* (San Francisco, CA: Harper and Row, 1981), p. 19.
22. Ibid., p. 163.
23. Ibid., p. 168.
24. Ibid., p. 170.
25. Ibid., p. 191.
26. Ibid., p. 192.
27. Katherine Sonderegger, *Systematic Theology. Volume 1, The Doctrine of God* (Minneapolis, MN: Fortress Press, 2015), pp. 156–57.
28. Keith Ward, *Christ and the Cosmos: A Reformulation of Trinitarian Doctrine* (Cambridge: Cambridge University Press 2015), p. 221.
29. Ibid., p. 227.
30. Ibid., pp. 230–31.
31. Ibid., p. 248.
32. Stephen H. Webb, *Jesus Christ, Eternal God: Heavenly Flesh and the Metaphysics of Matter* (Oxford: Oxford University Press, 2012), p. 269.
33. Ibid., pp. 97–101.

34. William Placher, *The Triune God: An Essay in Postliberal Theology* (Louisville, KY: Westminster John Knox Press, 2007), p. 78.

35. Ibid., p. 78. Placher is quoting Calvin, *Institues* 1.13.27; 1:156 and Irenaeus, fragment 53, Ante-Nicene Father 1:577.

36. Keith Ward, *Christ and the Cosmos* (Cambridge: Cambridge University Press, 2016) p. 81.

37. Most of the texts are found in the Gospel of John (see John 3:13, 31; John 5:36-38; John 6:46, 62; John 7:28-29; John 8:23; John 8:58; and John 17:24.

38. Kevin Giles, *Jesus and the Father: Modern Evangelicals Reinvent the Doctrine of the Trinity* (Grand Rapids, MI: Zondervan, 2006), p. 312.

39. Ibid.

40. Donald G. Bloesch, *The Battle for the Trinity: The Debate over Inclusive God-Language* (Ann Arbor, MI: Vine Books, 1985), p. 44.

41. Keith Ward, *Christ and the Cosmos* (Cambridge: Cambridge University Press, 2016) pp. 250–51.

42. William Placher, *The Triune God: An Essay in Postliberal Theology* (Louisville, KY: Westminster John Knox Press, 2007), p. 79.

43. See Genesis 1:2.

44. See Mark 1:10; Matthew 3:16; and Luke 3:22.

45. See Karl Barth, *Church Dogmatics: Volume 1 The Doctrine of the Word of God, Part 1* (Edinburgh: T&T Clark, 1936), pp. 98–111.

46. Ibid., pp. 111–24.

47. Ibid., p. 114.

48. It is worth noting that Barth takes issue with Paul Tillich, who wants to put some distance between Jesus as he appears in the Gospels and the essence of Jesus that is the revelation. Barth writes, "The essence of this person is identical with His language, action, and passion." This comment is one that Burridge, in his work on genre, would affirm: The purpose of the Gospel is to invite us to imitate a life, which handles death appropriately, and is seen in his words (language for Barth) and deeds (action for Barth). See Ibid., p. 156.

49. Ibid., p. 127.

50. Ibid., p. 127.

51. See Richard Burridge, *What are the Gospels? A Comparison with Graeco-Roman Biography*, revised and updated 2nd edition (Grand Rapids, MI: Eerdmans, 2004) and his sequel in ethics, *Imitating Jesus: An Inclusive Approach to New Testament Ethics* (Grand Rapids, MI: Eerdmans, 2007). For my own assessment of the significant of Burridge's work, see my article "Richard Burridge's Achievement," in *First Things*, January 2014.

52. Lewis Ayres, "The Word Answering the Word: Opening the Space of Catholic Biblical Interpretation," (unpublished paper).

53. See Macquarrie, *Principles of Christian Theology*.

54. See Augustine, *De consensu evangelistarum*, 1.2 (PL 34:1044).

55. Rowan Williams, *Meeting God in Mark* (London: SPCK, 2014), p. 18.

56. William C. Placher, *Mark* (Louisville, KY: Westminster John Knox Press, 2010), p. 3.

57. Ibid., p. 4.

58. See William Wrede, *Das Messiasgeheimnis in den Evangelien* (1901), translated into English as *The Messianic Secret*, 1971.

59. John R. Donahue S.J. and Daniel J. Harrington S. J., *The Gospel of Mark* (Collegeville, Minnesota: The Liturgical Press, 2002), p.28-9.

60. Rowan Williams, *Meeting God in Mark* (Louisville, KY: Westminster John Knox Press, 2014), p. 39.

61. Burridge, *What are the Gospels?*

62. Naturally, the tradition of the church links the Gospel with Mark, linked with Peter. I am less sure that such an identification should be made. There are several difficulties with tradition derived from Papias, bishop of Hierapolis; and internally, the text gives Peter a very hard time. For a good summary of the difficulties with the traditional ascription of authorship, see W. R. Telford, *Mark* (Sheffield, UK: Sheffield Academic Press, 1995), pp. 15–20. However, for a

defense of the traditional view, see James R. Edwards, *The Gospel According to Mark* (Grand Rapids, MI: William B. Eerdmans, 2002), p. 6.

63. See Morna D. Hooker, *The Gospel According to St. Mark* (London and New York: Continuum, 1991), p. 64.

64. Edwards, *The Gospel According to Mark*, p.56.

65. Morna D. Hooker, *The Gospel According to St. Mark* (London: Bloomsbury Publishing Plc, 1991), p. 65. Hooker goes on to suggest that given this use of the rebuke—"be silent"—the narrative could be read as a traditional and straightforward exorcism; however, she does not take that line. Instead, she thinks this term should be linked to the "secrecy concerning Jesus' identity."

66. Adela Yarbro Collins, *Mark: A Commentary* (Minneapolis, MN: Augsburg Fortress, 2007), p. 174.

67. Donahue and Harrington, *The Gospel of Mark*, p. 84.

68. Edwards, *The Gospel According to Mark*, p. 55.

69. Ibid., p. 58.

70. Francis J. Moloney, *The Gospel of Mark: A Commentary* (Grand Rapids, MI: Baker Academic, 2012), p. 54.

71. William L. Lane, *The Gospel According to Mark* (Grand Rapids, MI: Eerdmans, 1974), p. 74.

72. Charles Williams, *He Came Down from Heaven* (London: Heinemann, 1938), p. 63.

Chapter Six

Sacramentality

The Basics

Anafühl is the inability to see the textured nature of reality. It has roots in the mood of modernity—a mood that cannot see the multicolored and nuanced nature of reality (to return to the thought exercise that started the book). It is a mood that feels that a reductionist science has triumphed in explaining reality. Although this is scientifically false, it continues to hold a grip on the modern imagination. It is a mood that feels that there is nothing reliable to trust—no plausible account of revelation.

The response to *anafühl* is emerging. A new "social imaginary" is being proposed (to use the language of Charles Taylor). It is an "imaginary" that takes seriously the transformation in our understanding of the world through science; it advocates for the coherence and likelihood of spiritual causation; it has suggested a truth framework (Theological Traditioned Truth)—one that is critically realist yet admits the sociological reality of knowing; and it has argued for trust when it comes to the Christian claim that God is revealed in Christ.

The Christian task is to issue an invitation. It is an invitation to see how the spiritual infuses the material. Traditionally, this is the domain of the sacramental. We are now at the stage when the spiritually infused universe is being made visible. This chapter is focused on the claims that Christians want to make about the general connections between spirituality and materiality. This is the world of sacramental theology. Two distinct claims will be defended in this chapter: first, a general sacramentality that recognizes that grace is mediated in a multitude of ways in the world; and then, second, a particular sacramentality that recognizes that the church can mediate a particular grace through certain rituals.

118   *Chapter 6*

The problem of *anafühl* is our starting point in this chapter. We start by recognizing that, for many in our age, such talk is very implausible. We then move to the opposite extreme and consider a classical, pre-Vatican II defense of sacraments. There are three difficulties with this defense. These are (1) history, (2) efficacy, and (3) gender. Then we move to the constructive proposal, where the categories of general sacramentality and particular sacramentality will be defended.

THE CHALLENGE

Matter is pretty obvious. We touch and sit on matter; we are made up of matter. But spirit is much harder to see. What exactly is it? Where is it? The very categories in which we think about the world—location, space, time—do not, easily, accommodate the spiritual. This is all part of the cultural mood of *anafühl*.

For those of us infected with the mood of *anafühl*, the suggestion that the bread becomes the body of Jesus and the wine becomes the blood of Jesus has all the connotations of magic. We are finding the mystical assumptions that somehow the substance could change, while the accidents remain the same (to take a Roman Catholic account of transubstantiation) utterly implausible. One can understand the reaction that says, "Bread is bread, even if a priest says a prayer over the bread," or, "Examine the bread under a microscope and nothing has changed." Even the renowned historian Keith Thomas reveals his prejudice when he links sacraments with magic. Superstition, as examined in chapter 2, is the keyword that covers both magic and a sacramental view of the Eucharist. So, he quotes the Council of Malines in 1607, which describes as superstitious any effect that is not the result of natural causes or the church or ordination, and then writes, "There was, therefore, no superstition in believing that the elements could change their nature after the formula of consecration had been pronounced over them: this was not magic, but an operation worked by God and the Church; whereas magic involved the aid of the Devil."[1]

This is a prejudice. It is the dismissal of the possibility of spiritual causation a priori using the category of superstition. But this dismissal provides the challenge: How exactly do we give an account of a sacramental worldview that is plausible, coherent, and compatible with our scientific understanding?

Origin of the Term

We have Tertullian (b.260) to thank for the application of the term "sacraments" to baptism and communion. Sacrament is a Latin word—*sacramentum*. Originally, the term was a legal one involving the pledge of money—sometimes property—in a contractual arrangement, which took place in a temple. However, by the time of Tertullian, the Romans were using the term to mean "a sacred oath." Roman soldiers were required to take an oath of strict obedience and allegiance to the Roman gods and to their commander; so, by analogy, Tertullian saw the sacraments of baptism and Eucharist as equally binding loyalty symbols on Christians.

Although Tertullian might not have been the first, he used the word "sacrament" when translating the Bible. The Greek word *mysterion* ("a mystery"), he translated as sacrament. Everett Ferguson explains that the Greek *mysterion* carries a vast range of meanings. Ferguson writes, "From its principal usage for the secret rites of initiation in the Greek mystery religion *mysterion* came to be applied to many kinds of secrets or unexplained phenomena: a secret medicine, magical formulae, sexual relations, even philosophical teachings."[2] Perhaps, as a result, we see in Tertullian an application of the word *mysterion* that extends to the Trinity and saving work of God in history, but especially in the baptism and the Eucharist. "In baptism and in the Eucharist," Kenan Osborne explains, "Tertullian saw the mysterious presence of God."[3]

The Traditional View of Sacraments

One theme of this book is that many of the traditional defenses of these doctrines are highly problematic. Sacramental theology is no exception. Some of the pre-Vatican II Roman Catholic accounts are an extraordinary mixture of insights coupled with prejudice. Bernard Leeming, in his *Principles of Sacramental Theology*,[4] is a good example.

Starting with his insights, Leeming does recognize that the concept of sacraments has a deep connection with creation. He writes, "The sacramental idea is implicit even in Creation. Through material visible things, God's power and wisdom are manifest; and the earthly becomes a sign and an assurance of the heavenly."[5] He correctly grounds his exposition of sacraments in the Incarnation—"The Incarnation is a promise of sacraments."[6] And he wants to link his sense of sacraments throughout creation with the drama of salvation. So, he writes, "Sacraments are revelations of God: symbols, tokens, signs to us of the whole of God's dispensation of salvation."[7] He understands that grace is the key. And he correctly captures that grace is relational: so, he writes, "It should never be forgotten that grace is the intimate personal relationship between God and man, which changes not only man's thoughts but his being."[8] He rightly sees that this grace has power. He affirms that there is a real change in the person. Finally, he wants to link the sacraments with Christ. He writes, "Christians, with exceedingly few exceptions, have always believed that it was Christ who instituted the sacraments."[9] As we will see later in this chapter, this is good, although not easy. However, on all these points, Leeming is more right than wrong.

Then there are aspects of Leeming's account that are more problematic. First, he makes a social connection between doctrine and social practices that is both implausible and offensive. The best illustration of this was his description of marriage and the implications for Jewish and Muslim cultures. He explains: "The character of Christian Marriage is permanent image speaking of the love of Christ and the Church; and it is a significant fact that where Christian Marriage degenerates, there also the idea of God degenerates. Historically, polygamy and divorce have usually been found in societies which admit no Incarnation and no divine Trinity, as among Jews, Mohammedans, and many others."[10] Such parallels are widespread: Advocates of the social trinity have been known to argue that cultures that do not affirm the social trinity are more likely to have authoritarian regimes. All these connections are problematic. The relationship between any doctrine and social practices is often tenuous. The second difficulty is that he defends the sacraments in such a way that they are seen as utterly inflexible and, therefore, ironically, lacking grace. So, on marriage, he writes:

> Marriage of Christians must represent the union of Christ and the Church, which it would not do were it dissoluble by any human power after consummation. It is the enduring state which is the image of the union of Christ and the Church and not merely the cause of the state; and the state itself cannot subsist without supernatural aid.[11]

Any sacramental account of marriage must accommodate the complexities of human lives. Timothy Sedgwick is wise when he writes, "A vision of the Christian life and human sexuality must give form to our relationships in the world without an idealization and perfectionism which can be tyrannical and crippling."[12] The corollary that divorce is impossible does not recognize the complex ways in which the eternal touches human lives. The best of human intentions upon entering marriage can be eroded by the way humans change in the passing of time. Another illustration is his approach to the Eucharist. So, Leeming explains that the Eucharist is the way that "the faithful in receiving Holy Communion share in a special way the Church's union with Christ, the eternal victim, in his timeless self-offering for mankind."[13] Given it is a symbol of unity among Christians, Lemming explains that this is also the reason by those "disunited in faith cannot rightly communicate at the same altar."[14] Unity is complex. Unless it is one solitary Christian taking the Eucharist, some sort of disunity is inevitable. There are plenty of Roman Catholics who hold greater disagreements with the magisterium than Baptists do. Unless this is crudely tribal (i.e., those who call themselves Roman Catholic are in, everyone else is out), it is difficult to see how one can coherently justify the exclusion of other baptized Christians.

Setting Out the Parameters

Our parameters of our account of sacramental theology must include an appropriate historical sensitivity. So, it is not true to say that the seven sacraments of the Roman Catholic Church were instituted by Christ. Osborne attempts to make the case about the emergence of the sacraments when he writes:

> Baptism and Eucharist clearly go back to the time of Jesus and there is data for this in the New Testament itself. It is with the writings of Hermes (140–150) that we have the first clear reference to a rite of reconciliation after baptism. It is with the *Apostolic Tradition* of Hippolytus (c.215) that we have the first extant ordination ritual and a clear indication of ordination. In the same work we have the first clear indication of a blessing of oil for the sick. Around 400 we begin to see, on reliable historical data, that the Church officials begin to enter into the marriage rite. Since it was not until the time of Peter Lombard in the twelfth century that theologians acknowledged marriage as a sacrament, the first indication of marriage is placed in parentheses, indicating only a first step around 400 and a clear sacramental acceptance only in the twelfth century. The year 1000 for confirmation indicates that at that time, generally in the West, a separate rite, called confirmation can be found. Prior to 1000, in the West, less generalized situations on a separate rite of confirmation can be historically found.[15]

While Tertullian might be the first to use the word "sacramentus," the rich theology of the sacraments was developed in the eleventh and twelfth centuries. It was, explains Osborne, during this period that three factors came forward in our understanding of sacraments. The first was the link between sacraments and a sign or symbol. The second was the idea that grace is an intrinsic part of the invisible or sacred reality to which the sign points; and the third was the idea that these sacraments were in some way or another instituted by Christ. It is after the twelfth century that we have the popular definition: "Sacraments are external signs instituted by Christ to give us grace."[16]

So, how do we accommodate this complex history? Given Jesus is our authority for the nature of the spiritually infused universe, we clearly need to establish a link with Jesus. Now there are a couple of moves we need to make in response to the historical data. We should and can recognize that the Gospels are clearly sacramental, and that the historical Jesus did institute some sacraments. Baptism (clearly) and Eucharist (perhaps less clearly) can be linked with the historical Jesus. We have good reason to recognize that Jesus taught about marriage and forgiveness. Although this sounds messy, God's work in history is always going to be untidy. And an untidy link with the historical Jesus is a necessary building block of our sacramental theology.

Another helpful move is to recognize that Christians want to see Jesus as both sacramental in his life and as the source of a sacramental tradition. When we speak of Jesus as a sacrament of God, we are affirming that Jesus shows us God and establishes the principle that the material can show us God. Osborne is helpful on this point. He describes Jesus as "primordial sacrament" and explains, "When one speaks about Jesus as the primordial sacrament, a wholly new dimension appears. Jesus is the very reason why anything in the new covenant might be called and be in fact a sacrament. Jesus is in this view not simply another sacrament beyond the other seven, but Jesus is the primordial sacrament, the very reason for sacramentality."[17] In Jesus, we see how grace can be made visible in the world. Through the very materiality of the Incarnation, God can be seen. This is the basis of all sacraments. The Incarnation establishes the possibility of sacraments; the Incarnation establishes the criterion for determining a sacrament. In the same way as the Incarnation mediates the grace of the Creator, so we can and should look at ways in which there is an analogous movement in the Eucharist, in baptism, in marriage, and elsewhere.

On the sacramental nature of the tradition, we recognize that the tradition, established in liturgy, comes from Jesus and radiates through the church. It is Tyler Sampson who provides an Anglican read of the work of Yves Congar. Congar, in *Tradition and Traditions*, has a dynamic view of tradition, which is firmly grounded in the Incarnation. Congar affirms that Jesus is the source of tradition, yet Congar also recognizes that tradition moves through time. Sampson takes this insight and suggests that we should see tradition in a sacramental way. Sampson explains: "The sacramental nature of tradition means that the past, present, and future are held together as one reality. This sacramental reality is the work of the Holy Spirit in the history of the church. The past has a continuing presence in the present, thus making history a present actuality. The Spirit carries the tradition established by Christ in the principle of the Incarnation throughout time to its eschatological fulfillment."[18] The sacramental nature of tradition is seen most clearly in the liturgy. The implication of Sampson's work is that tradition could almost be defined as the work of the people in the liturgy who carry the Incarnation from Jesus through time. Given the Incarnation is the "primordial sacrament," tradition through the liturgy then assumes a sacramental quality. Sampson summarizes it thus: "The source of all tradition *is* Jesus Christ. Tradition, through liturgy, serves to keep us in contact with its source. Tradition is real access to the paschal mystery, the source of the Christian community, through a dynamic engagement with the past as it has come down through the generations."[19]

It is reasonable, then, to link Jesus (understood in three ways—historically, as incarnate, and as the one passed down in the Church through the liturgy) with our sacramental theology and with a recognition of particular sacraments.

We turn now to the question of the range and extent of the sacramental. It is the feminist theologian Susan A. Ross who argues for a broad definition of the sacramental that includes virtually everything. So, she writes, "On the most fundamental level, the sacramental principle means that creation is sacred: all of life—human, animal, vegetable, mineral—is potentially revelatory of the divine and is to be treated as such."[20] Although it is true that the sacramental ranges beyond the official sacraments, it is important that we do not simply equate the word "sacramental" with the word "revelatory." Ross is right to say that everything in creation is "potentially revelatory of the divine," but the word "sacramental" wants to say more than that. Sacramental implies a certain power—the power of divine grace—that can be mediated through the material. Now it is true that God can use a whole range of materials to mediate grace to a person. Rosary beads, a crèche, perhaps, and wood carvings that make up the stations of the cross are all potential examples of materials that convey sacramental grace. However, it is not helpful to use the term sacramental to describe the sense of awe arising from watching a bright red sky as the sun goes down. This latter experience is revelatory of divine power and beauty, but the sunset is not a particular vehicle of divine grace.

Ross is helpful in seeing how sacramental acts can be found in the entire community of the church and not restricted, at all, to those who are in holy orders. In a fascinating set of interviews that involved a group of lay Roman Catholic women, a broader view of sacraments emerged. Ross explains, "When pressed, these women said that their understanding of a sacrament was not, nor could it be, restricted to the 'seven sacraments' as officially defined by the Roman Catholic Church. While the official sacraments were not at all to be dismissed, they served as a center of what I call a 'constellation' of the official sacraments themselves and what one woman called 'sacramental moments,' times when these women's own pastoral skills were exercised in a way that they viewed as sacramental."[21] Ross provides an illustration: One of the interviewees described a combined first mass with a birthday celebration of a young Latina teenager, whose family could not afford a decent birthday celebration. Ross is right that this is more than a supportive community; this is the life of the church radiating out divine grace in this extraordinary and beautifully combined birthday and first mass. Indeed, Ross is right to want to see the definition of the sacrament broadened so they are "action of the community." What they are not is even clearer: Sacraments are not purely priestly actions; they are not restricted to the actual moment when the sacrament is "conferred." They are linked to an ongoing process of recognizing God's presence in all of life."[22]

Thus, I am arguing for the term "sacramental" to extend out from the incarnation, to the tradition (understood as the transmission of the incarnation in history), to a variety of materials in the world that can become vehicles of divine grace, whereby any person in the community can be used by God, to the particular sacraments that God has given the church.

A General Sacramentality

In an essay that has generated considerable interest, Mark Searle provides a helpful summary of the shift from a sacrament, focused on some particular divine action, to a sense of sacrament as grounded in the ecclesial connection of a person with Christ. He writes the following:

> During the past twenty or thirty years sacramental theology has undergone an enormous transformation. Undoubtedly the leading indicator if not the cause of this transformation is the abandonment of the questions and vocabulary of Scholasticism in favor of more existentialist and personalist approaches to understanding what sacraments are and how they function in the Christian life. What began as a recover of the ecclesial dimensions of the sacraments quickly led to further shifts: from speaking of sacraments as "means of grace" to speaking of them as encounters with Christ himself; from thinking of them primarily as acts of God to thinking of them mainly as celebration of the faith community; from seeing sacraments as momentary incursions from another world to seeing them as manifestations of the graced character of all human life; from interpreting them as remedies for sin and weakness to seeing them as promoting growth in Christ.[23]

Some of these shifts reflect the Western skepticism about particular divine action. We link the sacrament—in this case, infant baptism—to a general experience of Christ in the church rather than to a particular example of spiritual causation. However, it is also true that some of these shifts represent a healthy recognition that the sacrament is bigger than the particular instance of divine grace seen in baptism.

A number of theologians have explicated a general sacramentality that extends far beyond the two major ones (baptism and Eucharist) or even the Roman Catholic seven or even beyond the human. The idea of the entire world as a sacrament emerged in the writings of Alexander Schmemann, in his book *The Word as Sacrament*. For Schmemann, the argument is heavily Eucharistic. In the Eucharist, there is a thanksgiving for the world and the reminder that humanity has responsibility to care for the world. Schmemann writes, "The Eucharist is the sacrament of the cosmic remembrance: it is indeed a restoration of love as the very life of the world."[24] A more Christological argument, although interestingly one that is critical of a too Christological approach, is found in the work of Theodore Runyon.[25] He writes, "In the hands of the Creator, the world was itself the first sacrament, the first use of the material to communicate and facilitate the divine-human relation. Thus the world is the 'original sacrament.'"[26] In the universe, we see God, which God then gives the universe to humanity for appropriate care. In the act of redemption by Christ, the whole creation is part of the eschatological fulfillment.

As we noted above, such a broad definition of the sacramental is unhelpful. Certainly, the cosmos can be talked about as revelatory of God. And certainly, there are deep connections between the cosmos and Christology, especially in the Eucharist, that can be affirmed. However, it is important to make a distinction between the revelatory and the sacramental.

So, what exactly is that distinction? In brief, the revelatory shows us something of God, while the sacramental is a moment when God touches our lives. At this point, Augustine is most helpful. In Augustine's "Questions on the Heptateuch," he uses the word "sacrament" in very interesting ways. First, we have the sacrament of time. In his reflection on why was the Sabbath commandment given such prominence as Moses comes down the mountain, Augustine explains: "We do not have the slightest doubt that the other nine were commanded in some way or other to be observed in the new covenant too. But that one commandment about the Sabbath was always veiled among the Israelites in a figurative observance of the seventh day, and it was commanded in mystery and functioned as a kind of sacramental figure."[27] For Augustine, the Sabbath has a sacramental feel because "in that rest, when servile works are commanded to cease, there is a great depth of God's grace."[28] So the time of rest is a gift from God; in this respect, time can function in a sacramental way.

Second, we have the materials that a human, as directed by God, can turn into vehicles of holiness. This idea emerges as Augustine struggles with the phrase in Leviticus, where God tells Moses, "And you shall sanctify him" (Leviticus 21:8). Given later it is the Lord that makes the priest holy, how is it possible that Moses can do that? Augustine writes, "For Moses does not sanctify on behalf of the Lord, but Moses does so by invisible grace through the Holy Spirit, where the whole fruit of the visible sacraments is also present."[29] Now, presumably, the visible sacraments are the various mechanisms of worship in the temple (the firstborn males of the animals or the crops and animals that were sacrificed). For Augustine, these elements in the hands of Moses become sacraments.

Third, the sacrifices of the Old Testament can function as sacraments because they are anticipating the work of Christ. In Augustine's discussion of Numbers 19, he sees the washing of garments and the need to wait until evening a clear invocation of the impact of Christ and the promise of the full remission of sin. So, Augustine writes:

> What else does this show except the baptism of Christ, which the water of sprinkling signified and which was going to benefit the Jews and the gentiles, that is, the children of Israel and the foreigners, like natural branches and like the wild olive grafted onto the richness of the root? Whose attention would not be sieved by what is said about each one after the washing, *And he shall be unclean until evening*? This is said not only here but with respect to all or to almost all such washings. I do not know whether it can be understood as meaning anything but that, after the full remission of his sins, each person contracts something by remaining in this life, which is why he is unclean until the end of that same life, when this day is in some way ended for him, which is what *evening* means.[30]

These three principles create a basis for a general sacramentality. It is divine agency through either a gift (for example, time) or materials that can be used by God to bring us closer to God (and here I would include countless vehicles—the labyrinth, the crucifix, or the piece of music) or anything that points us to Christ.

Naturally, Christians want to go further and recognize, in certain respects, a more particular sacramentality. It is to baptism and the Eucharist that we need to turn next.

Baptism and the Eucharist[31]

For our purposes, we shall concentrate on the two sacraments of baptism and Eucharist. Historically, for Christians, especially those with a more Roman Catholic sympathy, it is at baptism and the Eucharist that God touches the material in a distinctive way. Again, stressing the contrast between the revelatory and the sacramental, it is not sufficient for a spiritually infused universe that baptism and the Eucharist are just showing us God or, more technically, just showing us what God has already done (the tendency in many protestant accounts of the sacramental). For the spiritually infused universe, baptism and Eucharist need to be divine actions, where spiritual causation occurs. Therefore, what follows is a defense of high sacramentality in respect to baptism and Eucharist.

So, let us start with baptism, in particular, focusing on the Roman Catholic account. For Roman Catholics, baptism is the "basis of the whole Christian life, the gateway to life in the Spirit, and the door which gives access to the other sacraments."[32] Baptism is grounded in Scripture. In the Hebrew Bible, the Jewish people escape from slavery in Egypt by crossing the Red Sea and receive the land by crossing the River Jordan. The point is one passes through water both to escape captivity and to receive the freedom of new life. So, by analogy, baptism plays the same role in the life of the Christian.

In being baptized, we are following the example of Jesus, who was baptized by John. In being baptized, the stain of original sin is removed. The Catechism claims that, "By Baptism *all sins* are forgiven, original sin and all personal sins, as well as all punishment for sin."[33] Both adults and infants can be baptized. This is clearly a divine action. It is a moment when the eternal consequences of our propensities to selfishness and cruelty are eradicated. Although we will still struggle with sins, the power of sin to be eternally destructive has been overcome. The act of water on a human life, with the appropriate Trinitarian formula, has a consequence that is far-reaching.

Now the fact it extends to infants is controversial. On infants, the Catechism writes:

> Born with a fallen nature and tainted by original sin, children also have need of the new birth in Baptism to be freed from the power of darkness and brought into the realm of the freedom of the children of God, to which all men are called. The sheer gratuitousness of the grace of salvation is particularly manifest in infant Baptism. The Church and the parents would deny a child the priceless grace of becoming a child of God were they not to confer Baptism shortly after birth.[34]

Some Christians object that given babies cannot yet decide for themselves, infant baptism is improper. However, the Roman Catholic response is convincing. There is an appropriation recognition that "faith must grow *after* baptism."[35] And they argue, rightly, that infant baptism is found in the New Testament because the author of the book of Acts wrote about entire "households" receiving baptism, which presumably would have included infants.

Because of its foundational character, any person can perform a baptism. Ideally, it should be a bishop or priest or deacon. However, "in case of necessity, any person, even someone not baptized, can baptize, if he has the required intention. The intention required is to will to do what the Church does when she baptizes, and to apply the Trinitarian baptismal formula."[36] Even today, there are many parts of the world where a devout midwife will take a sick baby and perform a discreet baptism. Although the Catechism does concede that God's mercy and Christ's injunction towards children "allow us to hope that there is a way of salvation for children who have died without Baptism,"[37] for the Catechism, it is clearly preferable that the stain of original sin has been removed and that the sick baby can be guaranteed its place in heaven.

The classic problem of the unbaptized person (whether child or adult) has haunted this original sin theology. The appropriate commitment to spiritual causation in the miracle of baptism leads to an immoral corollary. If God's mechanism for the eradication of original sin is baptism, then surely the unbaptized must face the consequences of original sin, which is eternal death. The mistake is in the premise. Christians do want to affirm that one of the mechanisms for the eradication of original sin is baptism, but there is no reason to assume that this is the only mechanism. The biblical witness clearly affirms that the great cloud of witnesses in Hebrews 11 are "saved," yet none were baptized. Baptism should be seen as a way that God can remove the consequences of original sin but not the only way.

Let us now turn to the Eucharist. The Eucharist is based on the Last Supper. Jesus brings his disciples together hours before he is going to be arrested (see Luke 22:7–20; Matthew 26:17–29; Mark 14:12–25; 1 Corinthians 11:23–26). In this meal, Jesus explains to the disciples that the bread is his body and the wine his blood. Paul, in 1 Corinthians, explains that Jesus took bread

> and when he had given thanks, he broke it, and said, "This is my body which is for you. Do this in remembrance of me." In the same way also the cup, after supper, saying, "This cup is the new covenant in my blood. Do this, as often as you drink it, in remembrance of me." (1 Corinthians 11:24–25)

At this poignant moment, Jesus asks his disciples to eat bread and drink wine in remembrance of him. From the time of Jesus onwards, the Eucharist (which means thanksgiving) or the Lord's Supper became a central Christian ritual.

Once again, we find that all three members of the Trinity are involved in the Eucharist. The Catechism explains:

> We must therefore consider the Eucharist as:
>
> - thanksgiving and praise to the *Father;*
> - the sacrificial memorial of *Christ* and his Body;
> - the presence of Christ by the power of his word and of his *Spirit*.[38]

It is a thanksgiving because we are celebrating the works of creation and salvation. God has given us the opportunity to become children of God by the gracious acts of creation and redemption. The memorial is not "merely the recollection of past events"[39] but the making present of Christ's sacrifice on the cross. And it is this work of "making present" that the Holy Spirit brings about. It is at this point we find the Catechism talking about transubstantiation. The Catechism quotes from the ruling at the Council of Trent, which was held in 1545–1563.

The Council of Trent summarizes the Catholic faith by declaring: "Because Christ our Redeemer said that it was truly his body that he was offering under the species of bread, it has always been the conviction of the Church of God, and this holy Council now declares again, that by the consecration of the bread and wine there takes place a change of the whole substance of the bread into the substance of the body of Christ our Lord and of the whole substance of the wine into the substance of his blood. This change the holy Catholic Church has fittingly and properly called transubstantiation."[40]

Transubstantiation is grounded in Aristotelian terminology and philosophy. Aristotle (384CE–322CE) distinguished between the "substance" and the "accidents." The essential nature is the "substance," while the shape, color, and general outward appearance are "accidents." Using this distinction, although the appearance of bread and wine remains the same, it does, nevertheless, become the body and blood of Jesus. The Eucharist, then, is a miracle of divine grace. In the act of taking the Eucharist, one takes into one's body the divine and redeeming power of God in Christ.

Now there are many obvious difficulties with any view that claims that the bread and wine are—in some real sense—the body and blood of Jesus. Bernard Prusak offers an interesting critique of the dilemma for medieval theology. The problem is easy to state: the glorified body of Jesus is located in heaven; insofar as Jesus is able to be everywhere, this is only possible in his divinity, not in his humanity. Therefore, how can the Eucharist be the presence of the body (and blood) of Christ?[41]

The solution for the church fathers was this: After the ascension, it was the spiritual Christ that is present in the world. For Augustine, explains Prusak, we see bread and wine; to the eyes of faith, we see an invisible reality. We become Christ in eating the bread. Now, in the eighth and ninth centuries, this clarity of description is less clear. Paschasius Radbertus, best known for his writing on the Eucharist, retains the idea that it is the spiritual resurrected Christ that is present, but he adds plenty of stories about bleeding hosts, as if it were the physical, historical Jesus. By the time we get back to Aquinas, we have a more Augustinian approach. For Aquinas, we are not eating the material body of Jesus. Instead, Christ's body is present in a spiritual way.

Reformation and Protestant views

One of Martin Luther's (1483–1546) targets at the Reformation was penance. It was the practice of indulgences that provoked his ire. However, as his views developed, he became increasingly suspicious of the use of Aristotelian philosophy in Christian doctrine. In "Babylonian Captivity of the Church" (1520), he insists that there are not seven sacraments. At the start of the tract, he implies there are three (baptism, Eucharist, and penance), but towards the end, he concludes the following:

> Nevertheless, it has seemed proper to restrict the name of sacrament to those promises which have signs attached to them. The remainder, not being bound to signs, are bare promises. Hence there are, strictly speaking, but two sacraments in the church of God—baptism and the bread. For only in these two do we find both the divinely instituted sign and the promise of forgiveness of sins.

> The sacrament of penance, which I added to these two, lacks the divinely instituted visible sign, and is, as I have said, nothing but a way and a return to baptism.[42]

So, for Luther, a sacrament needs to be a "divinely instituted visible sign." The sign is the "water" (in the case of baptism) and the "bread" and "wine" (in the case of the Eucharist). On baptism, Luther is equally committed as Roman Catholics to infant baptism. On the Eucharist, he wants Christ present in both the accidents and the substance. He draws an analogy with the doctrine of the incarnation: In the same ways Godhead permeated all of humanity, so Christ permeates all the bread. He writes:

> And why could not Christ include his body in the substance of the bread just as well as in the accidents? In red-hot iron, for instance, the two substances, fire and iron, are so mingled that every part is both iron and fire. Why is it not even more possible that the body of Christ be contained in every part of the substance of the bread?[43]

Luther, then, believes in the "real presence" or sometimes known as "consubstantiation." For Luther, it is because Jesus in the Bible states that "this is my body," it must be so. The power of the sacraments is made possible by God and received by the faith of the believer.

John Calvin (1509–1564) took the line that the sacraments were signs of a reality that God had already performed. When defining a sacrament, he writes:

> It seems to me that a simple and proper definition would be to say that it is an outward sign by which the Lord seals on our consciences the promises of his good will towards us in order to sustain the weakness of our faith; and we in turn attest our piety towards him in the presence of the Lord and of his angels and before men.[44]

The emphasis here is that sacraments are signs of work that God has already done. So, says Calvin,

> baptism should be a token and proof of our cleansing; or (the better to explain what I mean) it is like a sealed document to confirm to us that all our sins are so abolished, remitted, and effaced that they can never come to his sight, be recalled or charged against us. . . . Accordingly, they who regarded baptism as nothing but a token and mark by which we confess our religion before men, as soldiers bear the insignia of their commander as a mark of their profession, have not weighed what was the chief point of baptism. It is to receive baptism with this promise: "He who believes and is baptized will be saved" (Mark 16:16).[45]

This, then, is a nuanced account. Baptism is not simply a public witness but remains a moment that witnesses to a work that God has performed. On the Eucharist, the bread and wine witness to a spiritual reality of redemption. In both cases, for Calvin, the agent at work is the Holy Spirit.

Ulrich Zwingli (1484–1531) is the most radical of the big three reformers. For him, the sacraments are just "signs or ceremonials."[46] When baptizing a baby, one is simply saying this: "With this external sign you are to dedicate and pledge them to the name of the Father, the Son and the Holy Ghost, and to teach them to observe all the things that I have committed to you."[47] And on the Eucharist, he finds it absurd to say that "Christ is literally there." It would mean that Christ is literally "broken, and pressed with the teeth."[48] Instead, we should interpret the phrase "this is my body" more metaphorically. It is analogous, explains Zwingli, to a wife who shows someone her husband's ring and says, "This is my late husband."[49] In short, the Eucharist is a memorial.

While Luther, Calvin, and Zwingli were comfortable with infant baptism, it was the Anabaptists who insisted that it was wrong. Anabaptists emerged both in Saxony and Switzerland during this period of upheaval and reformation. Menno Simons, writing in 1539, claims that:

> Young children are without understanding and unteachable; therefore baptism cannot be administered to them without perverting the ordinance of the Lord, misusing His exalted name, and doing violence to His holy Word. In the New Testament no ceremonies for infants are enjoined, for it treats both in doctrines and sacraments with those who have ears to hear and hearts to understand. . . . Faith does not follow from baptism, but baptism follows from faith.[50]

Anabaptists (whose modern heir is the Baptist denomination) believed that a valid baptism involves an adult who wants to confess Christ in a public witness. It is simply a sign of a work of grace already performed in a life. It is not a vehicle of that grace.

Contemporary Debate

It is the Roman Catholic theologian Edward Schillebeeckx who has led the way in the modern debate. For Schillebeeckx, sacraments should be understood as a deep encounter with Christ. For the disciples in the presence of the historical Jesus, they had a sacramental encounter with God all the time. Schillebeeckx writes: "The man Jesus, as the personal visible realization of the divine grace of redemption, is *the* sacrament, the primordial sacrament, because this man, the Son of God himself, is intended by the Father to be in his humanity, the only way to the actuality of redemption."[51] Given Christ has ascended, today, we now receive that encounter through the seven sacraments. Schillebeeckx writes: "In an earthly embodiment which we can see and touch, the heavenly Christ sacramentalizes both his continual intercession for us and his active gift of grace. Therefore the sacraments are the visible realization on earth of Christ's mystery of saving worship."[52]

The modern debate around the nature of the Eucharist has been dominated by the introduction of two new terms to the debate. The first is "transfinalization." F. J. Leenhardt, in 1955, coined the term. Joseph Martos helpfully explains:

> The basic idea behind it was that the "final reality" of any created thing is determined by its maker and not by what it is made of. A carpenter who made a cabinet, for example, made something whose final reality was a cabinet even though he made it out of wood. He had actually produced something new, since before only the wood existed but now there was a new reality, brought into being through the intention of the creator.[53]

So, if you apply this idea to the Eucharist, then at the end of the prayer of consecration, the purpose of the bread and wine has changed. At the start of the service, it is just "bread" and "wine," but by the end, the creator, who is Jesus Christ, has made body and blood.

The second term is "transignification," which stresses significance and meaning. On this view, certain actions are symbolic. A slap across the face is on one level just a hand touching a face; but on another level, it can represent anger, even fury. The latter explanation is as real as the former: Indeed, one would completely misunderstand the slap across the face, if one interpreted as just a hand touching a face. So, by analogy, sacraments transignify a human and divine reality. On the human level, the practice of baptism involves a baby being marked by the sign of the cross with water; on a divine level, it is the life being transformed by grace. The latter is as real as the former.

These two terms are taking the debate to a new level. It should be completely clear: We are not talking about cannibalism—this is not the consumption of a human person. In fact, Christians do not consume the bread and wine for food but to enable the divine life to become part of their lives.

Keith Ward is very helpful at this point. He has clearly been influenced by the debate on transignification. Ward argues that one completely misunderstands the Eucharist if it is seen as simply bread and wine. It is symbolic; but in an echo of Paul Tillich, Ward then explains "a symbol, in this sense, participates in and conveys the reality which it symbolizes."[54] When Jesus initiates the practice, he

> gives the disciples a foreshadowing symbol of that revealing and redeeming act. The broken bread presents both the sacrifice of the faithful servant and the divine passion. The wine originates a new covenant, sealed by the sacrifice of Jesus, already completed in intention, by which the life of the eternal Word

begins to transform the lives of men and women. Every subsequent celebration of that supper makes present the same reality, whose significance is greatly enriched by knowledge of the resurrection and outpouring of the Spirit.[55]

The reality of the redeeming work of God, according to Ward, is made present every time we celebrate the supper. Ward believes that there is a real change in the bread and wine. However, unlike many mechanical accounts of the sacraments, he wants to advocate a relational model. He starts by suggesting that we need to revisit the meaning of the bread:

> A piece of bread, when perceived by a human consciousness, is not just a chemical compound. It takes on a complex set of symbolic associations. It is something to be eaten, with a certain taste and texture, perhaps to be shared, a product of sowing, growing, reaping, and baking, and so of a joining of natural forces with human cultivation. The chemical compound takes on the properties of its causal origin, its intended use, its relation to human senses, and its social context.[56]

He objects strongly to the view that these additional properties are not really part of the bread. Indeed, Ward argues the property of "having being prepared in order to be eaten"[57] is part of its Platonic Form. If this point is conceded, then Ward comes to the heart of his argument:

> One might then say that, if bread is used in a ritual context, its essence (its substance in the sense of that which defines what it essentially is) is significantly changed. The mode of preparation remains the same, and yet part of that preparation becomes its setting apart by an act of blessing. By that act, it is consecrated to God set apart from common use. It is no longer ordinary bread, and its intended purpose becomes quite different.[58]

The intended purpose is to enable the divine life to become part of the worshipper. The social context, purpose, and perception of the bread has all changed. For Ward, this can be called "transubstantiation." He writes, "If one means that the essential nature of the bread has been changed, even though all its essential properties remain the same."[59] And it has objectively changed: God has made it possible for the divine life to be "truly expressed and conveyed by the rite."[60]

How is it possible for Christ to be present in the sacrament? Ward suggests that the basic operation is the same as the incarnation. In the incarnation, the eternal Word (i.e., the second person of the Trinity) becomes present in the human life of Jesus. In the Eucharist, the eternal Word becomes present in the bread and wine. Ward writes:

> Even though the particular acts of the Word in Jesus are not exactly repeatable (there will never again be a young man teaching in a remote province of the

Roman Empire) there is a sense in which the liberating action of the Word in Jesus can be repeated in different contexts. What is present on the altar is the eternal Christ in the particular form he took in Jesus, acting to convey divine love and power as he did in Jesus.[61]

So, from the divine perspective, God, through the Spirit, is making the eternal Word present in a distinctive way in the bread and wine. From the human perspective, the liturgical context and the prayer of consecration imbues the bread with a new and distinctive purpose. In so doing, we can properly speak of the bread changing into the body and blood of Jesus.

A Spiritually Infused Universe and the Eucharist

One is now on the cusp of having a distinctive account of the Eucharist operating within the paradigm of the spiritually infused Eucharist. It is true that the purpose of the meal is important. When a priest, in a church setting, sets the bread and wine aside to be an encounter of divine grace, the very act does make an objective difference. When the epiclesis calls down the Holy Spirit to make Christ present to us, Ward's account is helpful. The eternal Word that entered Jesus of Nazareth is now entering these elements. However, this does not quite get to the claim of the tradition that Jesus is present in the elements.

At this point, the classical solution that invokes the spiritually present Christ makes perfect sense. The eternal Word makes the spiritual Christ present. The material does change. It is indeed the very presence of Christ. It is worth at this point of revisiting the primary metaphor for the spiritually infused universe. A study of the material brain can never see a thought. My thought of a beautiful flower is never detected or seen in the various nerve fibers moving around the brain. In the same way, a study of the physical bread and wine does not reveal the composition of the spiritual presence of Christ.

CONCLUDING INSIGHTS

This is a key chapter. A set of distinctions have been offered. First, much of the material can be revelatory of the divine. Nature—the sunset and the flower—all show us something of the Creator. But this is properly understood as revelatory, not as sacrament. Second, at certain points, the material becomes a vehicle for the spiritual—for the divine. This can be many things—a labyrinth, prayer beads, a church building. The spiritual is felt in these spaces. This is a generalized understanding of the sacraments. Third, at particular points, the material becomes so infused by the spiritual that it has a certain distinctive power. In this chapter, I defended both baptism and the Eucharist as such moments of particular sacramentality.

For the third particular understanding of the sacrament to be plausible, it is necessary to revisit one of the oldest and most puzzling doctrines in the church—the concept of apostolic succession. Grounded in the catholic (in the literal sense—the universal family of Christians) understanding of the world, the apostolic succession will be defended in the next chapter. The sense that there is a connection between Jesus (the disclosure of God to humanity) and those in Holy Orders today is a necessary part of the Christian understanding of how humans can interact with the spiritual realm. The church reveals and witnesses to the general sacramentality, where the sunrise and the blade of grass can mediate a sense of the divine; and the church is the vehicle for the particular sacramentality, through, in particular, the Eucharist. This is our task in the next chapter.

NOTES

1. Keith Thomas, *Religion and the Decline of Magic: Studies in Popular Beliefs in Sixteenth- and Seventeenth-Century England* (London: The Folio Society, 2012—originally published in 1971), Volume 1, p. 46.
2. Everett Ferguson, "Sacraments in the pre-Nicene Period," in Hans Boersma and Matthew Levering (eds.), *The Oxford Handbook of Sacramental Theology* (Oxford: Oxford University Press, 2015), p. 126.
3. Kenan B. Osborne, *Sacramental Theology: A General Introduction* (New York: Paulist Press, 1988), p. 22.
4. Bernard Leeming, S. J., *Principles of Sacramental Theology* (London: Longmans, Green and Co., 1958).
5. Ibid., p. xxxiii and p. xxxiv.
6. Ibid., p. xxxiv.
7. Ibid., p. xxxiv.
8. Ibid., p. 3.
9. Ibid., p. 385.
10. Ibid., p. xxxiv and p. xxxv.
11. Ibid., p. 369.
12. Timothy F. Sedgwick, *Sacramental Ethics: Paschal Identity and the Christian Life* (Philadelphia: Fortress Press, 1987), p. 70.
13. Leeming, *Principles of Sacramental Theology*, p. 376.
14. Ibid., p. 376. While taking issue with Leeming's view of other Christians and the Eucharist, I do agree with him on the unbaptized. For Leeming, the unbaptized cannot receive the Eucharist because "the Eucharist is for the nourishment of the Mystical Body; and hence one who is not in the body cannot profit by the food given to the body" (p. 376).
15. Osborne, *Sacramental Theology*, pp. 5–6.
16. Ibid., p. 7.
17. Ibid., p. 34.
18. Tyler Sampson, "Scripture, Tradition, and Resourcement: Toward an Anglican Fundamental Liturgical Theology," *Anglican Theological Review*, Vol. 96, 2 (2014): 318.
19. Ibid., p. 320.
20. Susan A. Ross, *Extravagant Affections: A Feminist Sacramental Theology* (New York: Continuum, 1998), p.34.
21. Ibid., p. 211.

22. Ibid., p. 213.

23. Mark Searle, "Infant Baptist Reconsidered," as reproduced in Maxwell E. Johnson, *Living Water, Sealing Spirit: Readings on Christian Initiation* (Collegeville, MN: The Liturgical Press, 1995), p. 395. Searle edited an earlier book where the essay appeared, *Alternative Futures for Worship, Volume 2: Baptism and Confirmation* (Collegeville, MN: The Liturgical Press, 1987).

24. Alexander Schmemann, *The World as Sacrament* (London: Darton, Longman and Todd, 1966), p. 42.

25. This criticism is well made by Dorothy C. Mcdougall in *The Cosmos as the Primary Sacrament: The Horizon for an Ecological Sacramental Theology*, (New York: Peter Lang 2003). Mcdougall writes, "What is disappointing about Runyon's approach is that he himself stays within the theological parameters of Christology to structure his own argument." (p.111). Mcdougall has a more radical account of cosmic sacramentality. She argues for the cosmos as the primary sacrament, where creation in its own right is worthy of affirmation, separate from the relationship with the human.

26. Theodore Runyon, "The Word as the Original Sacrament," in *Worship* 54 (November 1980): p. 500.

27. Augustine of Hippo, "Questions on the Heptateuch," in Boniface Ramsey (ed.), *The Works of Saint Augustine: Writings on the Old Testament*, Part 1: Volume 14, p. 174 (New York: New City Press of Focolare, 2016).

28. Ibid., p. 174.

29. Ibid., p. 259. It is worth noting that most modern renderings of the Hebrew in Leviticus 21:8 tend to the view that the obligation of Moses is to recognize their holiness not to make them holy. However, this does not detract from the general point about the depth of Augustine's view of the sacramental.

30. Ibid., p. 295.

31. Elements of what follows are drawn from my *Understanding Christian Doctrine*, (Oxford: Wiley Blackwell, 2017).

32. *Catechism of the Catholic Church* (Mahwah, NJ: Paulist Press, 1994) p. 312.

33. Ibid., p. 321 (italics in the text).

34. Ibid., p. 319.

35. Ibid., p. 320 (italics in the text).

36. Ibid., p. 320.

37. Ibid., p. 321.

38. Ibid., p. 342.

39. Ibid., p. 343.

40. Ibid., p. 347.

41. Bernard P. Prusak, "Explaining Eucharistic 'Real Presence': Moving beyond a Medieval Conundrum," *Theological Studies*, Vol. 75, 2 (2014): 239.

42. Martin Luther, "Babylonian Captivity of the Church (1520)," in James F. White, *Documents of Christian Worship: Descriptive and Interpretive Sources* (Louisville, KY: Westminster John Knox Press 1992) p. 131.

43. Ibid. p. 198.

44. John Calvin, *Institutes of the Christian Religion*, IV, 13, 1–26 (1559), found in James F. White, *Documents of Christian Worship: Descriptive and Interpretive Sources* (Louisville, KY: Westminster John Knox Press, 1992), p. 132.

45. Ibid., p. 172.

46. Ulrich Zwingli, *Commentary on True and False Religion* (1525), in James F. White, *Documents of Christian Worship: Descriptive and Interpretive Sources* (Louisville, KY: Westminster John Knox Press, 1992), p. 132.

47. Ulrich Zwingli, *Of Baptism*, found in James F. White, *Documents of Christian Worship* (Louisville, KY: Westminster John Knox Press, 1992), pp. 170–71.

48. Ulrich Zwingli, *On the Lord's Supper*, found in James F. White, *Documents of Christian Worship* (Louisville, KY: Westminster John Knox Press, 1992), p. 201.

49. Ibid., p. 201.

50. Menno Simons, *Foundations of Christian Doctrine* (1539) as found in James F. White, *Documents of Christian Worship*, p.169.
51. Edward Schillebeeckx, *Christ the Sacrament of the Encounter with God* (New York: Sheed & Ward, 1963), p. 15.
52. Ibid., p. 44.
53. Joseph Martos, *Doors to the Sacred: A Historical Introduction to Sacraments in the Catholic Church*, revised edition (Liguori, Missour: Liguori/Triumph, 2001), p. 263.
54. Keith Ward, *Religion and Community* (Oxford: Oxford University Press, 2000), p. 194.
55. Ibid., pp. 195–96.
56. Ibid., p. 197.
57. Ibid., p. 197.
58. Ibid., p. 197.
59. Ibid., p. 198.
60. Ibid., p. 198.
61. Ibid., p. 199.

Chapter Seven

Apostolic Succession

The Authority

> Here the Bishop lays hands upon the head of the ordinand, the Priests who are present also laying on their hands.
> *At the same time the Bishop prays* Therefore, Father, through Jesus Christ your Son, give your Holy Spirit to *N.*; fill *him/her* with grace and power, and make *him/her* a priest in your Church.

So goes the "Consecration of a Priest in The Ordination of a Priest," in the Episcopal *Book of Common Prayer*.

In terms of a spiritually infused universe, the moment that a person becomes a priest in the "one holy catholic and apostolic Church" is exceptional. Rich in pageantry and beautiful in structure, the liturgy quivers with expectation. Any participant in an ordination can feel that a person is changing. It is an ontological change. Barney Hawkins starts his beautiful book on ministry in the following way:

> Have you ever thought about what you would like to have written on your tombstone? If I were to have an old-fashioned tombstone, I would like my name and only one word: PRIEST. Being a priest has defined my adult life both personally and professionally. Being a priest is engraved on my very being. I really think God made me to be a priest. It is my authentic, true calling.[1]

Hawkins moves from the professional, to the ontological, and then finally locates it in a call, which he really believes God issued. The phrase "God made me to be a priest" implies a creation. This is much more than a career; it is his primary identity.

This is an elevated view of the priesthood. For Hawkins, a priest is a divine creation. It is a distinctive role—not better than a lay vocation but distinctive. And it happens with the tactile action of hands being laid on a person by a bishop and by his or her fellow presbyters. There is something that happens. Divine grace brings about a change.

This aspect of the spiritually infused universe is captured by the language of the apostolic succession—a complex doctrine with countless negative associations. In this chapter, we shall explore this complicated world. We will start by focusing on the many difficulties associated with the doctrine before moving to an account that affirms the spiritual reality while being ecumenically generous and historically sensitive.

Cuthbert Hamilton Turner wrote a short tract defending the apostolic succession in 1945. He starts by musing on the benefits of monarchy. The great advantages of such an institution are that it provides continuity of identity and belief. So, by analogy, Turner goes on to explain, the bishop plays the same role. He writes: "Emphasis on the apostolic succession is primarily an assertion of the external continuity of Christian history and witness, tradition and means of grace, as a real and precious thing, which no developments and no divisions must tempt us to overlook or under-estimate: it is a counterpart to our belief in the One Holy Catholic and Apostolic Church."[2] For Turner, the doctrine protects the church from schismatic tendencies because the bishop provides stability. Turner is aware of those critics who suspect that the historical data does not permit us to believe that there are unbroken lines of bishops back to the apostles. And, in response, he does discuss Eusebius, Hippolytus, and Irenaeus before reassuring the reader that the continuity is indeed safe and certain.

This is the sort of defense of a doctrine that gets a doctrine in trouble. The analogy with the monarchy will provoke the ire of all those who suspect the doctrine tends to hierarchal and undemocratic tendencies. Historians will get frustrated with the ease with which the initial two centuries of the church are treated. And anyone committed to ecumenism will find it puzzling why the issue of the validity of other reformed orders are not even considered.

Of all the unfashionable doctrines this book seeks to defend, the doctrine of the apostolic succession is one of the hardest. Indeed, the doctrine has almost assumed an esoteric quality. Defenders are confined to conservative Roman Catholics; and those attacking the doctrine are largely confined to conservative evangelicals. The rest of the church does not seem to be overly interested in the doctrine. It is almost too ridiculous to either defend or attack.

This lack of interest was not always the case. There have been two seasons when the doctrine got sustained attention in the Euro-American world. The first was provoked by the Tractarians in the 1850s, and the second was provoked by the ecumenical movement a hundred years later in the 1950s. Let us briefly look at these two debates.

It was John Henry Newman, the Vicar of the University Church of St. Mary the Virgin and a junior fellow at Oriel College, who credits John Keble's famous Assize Sermon, delivered on July 14, 1833, as the start of the Oxford Movement. Keble's great complaint was the legislation going through parliament to reduce the number of bishops in Ireland. His point was theological: Is the church a department of the state, or is it a divinely ordained institution? In short, what is the church? Naturally, for the Tractarians, apostolic succession mattered. Keble, in the fourth tract, provides a robust defense of the apostolic succession, when he writes:

> For it is obvious, that, among other results of the primitive doctrine of the Apostolical Succession, thoroughly considered and followed up, it would make the relation of Pastor and Parishioner far more engaging, as well as more awful, than it is usually considered at present. Look on your pastor as acting by man's commission, and you may respect the authority by which he acts, you may venerate and love his personal character; but it can hardly be called a *religious* veneration; there is nothing, properly, *sacred* about him. But once learn to regard him as "the Deputy of Christ, for reducing man to the obedience of God;" and every thing about him becomes changed, every thing stands in a new light. In public and in private, in church and at home, in consolation and in censure, and above all, in the administration of the Holy Sacraments, a faithful man naturally considers, "By this His messenger Christ is speaking to me; by his very being and place in the world, he is a perpetual witness to the truth of the sacred history, a perpetual earnest of Communion with our Lord to those who come duly prepared to His Table." In short it must make just all the difference in every part of a Clergyman's duty, whether he do it, and be known to do it, in that Faith of his commission from Christ, or no.[3]

For Keble, a priest is not a person commissioned by humans but rather a person commissioned by God. This changes the way in which a parishioner views the priest; it changes the way the priest sees himself (and, of course, we would now add herself).

Naturally, this provoked a reaction. Philip Cater was typical. In a response called *The great fiction of the times, or Apostolic succession, with other doctrines of Puseyism, proved to be unscriptural and absurd*, Cater summarized his position thus:

> Apostolic succession is the radical and distinguishing error of the system; for it not only contends with nearly all the clergy that the ordaining power has descended from the apostles in the line of bishops, but contends also for a succession of saving grace as well as ordaining power inherent in the line, and sent down from hand to hand, so that all the benefits of Christ to sinners must come exclusively through that descent. Let this one doctrine be disproved—let it be scripturally shewn that men of piety and of ability may be true ministers

of the gospel, and efficient administrators of its ordinances, though not episcopally ordained, then the foundation is undermined, and the whole fabric of Puseyism must necessarily fall to the ground. [4]

Cater had a whole range of objections. The doctrine is not found in Scripture. Technically, the apostles cannot have successors because they were directly commissioned by our Lord, unlike subsequent bishops.[5] He points out there is no single, unbroken succession.[6] He feels that it is deeply insulting to nonconformist clergy; and he stresses the fact that there were many popes and bishops that were ethically compromised.

Looking back on this debate, there is a strange sense of the two sides speaking past each other. For the Tractarians, the issue was authority. Has God, in God's providence, created a divine institution? For the opponents, the issues are history and ecumenism. Turning now to the debate in England in the late 1950s, we find a similar dynamic at work.

Defenders of the apostolic succession were, on the whole, critics of the drive towards ecumenism. Successors of the Tractarians saw with some horror the prospect of the Catholic view of holy orders being diluted or even denied by possible cooperation between nonconformist traditions and Anglicanism. Many in the 1950s were following the arguments of Charles Gore set out in his classic *The Ministry of the Christian Church*.[7]

Gore sets out his assumption early on. He explains that the apostolic succession "must be reckoned with as a permanent and essential element of Christianity."[8] He outlines his hypothesis that he wants to defend in the book as this:

> Let it be supposed the Christ, in founding His Church, founded also a ministry in the Church in the persons of His Apostles. These Apostles must be supposed to have had a temporary function in their capacity as founders under Christ. In this capacity they held an office by its very nature not perpetual—the office of being the original witness to Christ's resurrection and making the original proclamation of the Gospel. But underlying this was another—a pastorate of souls, a stewardship of divine mysteries. This office instituted in their persons was intended to become perpetual, and that by being transmitted from its first depositaries. It was thus intended that there should be in every Church, in each generation, an authoritative stewardship of the grace and truth which came by Jesus Christ and a recognized power to transmit it, derived from above by apostolic descent. The men, who from time to time were to hold the various offices involved in the ministry and the transmitting power necessary for its continuance, might, indeed, fitly be elected by those to whom they were to minister. In this way the ministry would express the representative principle. But their authority to minister in whatever capacity, their qualifying consecration, was to come from above, in such sense that no ministerial act could be regarded as *valid*—that is, as having the security of the divine covenant about it—unless it was performed under the shelter of a commission, received by the transmission of the original pastoral authority which had been delegated by

Christ Himself to His Apostles. This is what is understood by the apostolic succession of the ministry.[9]

Gore goes on to say that the shape of this apostolic succession is the threefold ministry—a single bishop, presbyters who constitute a "cooperative order,"[10] and deacons. Chapters 3 to 6 are then a substantial historical study making the case that an apostolic succession is there in our history. It is in the "Conclusions and Applications" where Gore makes certain corollaries explicit. Here, Gore reveals his Anglo-Catholic antagonism to nonconformists—a disposition that goes deep in the Anglo-Catholic tradition. He writes the following:

> But it will appear at once as a consequence of all this argument that the various presbyterian and congregationalist organizations, however venerable on many different grounds, have, in dispensing with the episcopal successions, violated a fundamental law of the Church's life. It cannot be maintained that the acts of ordination, by which presbyters of the sixteenth or subsequent centuries originated the ministries of some of these societies, were covered by their commission or belonged to the office of presbyter which they had duly received. Beyond all question they "took to themselves" these powers of ordination, and consequently had them not. It is not proved—nay, it is not perhaps even probably—that any presbyter had in any age the power to ordain.[11]

Leaving aside the lack of charity, there is also a failure of logic here. One can affirm the doctrine of the apostolic succession and completely recognize the validity of other orders in other Christian denominations in terms of *their own self-understanding* (i.e., the strategy taken in the last chapter on sacraments). However, Gore did not see this option. And his intransigence, dutifully followed by his disciples into the twentieth century, ended up creating an increasing indifference to the doctrine by the 1960s.[12]

This might sound harsh. But when Felix L. Cirlot, of Nashotah House in the United States, comes to the writing on his magnum opus *Apostolic Succession: It is True?*, he writes in his preface, "I want to pay tribute to his monumental book, and to express my own deep indebtedness to it at almost every turn."[13] Cirlot goes on to say that he is writing his book as his contribution to the crises in the Anglican Communion. He fears that proposals for the ecumenical "Church of South India" will undermine the Catholic faith. And he writes, "The cause of Christian unity is a great and worthy cause; and it is certainly God's cause. But the cause of loyalty to the Catholic Faith and to Catholic Order is also God's cause, and cannot give way to the cause of Christian unity."[14]

The 1950s was the wrong decade to be opposed to ecumenism. Ecumenism was in fashion. This was a period when there was real hope and optimism that the divisions between Christians might be overcome. The British

Council of Churches was formed in 1942, at a service where Archbishop William Temple preached. In 1952, Archbishop Geoffrey Fisher, in a sermon at Cambridge University, argued that the Free Churches should take the concept of episcopacy into their structures, thereby creating the possibility of common sacraments and a commonly accepted ministry. With proposals such as these in the air, the 1950s became the decade of focused discussion of episcopacy and governance. It was in 1959 that the *Expository Times* ran a series of articles on the concept of apostolic succession.

The bulk of the articles were rather unsympathetic to the concept. A key theme that has shaped much of the mainline ever since emerges in this period, namely, the doctrine is antiquated and irrelevant. So, for example, the Dean of St. Paul's Cathedral, W. R. Matthews, insists that we should recognize the grace in the leadership of the Presbyterians (he was thinking of the Church of Scotland) and not—contra Archbishop Fischer—insist they have bishops.[15] Ironically, the Methodist contribution is a little more generous to the concept. So, A. Gordon James celebrates the value of the language because it safeguards continuity, catholicity, and stability. But he then goes on to say: "It does not follow from what has been written above that the exaggerated claims made, for example, by the Church of Rome for an unbroken line of apostolic men existing from the beginning until now can be sustained. This is not historically credible. Nor does it follow that the episcopate as it functions to-day must forever be the only body competent to ordain by the laying on of hands."[16]

This captures the mood of the times. Noel Hall, writing in the *Scottish Journal of Theology*, makes the same case at greater length. The concept of the apostolic succession is unhelpful for ecumenical relations and impossible to justify or defend historically. He is brutal in his assessment and writes: "This brief and very inadequate, though I hope objective, marshalling of the evidence compels the acknowledgment that the Tractarian appeal to antiquity betrays a want of historical discrimination: many of St. Augustine's conceptions of the ministry were not shared by the ante-Nicene fathers and have always been repudiated by the Eastern Orthodox."[17]

When Anglicans are given a choice of being charitable or traditional, charity tends to win every time. Liberal Anglo-Catholics emerged, which retained all the enthusiasm for liturgy but none of the theology. Michael Goulder, Denis Nineham, and Leslie Houlden were typical.[18] They still identified with the Anglo-Catholic camp (partly to distinguish themselves from the evangelicals), but they distanced themselves very firmly from the traditional Anglo-Catholic theological framework. They were properly modernist. When it came to the apostolic succession, at best, it was a symbol of the church's unity. It no longer captured a truth beyond that.

Why is it important that the doctrine retains some truth? This is a study that affirms the Christian understanding of the spiritually infused universe.

There are certain points at which the spiritually infused nature of the universe is more visible than others. In the next chapter, we look at sacraments; in this one, the argument is being made that the ordination of a priest (and other orders of ministry) is a moment when divine grace touches a human life in a distinctive way, which enables the priest to be a vehicle to bring divine grace to others.

This is not to say that many of the themes emerging in ecumenical dialogues around the apostolic succession have not been helpful. In the Church of England report titled *Apostolicity and Succession,* there is an appropriate affirmation of the centrality of the doctrine—it is, after all, in our creeds. The language, the report argues, is intended to safeguard the continuity of witness to the God that sends forth Jesus Christ across the centuries. In addition, an important stress that "it is the Church *as a whole* that is primarily to be described as apostolic."[19] And the apostolic mission of the Church involves all Christians. The report states: "Every Christian has a unique place and role in this mission of the Church, because every Christian occupies a unique place in the world into which the Church is sent."[20] This emphasis on the whole church, and the significance of the lay, are important correctives to the propensity to limit the language of apostolic succession to the clergy. However, as the Report concedes, the succession should not be understood in the same way for everyone. The ministry of oversight is distinctive. It then stresses that the act of ordination implies continuity of witness. So, the Report writes, "The historic episcopal succession is an expression first of Christ's faithfulness to the Church, second of the Church's intention to remain faithful to the apostles' teaching and mission. It is a means both of upholding that intention and of giving the faithful the confident assurance that the Church lives in continuity with the Lord's apostles and in anticipation of a glory yet to be fully disclosed."[21]

All of this is true. However, I want to say that it is insufficient. The apostolic succession is intended to be a vehicle for divine grace. The liturgy does, indeed, make a difference. The touch makes a difference. It is only after a person has been ordained a priest that one can say the Eucharistic prayer and make a difference. In this sense, the Report has lost sight of a key idea behind the apostolic succession; it is the moment that God uses to bring the sacraments to God's people. A richer account of the apostolic succession needs to be defended. But what exactly do we mean by apostolic succession? What form of the doctrine, which includes touch as central, can be defended?

Apostolic Succession: A Definition That Can Be Defended

I am a father. It is one of the great joys of my life. Out of a loving relationship with my wife, a baby was born to whom I relate to as a father.

Fatherhood has real causal significance. The baby is made possible by the father providing the sperm. The genes of the father are part of the child: the father's genetic makeup will have a significant impact on the son and the shape of his life. But more ideally, the father is a presence in the child's life. Along with the mother, the father imparts values, aspirations, and some resources to help the child succeed.

When one moves from a person without a child to a parent, there is a significant change. It is not simply a change of function (i.e., you now have this child who keeps you awake at night that requires attention), but it is a change of causation (i.e., you have caused a child to come into existence, your genes are shaping the child, and you are forever a parent—even if you try and deny your responsibilities).

I want to defend the idea that when a person becomes a priest, there is an ontological change (i.e., a change in their very being), which is analogous to becoming a parent. Now all analogies are imperfect. When it comes to parenthood, the changes are less in the parent and more in the child. But parenthood does capture a change which includes relationship (with the mother or father and wider family), function (in terms of obligations to the child), and in terms of causation (your genes are passed along). When a person becomes a priest, there is an analogous set of changes. In terms of relationship, the community recognizes you as a person commissioned by God to deliver the promises that God has made to the community to be a vehicle of divine grace through the sacraments. In terms of function, you are called to serve the community in certain ways—at the Eucharist, in offering absolution, and in providing a blessing. And in terms of causation, God's chosen vehicle for the creation of a priest is the connection from the apostles to the bishops to the priest, which is mediated through touch.

The task now is to defend the doctrine in such a way that it is historically plausible, ecumenically sensitive, and consistent with modern science.

Historically Plausible

History is messy. The past is subject to so much uncertainty. We have the uncertainty of what exactly happened. Which sources do we trust? How reliable are they? Then we have the uncertainty of interpretation. How do we best understand this or that? What is really going on? Christianity is a religion deeply committed to God's engagement in history. The narrative of the Hebrew Bible tells of a God who intervenes in history—in an Exodus from captivity (where there are very few extracanonical sources to confirm its historicity), in a settlement in Canaan (which was almost certainly much more messy than depicted), to an exile and return (which again is highly over-simplified in the text). When it comes to the historical Jesus, there is a legitimate debate about almost every aspect of the narrative—save perhaps that there was a young man called Jesus who was killed by the Romans in the first century, we cannot be "sure" about his birth, his teaching, and the reasons for his death. We might wish that these historical complexities were not present. But the alternative is difficult to imagine. God's revelation to humanity needs to come in a certain time and in a certain place. Humans, as they receive this revelation, are bound to be located; they will be speaking a certain language, making certain assumptions about the world, and receiving information through a particular cultural lens. There is no alternative. The stories of the disclosure of God at the particular time and place will be shared and passed down. For most cultures, it will initially be oral and then, only later, in a text. All of this is inescapable. And at every step of the way, the uncertainty which is intrinsic to history will become part of the narrative.

The temptation is to despair. This is, indeed, the position of Denis Nineham in *The Use and the Abuse of the Bible*. We cannot know. The differences between one historical age and another are vast. Continuities of understanding are impossible to see. However, perhaps a better strategy is to revise our expectations. We recognize the messiness of the past, while at the same time allow ourselves to affirm the insight and encounter with God that is the seed of the experience described. So, the fact that there are historical objections to a belief that cannot be completely overcome to the satisfaction of a rigorous secular historian should not become a decisive reason for rejecting that belief. There does need to be a plausibility—a shape to the description of the past for which there is evidence that makes it probable that this event occurred. But one does not expect more than this. God does not grant us to have more certainty: this is what is meant when Paul writes, "For now we see in a mirror, dimly" (1 Corinthians 15:12). This is the inevitable limitation of being historically located.

One helpful assumption is that there are legitimate continuities between the past and the present. In other words, to assume a theology that works for the future church is unlikely to be historical is to assume a conniving church, which is having to hide the reality of the past to create a construct that serves the interest of certain people in the present. This is an unreasonable assumption. The Roman Catholic theologian Aidan Nichols is helpful when he explains that he is going to assume the opposite. He writes:

> If we accept the notion of a development of doctrine, whereby some features of Catholic faith, ethics and worship are regarded as legitimate outgrowths from New Testament origins, then we commit ourselves to what may be termed a "hermeneutic of recognition," whereby we who share the developed consciousness of the later Church come to the evidences of the earliest Church *in positive expectation of finding* the seeds from which the great tree of the *Catholica* has grown.[22]

Therefore, the argument goes, Nichols is trusting that what is true of us now has its roots in what was originally required of us. As a result, he believes that we can expect to find in the historical reality a sense that Jesus Christ really did intend to create an apostolic priesthood.

Working with these expectations, the question is now asked: In what sense is the doctrine of the apostolic succession true? When the Vatican issued a response to the *Final Report* of the First Anglican-Roman Catholic International Commission (ARCIC 1), the Vatican claimed that "the Catholic Church recognizes in the apostolic succession...an unbroken line of episcopal ordination from Christ through the apostles down through the centuries to the bishops of today."[23] Now, if by this, the Vatican meant that Christ appointed apostles who, in their turn, appointed a bishop for each congregation that the apostles founded, then this is almost certainly historically false.

Francis Sullivan, the Roman Catholic scholar, is correct when he writes:

> We must conclude that the New Testament provides no basis for the notion that before the apostles died, they ordained one man as bishop for each of the churches they had founded. The only person in the New Testament whose role resembles that of a bishop is James the "brother of the Lord," who was most likely designated for his position of leadership in the Jerusalem church by his relationship with Jesus and the special appearance with which he was favored by the risen Christ. It seems extremely unlikely that he was "ordained" as bishop of Jerusalem by St. Peter. Nor does the New Testament evidence support the idea that Peter, Paul or any other apostle became the bishop of any one local church or ordained one man as bishop of any local church. One looks in vain to the New Testament for a basis for the idea of "an unbroken line of episcopal ordination from Christ through the apostles down through the centuries to the bishops of today.[24]

The situation was much more complicated than our doctrinal retrospective would want. We want a simple situation where there were congregations created by apostles, in which a bishop is ordained as successor before the apostle died. Yet, as Sullivan shows, we should not go to the opposite extreme and conclude that there is no biblical foundation for the doctrine. This would be equally unfair. Close reading of the biblical text clearly shows a community deeply concerned about the authority, tradition, and leadership. Indeed, all the basic ingredients of the doctrine are clearly there in the tradition.[25]

First, it is clear that Paul's authority as an apostle was a matter of considerable debate. Paul did have criteria for the claim to be an apostle of Jesus. It must be someone who has seen Jesus—either as risen or on Earth (1 Corinthians 9:1–2). It must be a person who was called by Jesus Christ to be an apostle (Romans 1:1, 5). It must be a person whose ministry is effective—shows the "signs of an apostle" by the mighty deeds (1 Corinthians 12:12).

Now it might be true that Paul used the term "apostle" in a looser way earlier on in his ministry (see 1 Thessalonians 2:7), but as his authority becomes contested, he clarifies the criteria and meaning.

Second, there are clear moments of explicit commissioning. The best illustration is Acts 6:

> And the twelve called together the whole community of the disciples and said, "It is not right that we should neglect the word of God in order to wait at tables. Therefore, friends, select from among yourselves seven men of good standing, full of the Spirit and of wisdom, whom we may appoint to this task, while we, for our part, will devote ourselves to prayer and to serving the word." What they said pleased the whole community, and they chose Stephen, a man full of faith and the Holy Spirit, together with Philip, Prochorus, Nicanor, Timon, Parmenas, and Nicolaus, a proselyte of Antioch. They had these men stand before the apostles, who prayed and laid their hands on them. (Acts 6:2–6)

The situation is that the church in Jerusalem is increasingly complicated. In this narrative, the apostles needed co-workers. So, in the same way as Jesus appointed disciples, so the apostles appointed these seven "Hellenistic leaders." It is worth noting that there are criteria—persons who are of good standing, full of the Spirit and wise—and that there is a process, which includes the laying on of hands.

Moving into the so-called sub-apostolic period (67 CE to the end of the first century),[26] we learn from the Pastoral Epistles that there is real issue and concern about the commissioning of leadership. The text explicitly describes the appointment of leadership by Titus in Crete (Titus 1:5) and a list of criteria that Timothy should use in the appointment of leadership (1 Tim 3:1–13).

Third, there is a corporate dimension to leadership. Sullivan argues that certainly in those initial years, often the leadership passed to groups. He shows that actually both theological content and practices were passed on, but more often than not, they were passed on to groups of individuals. So, for example, in Ephesians, apostles might found churches, but their successors were prophets, evangelists, and teachers.[27] It is important to stress that these groups often included women (Romans 16:6 and Acts 18:18–19). It is likely, although we cannot be sure, that Paul appointed the leadership. After all, Paul repeatedly confirms the authority of those leading the congregations (1 Thessalonians 5:12 and 1 Corinthians 16:16).

Fourth, there is a process for deciding contentious questions that involved the gathering of apostles and presbyters. The best illustration of this is the so-called "first council," which, in actual fact, is probably two separate events (one dealing with circumcision, and the other dealing with which aspects of the Jewish law should still be observed by Gentile converts). The primary issue in Acts 15 was circumcision. Luke does want to convey that this key decision required the leadership of the early church to gather. Linked to this, Acts also depicts Paul, in his farewell address to the church in Ephesus, saying: "Keep watch over yourselves and over all the flock, of which the Holy Spirit has made you overseers, to shepherd the church of God that he obtained with the blood of his own Son" (Acts 20:28). The word "overseers" is of the Greek word *episkopous*, which becomes our word bishops. However, it is a plurality, but pastoral authority, especially, clearly resides with this group.

Various themes are emerging. There is an expectation that the Church will continue beyond the apostles. There is a concern with protecting the Gospel message from those who would distort it. There are processes and criteria for the appointment of leadership. It is untidy but in interesting ways. There is a pluralism in the leadership of "evangelists, prophets, and teachers" (depending on the gift given by the Spirit); and it is inclusive of women.

In much the same way as the Trinity is slowly discovered by the church (over the course of several centuries), so it is appropriate to see church structure being discovered by the church. The Didache, probably from the end of the first century,[28] provides basic instructions for new Christian communities, which highlights baptism, liturgical instructions, church order instructions, and predictions about the last day. And in 1 Clement (most certainly from 96 CE), there is the explicit recognition that the apostles "preaching both in the country and in the towns, they appointed their first fruits, when they had tested them by the Spirit, to be bishops and deacons for the future believers." Now it is true that there is a close connection between apostles and those appointed; it is true that the authority of those in leadership is supported by the apostles. The narrative is emerging that sees a succession as part of what is being offered to the future.

This trajectory becomes clearer as we work through Ignatius of Antioch. Sullivan observes that "we...have reliable information from the letters of Ignatius of Antioch that by the year 115 the church of Ephesus and the church of Antioch each had a single bishop as well as a college of presbyters."[29] We see some geographical variety as we move further into the second century. In the Letter of Polycarp from Philippi, the structure remains a group of presbyters, and there is no mention of a bishop over the whole community. In Rome, the Shepherd of Hermas does have a higher ecclesiology operating with the "church being in the mind and purpose of God and views the eschatological church as the goal for whose sake the world was created."[30] But again, there is no evidence of a single bishop operating. Justin Martyr is also in Rome, and in his Apology (defending the Eucharist), he does talk about the president at the Eucharist. Perhaps this is significant. Hegesippus is reported by Eusebius as providing a list of bishops and the succession. The likeliest explanation for this is that in the plurality of leadership, the presider at the Eucharist does have a higher rank. Even here, the threefold order of ministry is emerging.

Apologetics plays a significant role in the development of the succession.[31] It was a way of guaranteeing the veracity of teaching. So Irenaeus, Bishop of Lyons, as he takes on the gnostics, explicitly appeals to the tradition that came down from the apostles and was guarded by "succession of elders."[32] In Irenaeus, we now get a list of bishops who succeeded each other in Rome. And Tertullian, towards the end of the second century, seems to be almost assuming that the apostles founded churches that were then entrusted to bishops, which were appointed by them.

By the time we get to the end of the second century, we have a recognizable catholic order. However, before concluding this section, it is helpful to look at Cyprian, the Bishop of Carthage. He was converted in the 245 to Christianity, and he was elected bishop in 249. It was the persecution of emperor Decius that forced Cyprian to flee, leaving us, as a result, some eighty-two letters.

Cyprian is interesting because the Bishop serves as a symbol of unity. With schism a potential problem, the Bishop is the guarantor of the authenticity of the local congregation. In addition, a focus on unity means that the lay need to be fully involved in the appointment of a bishop. Cyprian is less hierarchal than he might appear. E. W. Fasholé-Luke explains:

> However, we cannot understand Cyprian's plea for unity in these terms; since he had a parallel horizontal theory of the unity of the local community, in which he gave a distinctive place to the laity and clergy, both in the appointment of a bishop and also in the rejection of unworthy bishops. We must now look at this horizontal stratum of his theory. First, Cyprian himself was appointed bishop of Carthage by the popular vote of the people; but he also explains that in the election of a bishop, the Old Testament precedents demand that the laity should approve of the choice that is made. He suggests that just as the vestments of Aaron were placed upon Eleazar in the presence of the people, so the bishop must be chosen in the presence of the laity, in order that they may ensure that the choice falls upon a person of good character.[33]

Cyprian locates the ministry of a bishop very firmly in the context of the ministry of all those baptized. There is a radical egalitarian dimension to his theology.

This brief historical survey has exposed the messiness of history. For Roman Catholic conservatives, it is virtually impossible to make the case that in every church planted by an apostle there was an appointment of one bishop. The three-fold order is not manifestly visible in the New Testament. Instead, we often have well into the start of the second century, a plurality of presbyters responsible for leadership.

However, this does not justify the opposite conclusion that the language of the apostolic succession is utterly misguided. All the ingredients for a succession are there: the safeguarding of the truth revealed in Jesus of Nazareth; a concern around commissioning; a recognition that some have authority as apostles and others do not; an expectation that the apostles and presbyters should gather to consider contentious issues; and slowly by the middle of the second century three-fold orders of ministry are the norm.

In addition, there is something attractive about the messiness. The inclusion of women as co-workers is an important witness to the need to include women as priests. The practice of working as a group of presbyters to determine the leadership of the church is an invitation to collegiality and cooperation. So, as we consider the historical data, we can arrive at an affirmation of the apostolic succession with a deep commitment to recognizing the authority of the lay, stressing the need for cooperation and collegiality with priests; and including all who have a sense of vocation. In other words, the history is supportive of the practice and polity of the Episcopal Church in America!

Francis Sullivan, at the end of his thoughtful and very balanced study, invokes the Holy Spirit. He writes, "we . . . have good reason to believe that the Spirit guided the development of the episcopate itself, for it was to play such a primary role in maintaining the Church in the true faith. Without the leadership of its bishops, the early Church could hardly have achieved a consensus on the canon of Scripture, recognizing the Old Testament as also Word of God for Christians and settling on the writings of the New Testament. Neither could it have overcome the very real threat Gnosticism posed to its unity and orthodoxy."[34]

To invoke the Holy Spirit, as an agent of Divine providence, is perfectly proper. However, I want to go further. The apostolic connection is true because it is a tactile connection with the disclosure of God in Christ. It is the reason why an ordination is so moving. When a person is ordained, the combination of the touch from the Bishop (representing the succession) and the immediate action of the Holy Spirit (in descending on the person) creates a priest. It creates the ontological change (to allude to the account of priesthood offered by Hawkins at the start of this chapter). It is the reason why a priest can provide the body and blood of our Lord to the people of God. It is the reason why a priest can pronounce the absolution with the words: "Our Lord Jesus Christ, who has left power to his Church to absolve all sinners who truly repent and believe in him, of his great mercy forgive you all your offenses; and by his authority committed to me, I absolve you from all your sins: In the Name of the Father, and of the Son, and of the Holy Spirit. Amen."[35]

Now, it might be objected: Why do you need the apostolic succession? Why cannot the coming of the Spirit descending on the person be sufficient for the "power" of the priest to do the work of bringing the sacraments to the people of God? The answer is that it is possible for God to have chosen several ways in which the spiritually infused nature of the universe is seen at an ordination. And certainly, part of the answer is that the Holy Spirit does indeed descend. But there is more to it than that. The Church teaches that while the Holy Spirit can and may descend on anyone, God has in God's providence safeguarded the revelation of God in Jesus through the apostolic succession. The commissioning that Jesus gave the seventy is now coming down to you and me through a bishop in continuity with the apostles.

But at this point, we should start worrying about our ecumenical partners. How do we view our ecumenical sisters and brothers?

Ecumenically Sensitive

Now, in terms of ecumenical sensitivity, let me state my position quite clearly. As an Anglican, I affirm the validity of all the ministries of our ecumenical partners. How is this possible? To answer this question, we need to consider the whole issue of difference and disagreement.

Disagreement in religion is widespread. The Qur'an teaches that Jesus did not die on the cross, while Christians affirm that Jesus did. Judaism does not recognize Jesus as the Messiah, while Christians do. Strands of Buddhism would not talk about a personal God, while the theistic traditions (strands of Hinduism, Judaism, Christianity, Islam, and others) would. Between Christian denominations, there are significant differences. Roman Catholics believe that the assumption and the immaculate conception of the Virgin Mary are part of the apostolic deposit of faith, while Anglicans are not persuaded. Baptists insist that baptism should only occur once the person is old enough to confess Jesus as Lord for herself, while Roman Catholics and Anglicans believe that it is perfectly proper for an infant to be baptized. Pentecostal Christians believe it is necessary to be baptized both in water (as a believer) and also in the Holy Spirit (for the receiving of spiritual gifts), while most Christian denominations do not talk about two baptisms. Fundamentalists have the view that the second coming of Jesus is "literal" language, while most mainline Christians believe it is metaphorical language capturing God's ultimate control of history.

There are three temptations we need to avoid. The first is to deny any possibility of truth. The second is to create a crude binary: my tradition is right; all other traditions are wrong. And the third is to say that what is claimed for my tradition is true of all other traditions. All three have an imperialistic tendency.

The first is imperialist because it imposes on disagreement the hubris of the relativism of European skepticism. In a binary between "science" and "metaphysics," a disposition emerged in European thought that saw science as factual and, therefore, disagreements as resolvable and metaphysics as speculative and, therefore, disagreements as irresolvable. The binary does not withstand close scrutiny. There are plenty of models in science that are not obviously factual or resolvable (e.g., the multiverse theory). And there are plenty of religious worldviews that can be judged in the same way as one would an "economic theory," using the tools of coherence and explanatory power. So, certain fundamentalisms, for example, are unlikely to be true because they are incoherent. If one can handle disagreements in economics or history, then metaphysical disagreements are not far away.

The second and third are imperialist because there are many more options than "wrong" or "same as me." It may be just different; it may be similar. Consider the Eucharist: When Baptists gather to participate in the Lord's Supper, I can, as an Anglican, entirely accept their self-understanding of the moment. They are gathering in the Lord's name to "remember his death, until he comes." It is a memorial. They make no other claim. When I join that community, I accept their self-understanding entirely. I participate fully in the moment. It is valid; it is efficacious. They are not claiming to create a "sacrament" (where the bread and wine in some sense become the body and blood of our Lord). So, I can fully participate in the moment, accepting their interpretation of the moment entirely, and indeed, as a Christian, appropriately "remember his death, until he comes." It is not wrong; it is just different.

One weakness in this debate is the propensity to treat traditions as undifferentiated entities. So, all Christians are right, and all Muslims are wrong. Alternatively, all Anglicans are right, and all Baptists are wrong. In respect to both Christians and Anglicans, we are right about certain things, wrong about others, and other traditions have insights from which we should learn. Muslims are right to insist that a discipline of five daily prayers is an excellent way of living faithfully, aware of our responsibility as creatures made by God. Christians should and could learn from this insight. We should all be encouraged observing the daily office. Baptists are handling a real and true insight about the nature of ministry in their emphasis on the priesthood of all believers and that ministerial leadership does not make a person "better" than the rest of the members. Anglicans need to listen and affirm this Baptist insight into the nature of ministry.

The Anglican witness is this. We join with our Roman Catholic and Orthodox communities in affirming that there is a connection between our bishops and the apostles. We recognize the story of that connection is complex and messy. But it is there. In addition, we affirm that because of this connection, we also share a recognition that in the sacrament of the Eucharist the priest can be a vehicle of God's grace that brings the presence of Christ to the believer.

Anglicans also affirm, uncomplicatedly, the self-understanding of Presbyterians, Methodists, Baptists, and others.[36] We note how their view of ministry shapes their view of the sacraments. We have no difficulty in entirely accepting their views of both ministry and the sacrament. When we participate in a Baptist service; the minister is not seeing herself as a person in succession from the apostles, nor is the minister believing that prayer over the sacraments is creating a change in those elements. As an Anglican, I have no problem at all in believing what they believe of themselves as true. Namely, the Baptist minister is a person called by God to serve a congregation, upon whom the Spirit rests, to lead the people of God by the preaching of the word and remembrance of the death and resurrection of Jesus in the Lord's Supper. In addition, this Baptist account of ministry is not only good, but it also has insights from which Anglicans can and should learn. There is a process in which every baptized believer participates. There is an appropriate emphasis on the authority of the local congregation that gives due recognition to the local context. There is a strong rejection of any implied status between the minister and the people; indeed, the word "ministry" embodies expectations of service to the congregation. As an Anglican, I do not simply recognize the validity of the ordination to ministry but also recognize that there are vitally important insights from which Anglican should and can learn.

Now, in one sense, the Baptists are easier than some of the denominations nearer to Anglican tradition. Some Lutherans and Methodists have a higher ecclesiology and a higher view of sacraments, yet they cannot trace an unbroken succession through bishops. However, the same principle outlined here applies. As Lutherans and Methodists provide an account of their ministry and the "powers" enabled by that ministry, as an Anglican, I can accept the integrity of their account. So, for Anglicans, Catholics, and Orthodox traditions, the apostolic succession, through a priest, is the vehicle of the divine promise to deliver the sacraments to the people of God. In God's sovereignty, God may have other vehicles of meditating divine grace—this is definitely true of other religious traditions. It is, therefore, perfectly possible that sacraments can be mediated through a Christian tradition without an intact apostolic succession. If this is what Lutherans and Methodists wish to claim, then as an Anglican, I can affirm the possibility and, therefore, the validity of their orders.

Scientifically Plausible in a Theological Framework

What sort of universe is plausible if we are imagining the idea of an ordination at which the Holy Spirit descends as a result of prayer and the Word (as embodied in Jesus) connects as a result of touch from a Bishop?

This question goes right to the heart of the argument of this book. We have already seen how words such as "magical" and "superstitious" were used to denigrate the concept of spiritual causation. The task now is to defend such a concept. In this section, we shall look first at the theological expectations that need to be in place. Then we shall examine ways in which the idea of the spiritually infused universe making a difference to a person might be intelligible within a scientific framework.

For those who are not persuaded that an apostolic succession is worth all this effort, it is worth noting that the same principle of touch bringing grace is not simply found at ordination. It is also found in baptism and confirmation. It was Kenneth Kirk who noted: "If there be those who speak disparagingly of 'apostolic succession by tactual transmission of grace,' and attempt to dismiss the doctrine . . . as 'magical,' 'mechanical,' or 'materialistic,' we need only observe that they will be hard put to justify baptism and confirmation. For certainly the matter of both sacraments is directly tactual, and in the case of confirmation (especially as administered in the Church of England), it involves personal contact between the bishop and the candidate; and what else do the two rites profess to effect than to usher the recipient, in exactly the same way as in the case or ordination, into a special and distinctive sphere of grace? It is not, indeed, that we should lay much theological stress upon the laying on of hands. It was the method chosen by the apostolic church to guarantee that the commission had been given by a member of the Essential Ministry; and as such we retain it and treasure it."[37]

In actual fact, the laying of hands has a deep biblical history. Albert Edward Johnson, back in 1911, does the simple exercise of documenting the biblical roots of the language. Strangely, most contemporary discussions of the laying on of hands focus on the immediate cultural context, rather than the biblical precedents.[38] However, Johnson is helpful and persuasive that the Old Testament is helpful here. He notes that when it comes to the Levitical sacrifices there is a requirement for the laying on of hands on the victims—for the burnt offering (Lev 1:4), for the peace offering (Lev 3:2), for the sin offering (Lev 4), for the Ram of consecration (Exodus 29:19), and for the so-called scapegoat (Lev 16:21). Johnson's view is that this created a connection between the worshipper, the animal victim, and God. However, more interestingly for the debate on ordination, we see the laying on of hands on Joshua. In one narrative, it is descriptive (Numbers 8:10); in the second, it provides power (Deut 34:9). In Deuteronomy, we find the text reads: "Joshua son of Nun was full of the spirit of wisdom, because Moses had laid his hands on him; and the Israelites obeyed him, doing as the Lord had commanded Moses" (Deut 34:9). Here, a causal connection is made between the laying on of hands and the resulting power. Johnson writes, "In the Old Testament physical contact is conceived of as the means of conveying status or spiritual energy from one person to another. Broadly speaking, we may say that this conveyance of status or energy was thought to take place mechanically."[39]

Once again, the Church of England has much that is right when in *Apostolicity and Succession*, there is an affirmation of the significance of the laying on of hands. The report writes:

> At the laying on of hands by the ordaining bishop and other representatives with prayer, the whole Church calls upon God in confidence of his promise to pour out the Holy Spirit on his covenant people. The biblical act of laying on of hands is rich in significance. It may mean (among other things) identification, commissioning or welcome. It is used in a variety of contexts: confirmation, reconciliation, healing and ordination. On the one hand, by the laying on hands with prayer a gift of grace already given by God is recognized and confirmed; on the other hand it is perfected for service. The precise significance or intention of the laying on of hands as a sign is determined by the prayer or declaration that accompanies it. In the case of the episcopate, to ordain by prayer and the laying on of hands is to do what the apostles did, and the Church through the ages.[40]

But, I want to go further. The touch is, in the tradition of Moses, a power; the touch is, in the tradition of the Fathers, a connection with our Lord.

Where *Apostolicity and Succession* is right, there is a context, which makes the "touch" happen (granted this is dramatic, but for the spiritually infused universe, this is when the spiritual is most visible). This is the old argument about under what conditions is an ordination valid. Norman Doe reminds us of the traditional Roman Catholic expectations when he writes:

> For the Roman Catholic Church the sacraments are "the actions of Christ and the Church"; requirements for their valid administration are determined by the supreme authority of the Church. A valid sacrament is one capable of producing the effects it is ordered to produce. The sacrament of holy orders is valid if it possesses the requisite (i) *matter* (action), the bishop's imposition of hands on the candidate's head; and (ii) *form* (words), the bishop's consecratory prayer 'asking God for the outpouring of the Holy Spirit and his gifts proper to the ministry' received; (iii) its *minister* is a validly ordained bishop: since ordination is 'the sacrament of the apostolic ministry, it is for the bishops as successors of the apostles to hand on the "gift of the Spirit"' (i.e., those "in the "apostolic line" "validly confer...the sacrament"); (iv) its *recipient* must freely consent and "Only a baptized man *(vir)* validly receives sacred ordination"; (v) *intention:* the bishop and recipient must intend what the Church intends.[41]

One problem for Anglican orders is that, according to *Apostolicae curae,* issued in 1896 by Pope Leo XIII, there is the deficiency in respect to (v) intention, and in respect to (ii) form. The argument, in brief, is that Anglicans did not intend to replicate a Roman Catholic "sacrificing" priesthood and, therefore, the words were deliberately modified. While Anglicans responded with an encyclical *Saepius officio* in 1897, the debate has become more complicated since the ordination of women. Indeed, there are significant numbers of Anglicans who want to protect the legitimacy of the "touch" by abstaining themselves from ordaining women. So, the whole concept of "gracious restraint" has arisen where bishops are present but not touching in an ordination. In a list where a bishop should exercise "gracious restraint," he suggests the following:

What would disqualify another Anglican bishop from laying a hand on a similar future candidate and thus trigger "gracious restraint"? One imagines a descending order of disqualification:

1. A female bishop.
2. A male bishop whose own chief consecrator had been a woman.
3. A male bishop who had once laid a hand on a woman being made a bishop.
4. A male bishop at whose consecration a female bishop had laid a hand on him.
5. A male bishop who had shared in the laying on of hands on another male bishop when a female bishop had also laid on hands.[42]

The purity of touch debate is interesting. Given the affirmation of women as leaders in the church in the New Testament, the focus is deeply misguided. Women can be priests. There is no good argument against this position. However, at least there is a recognition that "touch," in this moment, is important. So now we return to the important question: In what sense is "touch" in an ordination service really intelligible or plausible in our scientific age?

The primary argument, at this point, is the one developed in chapter 2 and 3. Christians are committed to the possibility of "spiritual causation." Following John Russell Robert[43] and Keith Ward[44], a picture is emerging that takes full advantage of the space created for nonmaterial causes in the universe. At the heart of the moment of touch is the agency of the Holy Spirit that both descends on the person and facilitates the connection between the person being ordained and our Lord's commission of the apostles.

However, the scientific literature on touch is considerable. Much of the literature speaks to the extraordinary capacity of touch to make a difference. From the weird to the important, touch is an important medical tool. So, on the weird end, here is an example: In rats, we know that touch can reduce the damage of strokes. At the University of California, a team of researchers induced strokes in rats, and then, through "touch"—sustained and frequent on their whiskers—actually reduced the impact of the stroke.[45] On the important end, we have known for a long time that touch is essential in childrearing. We know, for example, that babies raised in orphanages without affectionate touch would often die. And psychology provides the widespread explanation for this phenomenon. But now neuroscientists are involved. According to Lydia Denworth, we know that a set of nerve fibers, called C-tactile afferents (CT) seem to convey information about pleasant touch; these fibers are so attuned, they are crucial in creating a sense of social connections; and there is speculation that these nerves may help both treat and detect certain conditions such as autism and addiction.[46]

Perhaps closer to what we need, there is growing interest in the "healing touch." Rochelle B. Mackey, in the prestigious journal *The American Journal of Nursing*, offers a serious account of the therapeutic touch. It builds on the concept of "energy exchange," where one searches for the energy field being emitted by the patient. Mackey explains: "The goal is to restore balance to the patient's energy field, which allows the patient to recover his own healing powers."[47] The picture emerging is that touch has power. Used properly under a certain set of conditions, it can be a significant force for health and healing.

These illustrations are intended to demonstrate that the concept of the laying on of hands in an ordination and believing in some sense God is using that moment to make an ontological difference in a person are not manifestly implausible. Granted all the symbolism of the moment can be affirmed, but the claim in this chapter is that in an ordination, the spiritual realm is visible. God is at work. At the end of the liturgy, a person is changed and can serve the people of God in a way that is different.

Bringing the Threads Together

The doctrine of the apostolic succession carries considerable unhelpful baggage. It has been used as a weapon for exclusion and denigration. There are those who are most adamant that they are benefitted from the apostolic succession who treat the doctrine as grounds for superiority over others (other denominations and the rest of the lay). In truth, the doctrine was birthed with a set of values attached to it that are the opposite of the way it has been used. It was birthed with a commitment to collegiality and to service. For all its misuse, the fundamental insight of the doctrine of apostolic succession does make sense as a key theme of the church. Those of us in the episcopal and liturgical traditions do believe that there is a distinctive view of the sacraments made possible by the grace imparted at the ordination.

The argument of this chapter is that there are three elements at work in ordination. First, there is the relational element. A community relates to a priest in a different way. The second is the functional element. A priest now is called by God to serve the community in certain ways: she or he has a distinctive function within the community. And third (and most contentious) is the causation element. A priest is the vehicle that God uses to deliver on God's promise that the sacraments are available to the people of God. Therefore, there is a causal connection with the first apostles mediated through touch.

In a spiritually infused universe, where the divine and spiritual nature of the church are recognized, one should expect vehicles of divine grace to include the fragile and weak human vessel. This is ordination. This is the reason Hawkins can believe that "being a priest is engraved on my very being."

NOTES

1. Barney Hawkins, *Episcopal Etiquette and Ethics: Living the Craft of Priesthood in the Episcopal Church*, (New York, NY: Morehouse Publishing 2012), p.1.
2. Cuthbert Hamilton Turner, *Apostolic Succession* (London: Church Literature Association, 1945), p. 9.
3. John Keble, "Adherence to the Apostolical Succession the Safest Course," in John Keble, John Henry Newman, Edward Bouverie Pusey, William Palmer, Richard Hurrell Froude, Isaac Williams, *Tracts for Our Times: Nos. 1–46. Records of the Church, nos. I–XVIII* (J. G. F. & J. Rivington, 1839), p. 7.
4. Philip Cater, *The great fiction of the times, or Apostolic succession, with other doctrines of Puseyism, proved to be unscriptural and absurd* (Canterbury, 1844), p. 27.
5. Cater has a robust style. And he takes great pleasure in drawing a comparison between apostles and modern-day Bishops. He writes, "How cruel would it be to institute a comparison between them and the bishops of modern times. Can *they* make the blind to see,—the deaf to hear,—the dumb to speak,—the lame to walk, or the dead to live?" Ibid., p. 45.
6. He writes, "Through the successive ordinations of the last eighteen hundred years, our bishops claim a regular and uninterrupted descent from the apostle Peter. But really this notion is so puerile, and so destitute of any historic truth, that it deserves to be thrown aside at once as one of those endless genealogies or old wives' fables which Timothy was admonished to avoid." Ibid., p. 50. He makes much of the disputed chronology after Peter died and the fact that at one time there were two Popes in Christendom both ordaining bishops.
7. Charles Gore, *The Ministry of the Christian Church* (Waterloo Place, London: Rivingtons, 1889).
8. Ibid., p. v.
9. Ibid., pp. 69–71.
10. Ibid., p. 73.
11. Ibid., p. 345.
12. Gore's work was revised by C. H. Turner in 1919, which extended its impact.
13. Felix L. Cirlot, *Apostolic Succession: Is It True? An historical and theological inquiry*, (Louisville, KY: The Cloister Press, 1951), p. ix. The book appears to be self-published; the publisher was gleaned from the preface.
14. Ibid., p. xi.
15. W. R. Matthews, *The Expository Times*, Vol. 70, 11(January 1, 1959): 340.
16. A. Gordon James, "Apostolic Succession," in *The Expository Times*, Vol. 70, 6 (March 1959): 166.
17. Noel Hall, "Apostolic Succession," *Scottish Journal of Theology* Vol. 11, 2 (1958): 123.
18. Both Michael Goulder and Leslie Houlden were shaped by Austin Farrar. However, while Farrar remained a traditional Anglo-Catholic, Goulder and Houlden became progressives in their theology. They were both contributors to John Hick (ed.), *The Myth of God Incarnate* (London: SCM Press Ltd., 1977). Denis Nineham entrenched a version of extreme relativism in his book *The Use and the Abuse of the Bible*.
19. House of Bishops Occasional Paper, *Apostolicity and Succession* (London: Church House, 1994), p. 8.
20. Ibid., p. 8.

21. Ibid., p. 24.
22. Aidan Nichols OP, *Holy Order: Apostolic Priesthood from the New Testament to the Second Vatican Council* (Dublin: Veritas Publications, 1990). It is important to note that I am not persuaded on his views about women priests that forms an appendix in this book.
23. Origins 21/28 (December 19, 1991), p. 446.
24. Francis A. Sullivan, *From apostles to Bishops: The Development of the Episcopacy in the Early Church*, (Mahwah, NJ: Paulist Press, 2001).
25. It is important to note that this is a complex area. The list that follows does not discuss much of the complexity. Suffice to say, I am grateful for the study by Francis A. Sullivan. Much that follows is very dependent on his insights.
26. This is the phrase used by Raymond Brown, *The Churches the apostles Left Behind* (New York/Ramsey, NJ: Paulist Press, 1984), pp. 13–16.
27. Sullivan, From Apostles *to Bishops.*
28. There is considerable argument about the dating of the Didache.
29. Francis A. Sullivan, *From Apostles to Bishops,* chapter 6.
30. Ibid., chapter 7.
31. As the Christian tradition develops, apologetics remains central. Augustine of Hippo is a good example. When he is giving counsel to a priest who has received a letter from a Donatist priest, he makes authority central. The Donatist priest appeals to the Episcopal succession in his town; and Augustine, in response, appeals to the Episcopal succession of the entire church. Augustine writes: "For if the lineal succession of bishops is to be taken into account, with how much more certainty and benefit to the Church do we reckon back till we reach Peter himself, to whom, as bearing in a figure the whole Church, the Lord said: *'Upon this rock will I build my Church, and the gates of* hell *shall not prevail against it!'* Matthew 16:18. The successor of Peter was Linus, and his successors in unbroken continuity were these:— Clement, Anacletus, Evaristus, Alexander, Sixtus, Telesphorus, Iginus, Anicetus, Pius, Soter, Eleutherius, Victor, Zephirinus, Calixtus, Urbanus, Pontianus, Antherus, Fabianus, Cornelius, Lucius, Stephanus, Xystus, Dionysius, Felix, Eutychianus, Gaius, Marcellinus, Marcellus, Eusebius, Miltiades, Sylvester, Marcus, Julius, Liberius, Damasus, and Siricius, whose successor is the present Bishop Anastasius. In this order of succession no Donatist bishop is found. But, reversing the natural course of things, the Donatists sent to Rome from Africa an ordained bishop, who, putting himself at the head of a few Africans in the great metropolis, gave some notoriety to the name of *'mountain men,'* or Cutzupits, by which they were known." See Augustine, Letter 53, Chapter 1. Translated by J. G. Cunningham. From *Nicene and Post-Nicene Fathers, First Series, Vol. 1.* Edited by Philip Schaff (Buffalo, NY: Christian Literature Publishing Co., 1887.) Revised and edited for New Advent by Kevin Knight. http://www.newadvent.org/fathers/1102053.htm. Accessed July 10, 2016.
32. Edward R. Hardy, *Early Christian Fathers*, vol. 1, edited by Cyril C. Richardson (Philadelphia: Westminster Press, 1953), pp. 370–71.
33. E. W. Fasholé-Luke, "Christian unity: St. Cyprian's and Ours," in *Scottish Journal of Theology*, Vol. 23, 3 (August 1970): 316.
34. Francis A. Sullivan, *From Apostles to Bishops* (New York: Newman Press, 2011), chapter 11.
35. The Book of Common Prayer (the Episcopal Church), p. 448.
36. It is to the credit of K. D. Mackenzie that back in 1946 he attempted to learn from the different accounts of ministry in the non-episcopal communions. See K. D. Mackenzie, "Sidelights from the non-episcopal communions," in K. E. Kirk (prepared under the direction on), *The Apostolic Ministry: Essays on the History and the Doctrine of the Episcopacy,* pp. 461–91 (London: Hodder & Stoughton, 1947).
37. K. E. Kirk, "The Apostolic Ministry," in K. E. Kirk (prepared under the direction on), *The Apostolic Ministry: Essays on the History and the Doctrine of the Episcopacy* (London: Hodder and Stoughton, 1947), pp. 15–16. The entire volume is an interesting collection of essays, which primarily focuses on the biblical and historical. It shares the Anglo-Catholic concern with ecumenism as the motive for bringing together this edited volume of essays.
38. This is the reason I am not persuaded that the exercise of touch is simply another mode of prayer. This is the position of E. Ferguson, who argues thus: The basic idea in early Christian

ordination was not creating a substitute or transferring authority, but conferring a blessing and petitioning for the divine favor. Blessing, of course, in ancient thought was more than a kindly wish; it was thought of as imparting something very definite (as in the patriarchal blessings of the Old Testament). "Hand" in biblical usage was symbolic of power. The laying on of hands accompanied prayer in Christian usage. It was essentially an enacted prayer, and the prayer spelled out the grace which God was asked to bestow. As an act of blessing, it was considered to effect that for which the prayer was uttered. See E. Ferguson, "Laying on of Hands: Its Significance in Ordination," in *Journal of Theological Studies*, Vol. 26, 1 (April 1975), p 2. He is very selective in his choice of Old Testament text and does not give sufficient attention to the laying on of hands by Moses on Joshua.

39. Albert Edward Johnston, "The Laying on of Hands: Its Origin and Meaning," *The Irish Church Quarterly,* Vol. 4, 16 (October 1, 1911): 317–18.

40. House of Bishops Occasional Paper, *Apostolicity and Succession* (London: Church House, 1994), p.28.

41. Norman Doe, "Ordination, Canon Law and Pneumatology: Validity and Vitality in Anglican-Roman Catholic Dialogue," *Ecclesiastical Law Journal*, Vol.8, 39 (2006): 407.

42. Colin Buchanan, "Comment: Current Questions in Episcopal Consecrations," *Theology* 118 (July/August 2015): 279.

43. See John Russell Roberts, *Quantum Mechanics: Scientific Perspectives on Divine Action* (CTNS&Vatican Observatory/UNP, 1993).

44. See Keith Ward, *Divine Action* (London: Collins, 1990).

45. Mark Lescroart, "The Healing Power of Touch," *Scientific American Mind* Vol. 22, 7 (July/August 2011). Published online: June 23, 2011.

46. Lydia Denworth, "The Social Power of Touch," *Scientific American Mind* (July 1, 2015): 30–39.

47. Rochelle B. Mackey, "Discover the Healing Power of Therapeutic Touch," *The American Journal of Nursing*, Vol. 95, 4 (April 1995), p. 25.

Chapter Eight

Angels and the Communion of Saints

One peculiar argument embedded in this book is that recovering a sense of angels and saints should be part of our contemporary apologetic for faith. So, Serge-Thomas Bonino, the Roman Catholic theologian, is wrong to start his introduction in his defense of *Angels and Demons* with the following anecdote:

> A legendary but nonetheless tenacious anecdote relates that in May 1453, at the hour when Constantinople was falling into the hands of the Turks, an assembly of theologians had gathered in the very heart of the besieged city to debate about the sex of the angels—a quintessential Byzantine dispute, typical of a theology that was disconnected from reality. All the more reason why today, at an hour when Western culture is sinking inexorably into the night of massive unbelief, one might wonder whether the Christian theologian does not have something better to do than to expound upon an angelic other-world, the very existence of which is problematic in the opinion of some believers and whose relevance to everyday life seems almost nil.[1]

I am arguing that we need to rediscover a textured sense of the spiritual realm and, within this realm, angels are a key part. Our apologetic failure to advocate for angels is partly responsible for a perception that faith is just a matter of "believing in a creator God."[2] We have lost a sense of the animated nature of the spiritual realm.

So, the question arises: Are there angels? Is it plausible to believe in angels? The steps in the argument thus far are as follows. Reductionist science is implausible. There are good reasons for us to trust that God has spoken in Christ—that Jesus Christ is the eternal Word made flesh. The model for Christian decision-making is the Trinity. There are five principles, expounded in chapter 4, of Christian theological reasoning. These are:

1. An appropriate distinction between the eternal Word and the written Word. The eternal Word is a control on all our theological reasoning. In short, this is the witness of Christ as seen in the Gospels both in words and deeds.
2. We need to exegete Scripture with care, engaging with the best theology and philosophy, searching for appropriate unity across Scripture and taking seriously the patterns of language and worldview embedded in an individual book or author. In short, the witness of Scripture matters.
3. We reason within the church both present and past. We build on the past, as we engage with insights within contemporary culture. In short, the conversation with tradition matters.
4. We seek internal consistency—we aspire for coherence and compatibility with other truths. In short, the importance of rationality matters.
5. We acknowledge that there is an inevitability of pluralism within limits—there will be different ways of understanding the Incarnation or the Trinity. In short, the need for humility and conversation within the community of the church matters.

There is a sense in which these five principles are simple and straightforward: Christ, Scripture, tradition, rationality, and the church. If these are the principles that we need to shape our convictions as Christians, then we should apply these principles to contested areas of debates—such as angels and saints. It is to this task that we now turn.

INSUFFICIENTLY RIGOROUS EVALUATIONS OF ANGELS

Among theologians (even relatively conservative ones), skepticism about angels abounds. Brian Hebblethwaite, an incarnational, Trinitarian theologian, writes about angels:

> It is quite possible for Christians, without forsaking the heart of the Christian matter, to think of angels as symbolic personifications of God's own communications with the human world and of devils as projections of the evil tendencies which afflict us human beings individually and collectively just because of the necessary conditions of our formation.[3]

Hebblethwaite appeals to theodicy in support of this view. Christians, he explains, want to insist that the universe needed to be of this type and nature for the "formation of *any* finite creaturely persons."[4] For Hebblethwaite, sentient creatures with the capacity of moral discernment needed to be a result of "cosmic and biological evolution."[5]

Clearly, it would be advantageous if the emergence of all sentient creatures required evolution in a universe such as this; however, it is difficult to see why this is likely to be the case. Of all the conceivable universes, it sounds unlikely that the only possible way for sentient life forms to emerge is evolution. There is an irony in Hebblethwaite's position, for it is in the name of theodicy that many nineteenth-century Christians thought evolution was inconceivable—after all, it is a violent and cruel way to create the world. But my complaint is more fundamental. Hebblethwaite is guilty of assertion; he is not using the five principles identified above as the key way to reason appropriately as a Christian. The existence of angels complicating his theodicy is not a substitute for the hard work of thinking through the issue.

This failure not to take appropriate Christian reasoning seriously is also found with defenders of angels. Peter Williams, in *The Case of Angels*, lists nine arguments in favor of angels. The first four independent ones (by which he means not dependent on being a Christian) are:

1. Common consent (most of the population of the world believes in angels)
2. Authority, by which Williams means "the majority of the universally acknowledged great philosophers have believed in the existence of immaterial agents"[6]
3. Ockam's Razor and the occult (the simplest explanation for evil is demons)
4. Experience (the world over there are those who have experienced angels)

Then Williams shifts to nonindependent arguments, which assume the veracity of the Christian tradition. But, even here, he lacks historical sensitivity and shows little awareness of how carefully the tradition reasons. He lists eight reasons for believing that the Bible is God's Word (e.g., things like confirmation by archeology; the human conviction that they spoke with God's authority; the Bible's indestructability; and fulfilment of biblical prophecy) to justify the claim that the witness of Scripture can be trusted to prove there are angels. The Incarnation is justified by two premises which culminate in the argument that, therefore, "disciples of Jesus ought to believe in the existence of Angels and demons."[7]

If only Christian theology were so easy. But it is not so. We need to work much harder to establish that within the Christian tradition of enquiry it is appropriate to affirm the existence of angels.

Making the Case

This work is difficult to do. So, let us start that work. It begins with the primary authority in Christian theology, which is the eternal Word made flesh. We start, therefore, with the Gospels.[8] Now, interestingly, angels figure less prominently than demons. Angels tend to frame the narrative: They make key announcements (e.g., to Mary at the annunciation, Luke 1:26–38), they are present at the birth of Christ (e.g., also Luke 2:9–15), and they are prominent at the resurrection (Matthew 28:2–5).

In chapter 4, this text was considered central to the Christian claim. In the opening of Mark's Gospel, we find:

> They went to Capernaum; and when the sabbath came, he entered the synagogue and taught. They were astounded at his teaching, for he taught them as one having authority, and not as the scribes. Just then there was in their synagogue a man with an unclean spirit, and he cried out, "What have you to do with us, Jesus of Nazareth? Have you come to destroy us? I know who you are, the Holy One of God." But Jesus rebuked him, saying, "Be silent, and come out of him!" And the unclean spirit, convulsing him and crying with a loud voice, came out of him. They were all amazed, and they kept on asking one another, "What is this? A new teaching—with authority! He commands even the unclean spirits, and they obey him." At once his fame began to spread throughout the surrounding region of Galilee. (Mark 1:21–28)

The spiritually infused universe is the issue in this text. This first-century context is much closer to Africa than to the United States. In this richly textured world, spirits reside just underneath our experience of the world. Jesus provides a "new teaching—with authority." In this setting, to have authority, to have expertise, does not mean that one has been informed, but in the case of Jesus, having such knowledge means he can even control the spiritual realm. Jesus does not simply know what is going on in the spiritual realm but knows sufficient detail to control it.

This text suggests that the universe is spiritually infused, and some of this infusion is ugly and dangerous. This becomes a significant Markan theme (see Mark 3:15; Mark 6:7, where authority over demons is delegated; and Mark 11:28ff, where there is a debate over the authority of Jesus) and is picked up in the Synoptic parallels (see, for example, Luke 4:36 and Matthew 10:1). There is a difficulty here: For the Synoptics, there is much more interest in demons and less in angels. We shall return to demons in a moment. But for now, we note that angels do not need control in the way demons do. And, if the point of the narrative is to establish the authority of Christ over the spirit realm, then controlling demons is the way to do that. Angels provide a frame, often affirming the significance of Christ; demons illustrate the authority and knowledge of Christ over the complexity of the spiritual realm. As we move from the eternal Word to the written Word, we should exegete carefully and in the light of contemporary science and philosophy.

Working through the witness of Scripture, we get the following picture. There are a large number of angels (see Daniel 7:10; Matthew 26:53; Hebrews 12:22). Angels are incorporeal (Hebrews 1:14) but can assume human nature (Hebrews 13:2 and Matthew 28:2–4). Most of the time, they appear as men (Genesis 18; Mark 16:5; the sole exception may be Zechariah 5:9). Some angels may have wings (see Isaiah 6:2,6; Daniel 9:21). Angels are strong but not all-powerful (Psalm 103:20; 2 Peter 2:11). They have more knowledge than humans but are not omniscient (2 Samuel 14:20; Matthew 24:36). Angels do not marry or have sex (Matthew 22:30). The primary role of angels is to worship God, and some are especially chosen to make this their focus (1 Timothy 5:21; Matthew 25:31; Mark 8:38). Praising God is a key part (Isaiah 6:1–3; Revelation 4–5). They are messengers (Acts 7:52–53). They guide—see Joseph and the birth of Jesus (Matthew 1–2); the women at the tomb; Philip (Acts 8:26); and Cornelius (Acts 10:1–8). They can provide food (Genesis 21:17–20; 1 Kings 19:6; Matthew 4:11). They can protect the people of God from danger (Daniel 3 and 6). They can release Christians from prison (Acts 5; Acts 12). They play a pastoral support role (see 4 Ezra 4:1–11; Matt 4:11). They anticipate the future (Acts 27:23–25). They are the instruments by which God answers a prayer (Daniel 9:20–24; 10:10–12; Acts 12:1–17). They transport the dead to paradise (Luke 16:22), and they can be the vehicle by which God exercises judgment by slaughtering (185,000 Assyrians—2 Kings 19:20–34).

As we read Scripture, we might pause. This entire picture is read in the light of what we know about God in the eternal Word. So, perhaps, we desire to distance ourselves from the slaughter of the 185,000 Assyrians, but spiritual entities that worship God, interact with humans, and are a vehicle for divine action might be plausible.

Turning to the tradition, we suddenly realize how far we now are from the worldview of our Christian forebears. The Book of Enoch is a key text. It was purportedly written by Enoch (the grandfather of Noah) and tells the story of Enoch's visit to the heavenly realm. It is here that all the archangels of tradition are named:

> These are the names of the angels who watch. Uriel, one of the holy angels, who presides over clamor and terror.
> Raphael, one of the holy angels, who presides over the spirits of men.
> Raguel, one of the holy angels, who inflicts punishment on the world and the luminar.
> Michael, one of the holy angels, who, presiding over human virtue, commands the nations.
> Sarakiel, one of the holy angels, who presides over the spirits of the children of men that transgress.

> Gabriel, one of the holy angels, who presides over Ikisat, over paradise, and over the cherubim.

This goes far beyond the speculations of Scripture. And it gets better. The key text about "Angelology" is from Dionysius. According to a rather implausible tradition, Dionysius was told about the orders of angels by his friend Paul the Apostle. For Dionysius, there are three hierarchies. The first hierarchy comprises seraphim, cherubim, and thrones; the second hierarchy has dominions, virtues, and powers; and the third hierarchy has principalities, archangels, and angels. The first hierarchy is totally focused on the worship and love of God (so no interaction with the world); the second is involved in the government of the world; and the third interacts with human lives and appears to people. The third hierarchy is the lowest of the hierarchy and most commonly known order of angels.

The impact of this text is considerable. Thomas Aquinas follows the schema closely;[9] and it influenced both Dante and Milton. However, here I find myself in the company of Karl Barth. He counsels restraint with such speculation: "In this sphere there has always been a good deal of theological caprice, valueless, grotesque and even absurd speculation, and also of no less doubtful skepticism."[10] While Barth does not want the angelic world demythologized, he wants us to admit the limits of the revelation when it comes to this realm. One should affirm the reality of angels but not overthink the details of the heavenly order.

Does the idea of angels make sense? This is the issue of rationality. This is also our opportunity to consider the coherence and plausibility of angels.[11] Paul Griffiths is helpful at this point. He believes that Christians are committed to the view that angels have the same sense of location, spatial and temporal, as the souls of the departed. Although the tradition has wanted to stress that angels are spiritual and, therefore, do not have bodies, we must still locate them. He then suggests a set of distinctions. Griffiths writes:

> "Body" names capacity for spatio-temporal location, and thus for availability and responsiveness to other creatures with spatio-temporal location; any creature with that capacity has, or is, a body. Bodies come, however, in many kinds. There are, first, *fallen fleshly bodies,* of the kind common to all animate creatures (save the angels) in the devastation. Then, second, there are *risen fleshly bodies*, of the kind common to all animate creatures (save the angels) in heaven after the general resurrection....Third, there are *temporarily discarnate animate bodies*, which belong to humans between the separation of the soul from the fallen fleshly body and the general resurrection; these bodies may be purgatorial or heavenly. Fourth, there *permanently discarnate animate bodies,* which are those of the angels. Fifth, there are *inanimate material bodies* of various kinds; these have weight and continuous extension in timespace, and include things such as rocks and bodies of water. Sixth, and last, there are

discarnate inanimate bodies, which include at least quarks and other subatomic particles.[12]

We need to decide whether it is conceivable to envisage an entity that has "mass, but not, or not necessarily, matter."[13] Griffiths concedes that he is taking a different line from Aquinas. For Aquinas, one cannot distinguish different angels from each other; while Griffiths, in advocating for an angelic body (appropriately defined), can do so. Such a picture supports the biblical witness. When Mary was visited by the Angel Gabriel (Luke 1:26ff), the accounts seems to assume an entity that was present, albeit in a bodily form freed from the confines of physicality.

There is nothing incoherent about this idea. If one can step inside the Christian narrative and suspend our *anafühl*, this all makes sense. The God that has made a remarkable physical world has also intertwined that physical world with a spiritual realm that includes immaterial entities that have agency, can communicate, and are interacting with the physical realm in countless ways. There is not really any good reason to be skeptical of the idea.

Methodologically, we are almost there. We have lived in the Christian tradition; we are observing its method of enquiry. We have recognized that a central claim embodied in the disclosure of the eternal Word is the world animated by spiritual forces, and that Jesus has authority of disclosure (i.e., that these spirits are there) and control (i.e., that they obey him). We have looked at the sustained and significant biblical witness (and judged an aspect of that witness, the slaughter of Assyrians, as incompatible with what we learn of God in Christ), but we conceded it is a primary biblical theme. We have examined the tradition and express some nervousness about the extent of the speculation. We have noted the logical possibility of spiritual entities with distinctive bodies and emphasized that such a possibility is not incompatible with a modern scientific worldview. The result is that it seems appropriate for Christians to affirm the reality of angels.

One cannot leave angels without some discussion of demons. Demons abound in the New Testament, with the Greek word δαιμονιον appearing some sixty-three times. In the Gospels, they are represented as a force opposed to Jesus (e.g., Matthew 8:31; Luke 8:30); in many cases, Jesus frees a human life from the bondage created by the demon. In 1 Timothy, the demons are responsible for false teaching (1 Timothy 4:1); and Paul, writing in Corinthians, talks about the sacrifices of pagans are being offered to demons, not to God (1 Corinthians 10:20). For the church fathers, the two most important New Testament texts were probably 2 Peter 2:4 and Jude 6. In Peter, it is written: "For if God did not spare the angels when they sinned, but cast them into hell and committed them to chains of deepest darkness to be kept until the judgment." And in Jude, we have: "And the angels who did not keep their own position, but left their proper dwelling, he has kept in eternal chains in deepest darkness for the judgment of the great day." These texts gave explicit justification for the view that certain angels had sinned and that they will be judged.

Certain texts in the Old Testament have been interpreted within the framework of fallen angels. The Nephilim (arrogant giants) of Genesis 6 were interpreted by intertestamental Judaism as the offspring of lying angels. Isaiah 14, which is all about the fall of the Babylonian king, is simultaneously linked with the original sin of the fallen angels. Ezekiel 28, which concerns the demise of the king of Tyre, gets similar treatment.

The tradition emerged that linked all these biblical dots into a pattern. Considerable debate centered on how exactly it was possible for angels to sin. This is a good question, partly because it touches on a conundrum around redemption—if angels in the presence of God were able to fall, then what is to stop redeemed humanity in the presence of God from falling? However, the standard line, courtesy of Augustine, was pride. Bonino explains:

> Pride is the disordered love of my own excellence—in other words, of my good, not because it is a good but because it is mine and distinguishes me from others. Pride is therefore love of the *bonum privatum* to the point of contempt for the *bonum commune*—it is love of self to the point of contempt for God.[14]

The results are spiritual entities who are opposed to virtue and love and who create mayhem on Earth. And before very long, we find ourselves in the world of demon possession. A veritable industry specializing in exorcisms has emerged ranging from the relatively subdued to the utterly outlandish.[15]

At this point, the author needs to confess to the sense of *anafühl*. One does not necessarily want to keep the company of those who spot the demonic everywhere. One is aware of how mental illness can easily be misdiagnosed as demon possession and lead to horrendous and deeply misguided decisions. One is tempted to suggest that some type of scientific explanation for ostensible evil phenomenon is more plausible than to argue for demons.[16] But, these are not arguments against the possibility of the demonic. In the same sense that the inappropriate actions of Westboro Baptist Church[17] in the name of God are not arguments against the existence of God; so, one should not take the misuse of an idea as decisive evidence against the possibility of that idea. So, let us go back through the process. There is no question that the eternal Word witnesses to the reality of spiritual forces being evil. It is confirmed in the witness of Scripture and the tradition.

On rationality, one might want to challenge the picture of demons as monochromatic. All demons are just completely evil, and that is it. It is puzzling why Jesus responded to the pleas of the demons to be cast into the herd of the swine (Matthew 8:28–34). Perhaps not all demons are the same. And Griffiths suspects that the sin of the fallen angels is comparable to an inability to completely understand a mathematical proof, which leads him to write:

> If something like this is right—and we are at a speculative height now that will not be exceeded in this book—then demonic existence need not be seen as Augustine and the long tradition mostly do, which is as a kind of simple stasis. Rather it may be seen as a continuum along which individual demonic angels may move, whether by embracing lack or by struggling against it. And if that is right, the most radical, fully Satanic, embrace of lack would inevitably lead to nonbeing, to angelic annihilation. This seems a possibility. And if it is, it carries with it another, which is the possibility of demonic redemption.

This makes sense. Griffiths is focused on the ultimate end of angels. He is here postulating that a completely evil fallen angel ends up facing annihilation, while other angels who are only missing parts of the mathematical puzzle (to stay with his analogy) may ultimately be redeemed. And working with this model, one might then suppose that the willingness of Jesus to take the merciful line with the demons being moved into the swine (although it should be noted less merciful for the swine themselves) was a recognition that these demons were more open to redemptive possibilities than other demons.

To the obvious question, is it possible that angels (those which did not fall) are also on a spectrum? The answer is that the biblical witness does talk about different types of angels, with different roles; and, therefore, in terms of function, there might be a spectrum, but generally, these angels are all fully aware of the divine presence and, therefore, none are tinged with evil.

So, we arrive at the following picture of the spiritual realm. There are angels that are messengers of God; there are fallen angels that are on a spectrum, with some more evil than others. As humans interact with the spiritual realm, we should "test the spirits." We should engage prayerfully with the forces that we sense around us. In my view, rarely is an exorcism necessary. Instead, the following very Anglican account of a house exorcism by Martyn Percy is, in my view, a perfect model:

> Quite recently I was invited to a house to perform an exorcism. If at once this sounds a little too dramatic, let me explain. Someone connected to the parish asked if the church could help with a matter that they were finding both puzzling and disturbing. A young couple with their two-year-old son had recently moved into the neighbourhood. But after a while the child started to complain about "seeing things" and had started to become disturbed and frightened. The boy reported seeing an elderly man wandering around the upstairs of the house, although no one else could see this. Added to which, the rooms where the appearances took place were unusually cold, in spite of central heating. The couple called the church, because they knew that I had worked with this sort of thing before.

Percy realizes the account may sound a little strange to some contemporary readers, and states the following:

> What is one to make of this? I am well aware that there are potential social, psychological and psychotherapeutic angles that could be explored. However, after an interview in the home, it seemed that there were no obvious reasons for what one might call "a lingering, disturbing and unexplained presence." There were, for example, no deaths in the house reported by the previous occupants. Under such circumstances, I take the view that there are two priorities. First, take the presenting situation seriously as a point of pastoral need; the unexplained should not be over-dramatized, or talked up as something to be feared unduly. Second, religious-type problems tend to be best addressed by religious rejoinders. Correspondingly, I sprinkle the rooms with holy water, saying the Lord's Prayer and various collects in all the rooms where there has been disturbance. After that, I have a cup of tea with the family, play with the child a little, and go home. Two weeks later, the mother mentions to me that the child slept soundly from that night, and there have been no further instances of disturbance. "Fine," I said, "and thanks for the tea."

Percy does not deny the possibility; he does consider other dimensions of the situations; and then, with appropriate seriousness, as a priest, he works through the rooms affected. This is a good example of appropriate engagement with the spiritual forces that are opposed to God and, therefore, create a malignant presence in the world.

Let us now try a second exercise. What about "saints" in heaven interceding for us?

Turning to the Saints

Starting with the Bible works well with angels. However, with the saints, it does not. In many ways, the most visible witnesses to the saints are the tradition and the Roman Catholic Church. And this creates for us a problem. Starting with the tradition, the sense that the faithfully departed are interceding on our behalf has its roots in late antiquity.[18] The idea of those martyred for the faith shattered the cosmology of the ancient world. They passed from Earth to heaven. In Hellenistic and Roman times, the cult of the saints was a natural evolution of the cult of the heroes. Within this fertile soil, the cult of the saints generated its own extraordinary energy. It had a remarkable impact socially. This practice led to the dismembering and the adoration of every part of the saint—from bones to fingernails. The cult of the saints slowly assumed the same role as the ancient Roman practice of patronage. Where a patron would have a client and create a mutually agreed upon set of expectations in the relationship, so a Christian would have a saint that played a comparable protective and advocacy role. The result is dramatic. Peter

Brown writes: "[B]y the mid-fifth century, the cult of the saints had ringed the populations of the Mediterranean with intimate invisible friends."[19]

We turn now to the Roman Catholic Church. The Roman Catholic Church established a formal process for naming saints in 1234. Prior to this, it was the "vox populi" or "spontaneous local attribution" that led to the proclamation of a saint. However, such simple acclamation by the faithful was not always reliable and was easy to manipulate for political purposes. The Congregation for the Causes of Saints was instituted in 1588 by Pope Sixtus V. It is not necessary for us to rehearse all the steps to sainthood—from servant of God, to Venerable, to Beatification, to Blessed, to Saint. However, it is worth highlighting that the Roman Catholic Church does not make saints but recognizes those in heaven who live a life worthy of imitation.

One temptation at this point needs to be named and confronted. Brown documents how the cult of the saints emerges in a culture familiar with the veneration of the hero and is used politically by the bishops for certain economic ends. Add to this analysis the need for the Roman Catholic Church to create a system for identifying saints, and it is tempting to reduce the idea of saints to a social construct of the Hellenistic and Roman world, which was used by bishops and finally the Roman Catholic for political ends. If this is what the cult of the saints is, then clearly it cannot be true.

The Genetic Fallacy always haunts the social sciences. It is perfectly possible that there is a social narrative that made the idea of saints plausible and that a discovery is made about the truth of the saints. In one sense, this must always be true about the knowing process. Sociologically, the ground for any belief must be conducive to that belief taking root. That process is logically separate from the possibility that the belief is true. For example, a teenager becomes an atheist at university because she is so appalled by the intolerance of her fundamentalist upbringing. The reality that there is a sociological narrative of her belief does not determine the truth or falsehood of atheism. Many Christians turn this objection into a theological doctrine: It was in God's providence that Hellenistic culture gave the church the vocabulary to formulate the doctrine of the Trinity or, for our more Reformed brothers and sisters, God created the environment where European princes were ready to defy the Pope and enable an authentic renewal and reformation of the Church. It is, then, perfectly possible that God knows the truth about the presence of the faithfully departed to intercede for us on earth and that it would most effectively be discovered in a Hellenistic and Roman environment of the early centuries of Christianity.

But is it true? This is now our question. Once again, we turn to our five principles developed as a model of Christian reasoning. We start with what we can learn from the eternal Word—the life, death, and resurrection of Jesus. At this point, we need to add the category "ascension," the moment when the resurrected body of Jesus passes into the presence of God.

The reason why the ascension is key is that the participation of Christ in the world is the basis for the participation of any "saint" in the world. The biblical witness is clear. The physical body of Jesus died. The physical body was then recomposed to form a resurrection body with significant freedom from the traditional limitations of the physical body. We see this from the empty tomb (which is certainly part of the narratives of the Gospels even if it is less clear in 1 Corinthians 15). The resurrection appearances capture a body that can appear, disappear, and move through locked doors. Then, after forty days, in a moment pivotal for the movement of Luke/Acts, Jesus ascends into the air and disappears into heaven.

The cosmology of Scripture right up and through the Ptolemaic cosmology had little difficulty with the idea that heaven is a location where the resurrected body of Christ now resides. John Shelby Spong is fond of reminding us all that Carl Sagan took the view that if Jesus ascended from the Earth 2,000 years ago at the speed of light, then he still would not have left this solar system. The point was made earlier that every age has a limited cosmology, and so it is unfair to judge a doctrine because of the inevitable attempt to understand that doctrine within their limited cosmology. However, it is true that the sense of heaven as location spatially related with our universe is a problem.

We need to make a shift. T. F. Torrance is helpful when he observes, "We must not abstract the notion of space from that which is located in space—for space concretely considered is place, but place not abstracted from purpose or content, and place not without ends or purposeful limits. Time and space must both be conceived in relational terms."[20] The point here is the modern scientific insight that space, time, and motion are not concrete and fixed but have a complex interplay through relationships between things. I want to avoid talking of heaven as a parallel universe because there is no relationship with that universe and this one. Instead, heaven as a dimension that continues to intersect with this universe is more helpful. This seems to be where Torrance ends up, when he suggests that heaven is more appropriately described as a place rather than space. Space is where you put things; God's place emphasizes the inhabitant. To conceive of the ascension as a passing from this dimension to an alternative dimension seems possible.

Now, I want to suggest it is perfectly possible and proper to believe that the resurrected and ascended Christ is in the presence of God in heaven. Paul informs us in 1 Corinthians 15:20 that Christ is the first fruits of those who have died. The promise of the resurrection is that we too will participate in the glorification that God has given Christ (Romans 8:17). Herein is our model of the saints. We learn this as a disclosure from the eternal Word made flesh and in particular, the Ascension.

Now, we need to work through the other four principles. When it comes to the biblical witness, the practices of prayer—praying for others—and asking others to pray for you are well established. The author of 1 Timothy stresses the importance of praying for others (1 Timothy 2:1–5); Paul often exhorts others to pray for him (Rom 15:30–32; Eph 6:18–20; Col 4:3; 1 Thess 5:25; 2 Thess 3:1); and Paul prays for others (2 Thess 1:11). The obvious question arises: What difference do all these prayers make? Is God more likely to answer a prayer when ten people pray rather than just one? This puzzle is not made any greater by postulating that the saints are able to pray for us. It is a conundrum at the heart of the Christian view of divine action. My own view is heavily shaped by Keith Ward, who argues that prayers work with the contours of creation by creating space through which God can work.[21] And if this is true, then asking the saints to pray for us makes perfect sense.

There is one place in the text of Scripture that seems to allude explicitly to the prayers of the departed. The clearest is Revelation 8:3–4:

> [An] angel came and stood at the altar [in heaven] with a golden censer; and he was given much incense to mingle with the prayers of all the saints upon the golden altar before the throne; and the smoke of the incense rose with the prayers of the saints from the hand of the angel before God.

This establishes that the saints are able to pray and that their prayers are received.

In respect to the tradition of the church, we have already noted, as a potential difficulty, the emergence of the cult of the saints. However, more positively, there is an abundance of affirmation that the faithful departed have consciousness and are able to pray for us. As with angels, the extent of the speculation (St. Amelia is responsible for bruises; St. Lawrence for comedians) is not justified.

In terms of coherence and compatibility with truths known elsewhere, the key idea we need to affirm is that a resurrected body in the presence of God can be aware of our prayers. The idea of the mind of a person in a different and improved body, located in a shadow dimension, is not manifestly incoherent. And, in respect to other truths known elsewhere, this is an interfaith moment. Ancestor veneration is widespread. Perhaps this impulse is evidence of its validity.

There are plenty of religious cultures in the world that do need these arguments. They live their lives deeply aware of the angelic, the demonic, and the willingness of those gone before to respond to the request for prayers. We are in the world of the most devout. *Anafühl* haunts those who have lost this connection with the textured nature of reality, which is, at the deepest level, simply felt. Our supposed sophistication has made all this seem implausible. But at the level of good arguments, there are none. We do not have reasons for our skepticism. The steps are clear: If you trust that God has spoken in Christ, then saints and angels just follow.

NOTES

1. Serge-Thomas Bonino, *Angels and Demons* (Washington, DC: Catholic University of America Press, 2016), p. 1.
2. Dylan David Potter, in *Angelology* (Eugene, OR: Cascade Books, 2016), argues that the Reformation theologians lost interest in angels because of their emphasis on "the centrality of Christ in God's reconciliation of the world to himself" (p. 186). This is helpful and true, although it is true, as Potter admits, that angels remained very firmly part of their worldview.
3. Brian Hebblethwaite, *The Essence of Christianity: A Fresh Look at the Nicene Creed* (London: SPCK, 1996), pp. 75–76. Although I disagree with Hebblethwaite, I do concede it is possible to believe in the creed and not believe in angels. I think angels exist, but I understand that some Christians will not.
4. Ibid., p. 76.
5. Ibid., p. 76. He goes on to list further reasons why the Devil is problematic. He writes, "Literal belief in the devil is not really an intelligible belief. For what could possibly tempt a pure spirit, unencumbered with the lures of physical origin, to fall from grace? Why should such fallen spirits be permitted to wreak havoc in nature or the human world? What is the point of keeping them in being, let alone in active interference with the world, if they have rendered themselves wholly unredeemable?"
6. Peter Williams, *The Case for Angels* (Carlisle, UK: Paternoster Press, 2002), p. 120.
7. Ibid., p. 139.
8. Now, one could start with any significant Christological passage in the New Testament (for example, Hebrews). However, for the purpose of the argument that follows, the Gospels are a good place to start.
9. Most discussions of angels in the literature tend to focus on Aquinas. It is worth noting that although Augustine did not write a treatise on angels, they are very present in his writing. For an excellent discussion, see Elizabeth Klein, *Augustine's Theology of Angels* (Cambridge: Cambridge University Press, 2018).
10. Karl Barth, *Church Dogmatics, Vol. III.3 § 51.1* ("The Limits of Angelology"), p. 369.
11. This is where Williams, *The Case for Angels*, is better; see pp. 78–103. See also Mortimer J. Alder, *The Angels and Us* (New York: Collier, 1982).
12. Paul J. Griffiths, *Decreation: The Last Things of All Creatures* (Waco, TX: Baylor University Press, 2014), pp. 121–22.
13. Ibid., p. 122.
14. Bonino, *Angels and Demons*, p. 203.
15. For a Roman Catholic example, see Anthony Finlay, *Demons: The Devil, Possession and Exorcism* (London: Blandford Press, 1999).
16. David Bradnick occupies a very distinctive position in the debate about the notion of demons. Drawing on the work of the Pentecostal theologian Amos Yong, Bradnick argues for an account of the demonic that emerges from the processes of evolution and results in a causal impact that is top-down. This is an intriguing study that takes seriously the witness of Scripture and the tradition. The possibilities in emergentist philosophy for an account of the interaction of the spiritual and the physical are intriguing, the potentially reductionist implications that denies the autonomy of the spiritual realm (as none derived from the physical) is more problematic. For Bradnick, see *Evil, Spirits, and Possession: An Emergentist Theology of the Demonic* (Leiden, Netherlands and Boston: Brill, 2017).
17. Westboro Baptist Church is the small church that became famous for their demonstrations at the funerals of soldiers who died overseas. They were demonstrating because they believed that God was letting these soldiers die because the United States tolerated LGBT persons, along with other sins against Scripture.

18. What follows is a very abbreviated summary of the argument found in Peter Brown, *The Cult of the Saints: Its Rise and Function in Latin Christianity* (Chicago: The University of Chicago Press, 1981).

19. Brown, *The Cult of the Saints*, p. 50.

20. T. F. Torrance, *Space, Time and Resurrection* (Grand Rapids, MI: Eerdmans, 1976) pp. 130–31.

21. Keith Ward, *Divine Action* (London: Collins, 1990), chapter 9.

Chapter Nine

Inclusion, Justice, and the New Apologetics

Objections and Replies

I am grateful for the reader who has managed to stay with the argument and has finally arrive at chapter 9. Now, let me engage with a set of issues that might be on the reader's mind. The primary issue is the relationship of this rarefied (perhaps) theology with the fundamental issues that face our society around inclusion and justice. Then, let me consider a set of "objections" and formulate some response to those objections. I appreciate this argument is distinctive and, in many ways, running counter to the primary trends in the academy and the church. Therefore, this chapter seeks to persuade the reader that there is a need for this argument.

We start with the issues of inclusion and justice. For some, traditional theology is just too damaged. Too many human lives have been destroyed on the altar of an "orthodoxy," they argue. The victims are many. Women, African Americans, and LGBT persons have all been crushed by a theology that discerns that God's providential pattern is hierarchal, white, heterosexual, and male. In this chapter, we will consider this perspective.

Let me start with patriarchy. It is still the case that gender inequality persists. The World Health Organization (WHO) estimates that 35 percent of women around the world have experienced "either physical and/or sexual intimate partner violence or non-partner sexual violence in their lifetime."[1] If you take into account unpaid work (caring for children and household chores), women work longer days—"an average of 30 minutes a day longer in developed countries and 50 minutes in developing countries."[2] Only half of the women in the world are in the labor force, while over three-quarters of the men are. Pay inequality persists. In the United States, in 2017, "female full-time, year-round workers made only 80.5 cents for every dollar earned by men, a gender wage gap of 20 percent."[3]

Feminist theologians made a simple and incontrovertible case that patriarchy has deep roots in cultural sexism. From even in the writings of Aristotle, we find a hierarchy that justified a social structure where citizenship is confined to the free male who owns property. Aristotle saw the world through a set of subordinations: the soul should govern the body, the master should govern the enslaved person, and the male should govern the female. Aristotle argues that the first is superior, "the other is inferior, for one governs and the other is governed."[4] One reason why feminist theologians contest the dualism of body and soul is because of the role it seems to play in justifying a politics of male superiority.

The New Apologetics is seeking to engage feminism in two ways. First, the account of God underpinning this project is engaged closely with the creation. The insights of Sallie McFague and others are being assumed.[5] God does embrace the world within God's being. There is a temporal life within the life of God. There are some differences: Unlike McFague, the model of God is not simply a human construct, although I concede the model of God can have political implications. In addition, I am committed to *creatio ex nihilo* ("creation out of nothing"); the creation is within the life of God, but God transcends the creation.[6] The image of creation within the body of God has power: creation is analogous to the embryo—it can move, has some independence, and can fall sick, and all of this is felt by the mother. Naturally, all analogies have limitations; God is not then understood as material, but the Spirit of God embraces the material, enables it to be, and feels everything that is happening within creation.

The second way is that the New Apologetics is inviting women to be ordained into the richness of the tradition. It is ironic that as the status of the church declined in Western societies, women were invited into the church. In addition, many of the advocates for the inclusion of women did so because they were skeptical about doctrine generally and ecclesiology in particular. John Shelby Spong has been a tireless campaigner for the ordination of women. He has also been a tireless campaigner for a faith without a traditional Incarnation, one that does not involve the Trinity, and one that sees the church as primarily an association.[7] The argument of this book is that justice is not progressed when the invitation to holy orders for women is simply an invitation into a leadership role in the church. We need to retain a robust account of ordained ministry that protects the invitation of women into the sanctuary. Advocates for the ordination of women need to state clearly that women are being invited to be part of the richness of the apostolic succession. The line that Jesus started permitted women to emerge in leadership positions even in the New Testament (e.g., Phoebe was a deacon of the church at Cenchreae—see Romans 16:1–2). Defending a traditional view of Anglican ministry makes the inclusion of women in that ministry all the more significant.

Having made the case that the argument of this book is compatible with a feminist theology, let me now turn to the issue of the New Apologetics and racism. Racism puzzles me deeply. To believe in the legitimacy of the slave trade is a deep moral blindness. As David Eltis, in the remarkable resource called the *Trans-Atlantic Slave Trade*, puts it:

> It is difficult to believe in the first decades of the twenty-first century that just over two centuries ago, for those Europeans who thought about the issue, the shipping of enslaved Africans across the Atlantic was morally indistinguishable from shipping textiles, wheat, or even sugar.[8]

And then, as one explores this complex database, the sheer scale of the trade is deeply disturbing. From 1501 to 1866, 12,521,337 human lives are uprooted and turned into property. The scale of human misery that this number represents is impossible to imagine. When one reads Zurara, the chronicler for Prince Henry of Portugal in 1444, one can see that the anguish at the point of capture was deep and real. Zurara writes:

> But what heart could be so hard as not to be pierced with piteous feeling to see that company? For some kept their heads low and their faces bathed in tears, looking one upon another; others stood groaning very dolorously, looking up to the height of heaven, fixing their eyes upon it, crying out loudly, as if asking help of the Father of Nature; others stuck their faces with the palms of their hands, throwing themselves at full length upon the ground; others made their lamentations in the manner of a dirge, after the custom of their country. And though we could not understand the words of their language, the sound of it right well accorded with the measure of their sadness.[9]

To take a human life and enslave that life, treat that life as property, and deny that life the right to freedom was from the start a recognizable and wicked sin.

There is a link between traditional theology and the trade in enslaved persons. There are, of course, biblical passages that were used to justify the trade. From the "curse of Ham" in Genesis 9:18–27 to the injunction in Ephesians 6 for slaves to obey their masters, the text of Scripture was used to explain why the trade was compatible with the Gospel. In 1788, Raymond Harris wrote a pamphlet entitled *Scriptural Researches on the Licitness of the Slave-Trade Shewing its Conformity with the Principles of Natural and Revealed Religion Delineated in the Sacred Writings of the Word of God.*[10] It is a painstaking analysis of all the relevant passages that discuss slavery.

Many Christians who have loved the Lord Jesus thought that slavery was legitimate.

There were always some who saw that the principle of Galatians meant that slavery was an evil. When Paul wrote, "There is no longer Jew or Greek, there is no longer slave or free, there is no longer male and female; for all of you are one in Christ Jesus" (Galatians 3:28), the debate over slavery was theologically resolved. There is a fundamental human equality and dignity in Christ. There is no longer a hierarchy. There are no longer differences in economic status. The poor are as important as the rich; the enslaved person as important as the owner; and different ethnicities are equally important. This was a shocking teaching. How can the holder of enslaved persons be as important as the enslaved person? But this is the Christian claim; this is the Christian assumption.

Galatians is important. It is important to note that from the start of Christianity, there was a faith that, in its logic and self-understanding, repudiated any teaching that approved of enslaved persons. A traditional faith always had the resources to oppose slavery. The tragedy is that the church took too long to see the logic of Galatians.

Although the Civil War in the United States liberated some four million slaves, Black Codes were introduced in many states. These were intended to guarantee that African Americans continued to be a source of cheap labor. African Americans had to sign employment contracts, which if they refused could lead to arrest and penalties. In addition, these codes determined housing options. Black Codes were soon followed by the so-called "Jim Crow laws" that entrenched segregation. From schools to neighborhoods to recreation, whites and blacks had to be kept separate. In 1896, in the case of *Plessy v. Ferguson*, the Supreme Court of the United States ruled that segregation was constitutional.

The creativity that went into keeping the options for African Americans limited was extraordinary. So, although, in 1917, the Supreme Court ruled that zoning laws prohibiting African Americans moving into white neighborhoods were illegal, in 1920, a federal zoning committee was created that prevented poorer families from moving into middle-income neighborhoods. Inevitably, because of the history of African Americans, this meant that neighborhoods would remain segregated. The practice of "red-lining" (where the Federal Home Loan Bank Board and Home Owners' Loan Corporation identified districts that were unsuitable for mortgages) persisted from the 1930s until the late 1970s. It was overt discrimination: African American neighborhoods had either no access or extremely expensive access to loans. It is no surprise that this led to a higher rate of foreclosure.

Major problems persist today. Jacqui Ballou documents the problem of incarceration:

Out of 10.4 million U.S. Black adult males, nearly 1.5 million are in prisons and jails, with another 3.5 million more on probation or parole, or who have previously been on probation or parole. Black males make up nearly 75% of the total prison population, compared to 7.7% of Hispanic men and 2.6% of White men, and due to either present or past incarceration.[11]

The consequences, as Ballou points out, are tangible. This means that there are fewer marriages, fewer family units, and a higher likelihood of children having fewer opportunities. The white majority continue to make life brutally hard for the African American minority.

So, how does the New Apologetics engage with the African American experience? The first is that opposition to racism is fundamental. There can be no ambiguity: Racism is a deep and abiding sin of the whole church. The propensity of the church to either avoid discussing racism or to provide, often subliminal, justifications for racism is wicked. All forms of Christianity must be unequivocal. There is no room for racism in the church. The second is that this project is deliberately drawing extensively on the African experience of the transcendent as a key part of the argument. Instead of patronizing and, therefore, overlooking the African sense of the divine, this book is arguing it is key datum. Margarita Simon Guillory, in her impressive study entitled *Spiritual and Social Transformation in African American Spiritual Churches: More than Conjurers*, argues that the spiritual churches in her study in New Orleans would combine traditional religion with intense spiritual experiences. Guillory notes that these churches "combine elements of Catholicism, Protestantism, Spiritualism, Voodoo (derivative of Haitian Vodou), and Hoodoo, and their dynamic ritual practices concerning healing."[12] Guillory goes on to say that it is precisely this syncretistic spirituality that leads these churches to orchestrate "many social initiatives to address poverty, homelessness, and gender inequality in New Orleans."[13] In addition, she writes that "these same churches also have employed diverse doctrines of wholeness and healing rituals to attend to the spiritual needs of both their adherents and community members at-large."[14]

We can and should agree that a theology should be evaluated on its commitment to justice. The New Apologetics believes that a rediscovery of the richness of the Christian tradition coupled with a recognition that the world is genuinely textured and the spiritual realm is real can lead to a robust resource for a theologically grounded justice. This taps into the experience of African religion; and this is the experiential basis of many African American churches.

Taking the spiritual as real is not evading the obligation to fight for justice but rather a foundation for the epic struggle. "Academic and intellectual" liberalism may not always connect with the Christian experience of those who are struggling for justice. Recovering this sense of God permeating the universe is part of our commitment for justice and inclusion.

OBJECTIONS AND REPLIES[15]

I appreciate that the argument of this book is contentious. The mood of the academy is not sympathetic to a liberal defense (in that science and ecumenism are taken seriously) of traditional catholic doctrines. The mood of those sympathetic to traditional catholic doctrines will not appreciate my liberal defense. So, this is a book that is likely to irritate everyone. Therefore, in this section, let me attempt to persuade the contemporary skeptic that there is some merit in this approach. To do this, I will formulate the key objections to my approach and outline a response.

We need to start with a summary of the steps in the argument. First, contemporary skepticism is more of a mood than a rational rejection of theism. Second, the basis for that mood—namely reductionist, mechanistic science—is increasingly rejected by scientists. Third, we need to recover a spiritually infused universe. Fourth, we are trusting revelation to disclose what this spiritually infused universe is really like. Fifth, we utilized the Trinity as a model of theological reasoning and applied that to the concepts of angels and saints. Sixth, the language of spirituality is key. Seventh, the conviction that we are in a church where God has promised to deliver certain sacraments through the apostolic succession can make sense. And, finally, we are entitled to conclude that angels and saints are part of the Christian claim about this spiritually infused universe. This all means that the New Apologetics is an invitation to discover Christian practices, which then opens up an experience of the world as textured. This is not an invitation to the spiritual in the abstract. This is spirituality grounded in the revelation of God, as seen in the eternal Word made flesh.

Let us now consider the major objections to this argument.

> Objection one: *The key problem with this book is that it is a call to return to a premodern worldview. Whereas Charles Taylor wants a reinterpretation of the symbols of the enchanted world, this book is calling for a reaffirmation of the reality of enchantment. This is simply impossible and unavailable to any person living in the twenty-first century.*

We all recognize that religion is in trouble. It is true that there are a variety of responses to our religious predicament. At one extreme, we have those who reject the language of the transcendent and spiritual. God is demythologized into a symbol for good.[16] At the other extreme, we have a fundamentalist reaffirmation of traditional doctrinal claims.[17] Both extremes are misguided. The demythologized God is a surrender to a secular world; the fundamentalist reaffirmation fails to engage with the truth of the modern scientific worldview. The New Apologetics seeks to reframe traditional affirmations in a way that is scientifically plausible and sensitive to our current mood. Science is now more friendly to a "spiritually infused universe" than ever before. There are good reasons to trust the revelation of God that is found in Jesus of Nazareth. Accounts of angels and saints can be constructed that make sense. So, it is not a return to a premodern worldview, but it is also more than just a reinterpretation of a universe of symbols. In a "critically realist" sense, the world is really to be understood as spiritually infused. Part of the evidence for this is the account of the universe emerging from modern science.

> Objection two: *The argument is a reassertion of traditional metaphysics. Can a truly scientifically sensitive account accommodate this reassertion of traditional metaphysics?*

Metaphysics is inescapable. Even scientists skeptical about religion are making a metaphysical claim. Materialism is a claim in the realm of metaphysics that most contemporary philosophers find very hard to defend. It is interesting to note that many scientific innovations are making fascinating metaphysical assumptions. Just to take one interesting example: It was the philosopher Nick Bostrom who made the case that our universe might be the result of an advanced civilization creating a complex computer simulation. At the University of Washington, a group of physicists is attempting an empirical experiment to determine the validity of the simulation hypothesis. Preston Greene summarizes the experiment thus:

> The details are complex, but the basic idea is simple: Some of today's computer simulations of our cosmos produce distinctive anomalies—for example, there are telltale glitches in the behavior of simulated cosmic rays. By taking a closer look at the cosmic rays in our universe, the physicists suggested, we might detect comparable anomalies, providing evidence that we live in a simulation.[18]

Now Greene's own view is that it would be very unwise for humans potentially to undermine an experiment of an advanced civilization by becoming aware that we are in a computer simulation. However, my point is that this hypothesis is a metaphysical claim that is being taken very seriously by a prestigious university and presumably some funding agency. Alternative hypotheses are very much back in vogue. Now, the metaphysics I am defending are grounded on revelation. So, as one evaluates metaphysical options, one needs to weigh ideas such as we are in a computer simulation with the possibility that at the heart of the universe is goodness and love revealed in Jesus of Nazareth. The argument of this book is that revelation is defensible and plausible. If the choice is a computer simulation or Jesus, I think most people should concede that Jesus deserves a hearing.

> Objection three: *Why not stop at spirituality and stay away from particulars, such as the sacraments and apostolic succession?*

This was a temptation. It would have been an easier book to write, if it had joined the many other texts that affirm the reality of the spiritual dimension. The idea of a book that defended the reality of the spiritual realm and, perhaps, the efficacy of intercessory prayer would have been easier to write and less likely to provoke surprise.

The goal of this book, however, was to move away from a generalized defense of spirituality. The argument needed to be concrete. Angels really exist. It is appropriate to ask the saints to pray for us. And, as a seminary dean training women and men for holy orders, this is how I understand their vocation. The spiritual needed to be made concrete, not simply be in the abstract.

> Objection four: *The whole liturgical renewal movement was intended to find a way to use the language without the burden of believing in such things as the apostolic succession.*

The relationship of this book with the liturgical movement does require some comment. We tend to date the liturgical renewal movement from the 1870s. It is Dom Prosper Guéranger, the leader of the Benedictine community at Solesmes, France, who developed a research interest in Christian liturgy. Ancient resources were rediscovered; and these documents were studied with appropriate scholarly attention. In 1909, Dom Lambert Beauduin, in a key address at the National Congress of Catholic Action, argued for the full participation of the lay. These initiatives within the Roman Catholic Church spread out to other denominations. Indeed, the 1979 *Book of Common Prayer of the Episcopal Church* was a direct result of the liturgical renewal movement.

The New Apologetics is in conversation with the liturgical renewal movement. The emphasis on the participation of the laity; the growth of ecumenical awareness; and the desire to use a range of resources are all compatible with the movement. The desire to reengage with the doctrine of the Apostolic Succession would be seen to run counter with the movement. Yet the account offered in this book does seek to be sensitive, both ecumenically and scientifically.

Conservatives have long complained that the liturgical renewal movement had a "liberalizing" effect on the church. The truth is much more complicated. Many liturgical innovations were actually drawing on older and more ancient traditions; they were a recovery of the old, not the creation of something new. However, there is a risk that a liberalizing tendency could be the basis for some liturgical proposals. In the Apostles' Creed, the shift from the "descent into hell" to "descend to the dead" could reflect an anxiety about the "harrowing of hell." To lose the "harrowing of hell" would be tragic. The cosmic consequences of the Incarnation of God dying at the hands of the creation that God made must include the reach of love to the places where love is not: All of this is captured by the "harrowing of hell." Earlier in the book, I argued against turning the Trinity into three activities—Creator, Redeemer, and Sustainer—and instead expressed my sympathies for William Placher's suggestion of "Father, Son, and Holy Spirit, One God, Mother of us all."

Reengaging with the doctrine of the Apostolic Succession affords the liturgical movement an opportunity to illustrate that it wants to affirm the richness of the tradition and to make that tradition available to the people of God.

> Objection five: *The truth about the witness of the Gospel is that there is much more interest in the activity of demons and rather less interest in the activity of angels. Yet, the argument of this book has made angels central but has been rather cursory in the treatment of demons. Given that the argument is grounded in the authority of the revelation of God in Jesus Christ, is not this a key weakness in the entire argument?*

It is true that the healing ministry of Jesus involves many exorcisms. However, the witness of the Gospels does afford considerable space for angels. From the nativity to the temptation to the resurrection, angels play a major role. The central argument in this book is that spiritual entities such as angels and demons are plausible; and given an assumption of trust in the revelation of God in Jesus Christ, their existence should be affirmed by Christians.

On the basis of such trust, I have affirmed the reality of spiritual entities that are tormented and more destructive (i.e., demons). However, I concede that there is a nervousness here. The church can turn the demonic into a destructive preoccupation. So, one should tread carefully; we should acknowledge the reality of such forces and seek to locate them in the wider narrative of human sinfulness and our own fascination with destructive sinful behaviors.

This concludes this exercise where we have engaged with a set of potential objections to my argument. The craft of theology is always an attempt to engage with the resources of our tradition and to seek to illustrate the coherence and plausibility of the Christian narrative about life. Every theologian should offer our engagement with the mysteries of the faith with some humility and awe. We are writing about the intersection of heaven and Earth, and we offer our reflections to the church trusting that the people of God will be able to sift the illuminating from the confusing.

NOTES

1. World Health Organization at https://www.who.int/news-room/fact-sheets/detail/violence-against-women (accessed August 19, 2019).

2. United Nations Statistics at https://unstats.un.org/unsd/gender/chapter4/chapter4.html (accessed August 23, 2019).

3. Institute for Women's Policy Research at https://iwpr.org/issue/employment-education-economic-change/pay-equity-discrimination/ (accessed August 23, 2019).

4. Aristotle, *Politics and Economics,* translated by Edward Walford (London: George Bell and Sons, 1885), part 1, "Politics" or the "Treatise on Government," book 1, chapter 5, 12–13.

5. See Sallie McFague, *Models of God: Theology for an Ecological, Nuclear Age* (Philadelphia: Fortress Press, 1982).

6. For an excellent discussion and defense of *creatio ex nihilo* and feminist theology, see Janice McRandal, *Christian Doctrine and the Grammar of Difference: A Contribution to Feminist Systematic Theology* (Minneapolis, MN: Augsburg Fortress 2015).

7. See John Shelby Spong's autobiography, *Here I Stand: My Struggle for a Christianity of Integrity, Love, and Equality* (New York: Harper One, 2001).

8. David Eltis, "Introduction to the Methodology," on the *Trans-Atlantic Slave Trade – Understanding the Database*, at https://www.slavevoyages.org/voyage/about (accessed July 2, 2019).

9. Gomes Eanes de Azurara, *The Chronicle of the Discovery and Conquest of Guinea,* as quoted in Willie James Jenning, *The Christian Imagination: Theology and the Origins of Race,* (New Haven, CT and London: Yale University Press, 2010), pp. 18–19.

10. See Reverend Raymond Harris, *Scriptural Researches on the Licitness of the Slave-Trade Shewing its Conformity with the Principles of Natural and Revealed Religion Delineated in the Sacred Writings of the Word of God* (Liverpool: printed by H. Hodgson, Pool-Lane, 1788). An extract is reproduced in my *Do Morals Matter*, second edition (Oxford: Wiley Blackwell, 2018).

11. Jacqui Ballou, "Is there Liberation for the Single, Saved, and Sexually Repressed," in Brittany C. Slatton and Carla D. Brailey (eds), *Women and Inequality in the 21 st Century*, p. 224 (New York: Routledge, 2019).

12. Margarita Simon Guillory, *Spiritual and Social Transformation in African American Spiritual Churches: More than Conjurers* (New York: Routledge, 2017), p. 4.

13. Ibid., p. 4.

14. Ibid., p. 5.

15. I am grateful to Jeffery Stout in his *Ethics after Babel: The Language of Morals and Their Discontents* (Princeton, NJ: Princeton University Press, 2001), chapter 2. I have taken from this chapter the simple idea of stating potential objections and constructing appropriate replies.

16. This is the position of Don Cupitt in *Taking Leave of God* (London: SCM Press, 1980).

17. See, for example, John Warwick Montgomery in *Fighting the Good Fight: A Life in Defense of the Faith* (Eugene, OR: Wipf & Stock, 2016).

18. Preston Greene, "Are We Living in a Computer Simulation? Let's Not Find Out," in *The New York Times*, August 10, 2019.

Concluding Reflections

The Irish talk about "thin places." When one walks into a cathedral where the agonies of the human heart have been poured out to God, one is in a thin place. As one stands on the island of Iona breathing in the air where pilgrims have encountered God, one is in a thin place. These places feel different. Timothy Sedgwick defines a "thin place" thus:

> There are some physical locations that are called "thin places." People speak of these as where heaven and earth collide, where you fall from the everyday world into another. They may be still, but they are not necessarily tranquil. In these places, we are touched in ways that draw us beyond our immediate worries and concerns. We feel connected beyond ourselves.[1]

There is a power in these spaces. It feels different. Timothy George makes the point in this way:

> Thin places—not because the air is rarified or the land is narrow but because the distance between heaven and earth shrinks, and time and eternity embrace. A thin place is where the veil between this world and the next is lifted for a moment, and it may be possible to get a glimpse of what one's life is all about—perhaps of what life itself is all about.[2]

With the growth of Celtic spirituality, the term is widely used. Often, it is where the natural beauty of the world coincides with the deep presence of the faithful to create a place that has a palpable feeling of the transcendent. Ann Armbrecht, in her moving book *Thin Places: A Pilgrimage Home*, extends the concept of thin places to the spaces that make us authentic. She even talks of "every birth is a thin place."[3] All these moments that help us see that we are more than just a "bundles of atoms" can be, if we let them, "thin places."

The argument of the "New Apologetics" is that all of life can be a "thin place." There will always be some places thinner than others. In a world where spiritual causation is real, there are spaces where the spiritual is more visible than others. Places of worship or pilgrimage are venues of spiritual energy. But, theologically, the God at work in a holy site is the same God who aspires to be at work in every site—at work, on the train, in the home, or at the Starbucks. Life is always textured; we just need the gift of faith to see that truth.

The mainline churches in the United States are at a crucial crossroads. We have been defending an increasingly impoverished faith. In response to the insights and truths emerging from modern science, we surrendered the world; we conceded that materialist explanations for the natural world are sufficient; and we turned God into a semi-intellectual act of assent that makes little difference to living and life. "Moral, therapeutic deism" became our impoverished understanding of Christianity. A mood—*anafühl*—made faith just feel unlikely. All of this coincided with urban life, making civic association and participation harder (we all stopped joining things), and a precipitous decline has affected every mainline church.

The mistake was our response to science. Cutting-edge science has long since rejected the mechanistic and materialist model of the universe. Spiritual causation is a possibility. So, all those things that the mainline became nervous about (another symptom of *anafühl*) need to be revisited. If there are material entities and, as is likely, life on other planets, then why not spiritual entities (so bring back angels)? If prayer taps into spiritual causation, then why not the Eucharist? If there is a life beyond the grave, then why not ask the saints to pray for us? Stop using the language of superstition. There are ways that these ideas can be defended. Let us invite again the people of God into the deeper sense of God's world.

These ideas can be defended with a scientific awareness (this is not a New Age tract) and ecumenical sensitivity. The goal is to invite the people of God into practices that help them sense the textured nature of reality—the "thin places"—and the awareness that God is and that we are loved by God.

Church can be hard work. The quality of the music and the sermon is often uneven. One does not go to church for entertainment. Instead, one goes to church because it is true. There really is a God. The spiritual realm is real. We need to practice the skill of participating and entering into the spiritual. We need to feel the textured nature of reality. This book started with a thought exercise: Our capacity to see colors has been eroded. The invitation of this book is that we learn afresh how to live closer to nature, live closer to God, and, therefore, live closer together.

This is the timeless invitation of the Gospel. God is; Jesus has shown us what God is like; and the church is the place where we experience the transforming love of God. Let us all "Go into the world and preach the Gospel."

NOTES

1. Timothy F. Sedgwick, *What Does It Mean to Be Holy Whole?* (New York: Church Publishing, 2018), p. 2.
2. Timothy George, "Thin Places." *First Things*. February 2, 2015, found at https://www.firstthings.com/web-exclusives/2015/11/thin-places. Accessed August 24, 2019.
3. Armbrecht, Ann, *Thin Places : A Pilgrimage Home*. New York: Columbia University Press, 2008. http://0-search.ebscohost.com.librarycatalog.vts.edu/login.aspx?direct=true&db=nlebk&AN=953941&site=ehost-live&scope=site.

Bibliography

Alder, Mortimer J. *The Angels and Us*. New York: Collier, 1982.

Aquinas, Thomas. *Summa Theologiae*. II, II, Q. 92, art 1.

Aristotle. *Politics and Economics,* translated by Edward Walford, London: George Bell and Sons, 1885, part 1, "Politics" or the "Treatise on Government," book 1, chapter 5, 12–13.

Armbrecht, Ann. *Thin Places: A Pilgrimage Home.* New York: Columbia University Press, 2008. http://0-search.ebscohost.com.librarycatalog.vts.edu/login.

Astuti, Rita and Maurice Bloch. "Are Ancestors Dead?" In *Wiley Blackwell Companion to Anthropology : Companion to the Anthropology of Religion,* edited by Janice Boddy and Michael Lambek, 104. Somerset, NJ: Wiley-Blackwell, 2014.

Atkin, Peter. "The Limitless Power of Science." In *Nature's Imagination,* edited by John Cornwell, 125. Oxford: Oxford University Press, 1995.

Augustine. *De consensu evangelistarum.* 1.2. PL 34:1044.

Augustine of Hippo. "Questions on the Heptateuch." In *The Works of Saint Augustine: Writings on the Old Testament, Part 1: Volume 14*, edited by Boniface Ramsey, 174. New York: New City Press of Focolare, 2016.

Augustine. "Letter 53, Chapter One." Translated by J. G. Cunningham. From *Nicene and Post-Nicene Fathers, First Series, Vol. 1*, edited by Philip Schaff. Buffalo, NY: Christian Literature Publishing Co., 1887. Revised and edited for New Advent by Kevin Knight. http://www.newadvent.org/fathers/1102053.htm. Accessed July 10, 2016.

Ayres, Lewis. "The Word Answering the Word: Opening the Space of Catholic Biblical Interpretation." Unpublished paper.

Ballou, Jacqui. "Is there Liberation for the Single, Saved, and Sexually Repressed." In *Women and Inequality in the 21st Century*, edited by Brittany C. Slatton and Carla D. Brailey, 224. New York: Routledge, 2019.

Barbour, Ian G. *Religion in an Age of Science.* San Francisco: Harper San Francisco, 1990.

Barnes, Julian. *Nothing to Be Frightened Of.* London: Jonathan Cape, 2008.

Barr, James. *Fundamentalism*, second edition. London: SCM Press, 1981.

Barth, Karl. *Church Dogmatics: Volume 3.3 § 51.1 ("The Limits of Angelology").* Edinburgh: T&T Clark, 1936.

Barth, Karl. *Church Dogmatics: Volume 1 The Doctrine of the Word of God, Part 1.* Edinburgh: T&T Clark, 1936.

Bates, Matthew W. *The Birth of the Trinity: Jesus, God, and Spirit in the New Testaments & Early Christian Interpretations of the Old Testament.* Oxford: Oxford University Press, 2015.

Bauckham, Richard. *God Crucified: Monotheism and Christology in the New Testament.* Carlisle, UK: Paternoster, 1998.

Bhaskar, Roy. *The Possibility of Naturalism: A Philosophical Critique of the Contemporary Human Sciences*, third edition. London: Routledge, 1998.

Bloesch, Donald G. *The Battle for the Trinity: The Debate over Inclusive God-Language.* Ann Arbor, MI: Vine Books, 1985.

Bonhoeffer. *Christology*, translated by John Bowden. London: Collins, 1966.

Bonino, Serge-Thomas. *Angels and Demons.* Washington, DC: Catholic University of America Press, 2016.

Bradnick, David. *Evil, Spirits, and Possession: An Emergentist Theology of the Demonic.* Leiden, Netherlands and Boston: Brill, 2017.

Brooke, John Hedley. *Science and Religion: Some Historical Perspectives.* Cambridge: Cambridge University Press, 1991.

Brown, Bridget. *They Know Us Better Than We Know Ourselves: The History and Politics of Alien Abduction.* New York: NYU Press, 2007.

Brown, Peter. *The Cult of the Saints: Its Rise and Function in Latin Christianity.* Chicago: The University of Chicago Press, 1981.

Brown, Raymond. *The Churches the Apostles Left Behind.* New York/Ramsey, NJ: Paulist Press, 1984.

Brunner, Emil. *The Christian Doctrine of the Creation and Redemptions: Dogmatics Vol. II*, translated by Olive Wyon. Eugene, OR: Wipf and Stock Publishers, 1952.

Bryson, Bill. *A Short History of Nearly Everything.* New York: Broadway Books, 2004.

Buchanan, Colin. "Comment: Current Questions in Episcopal Consecrations." *Theology* 118, July/August (2015): 279.

Burridge, Richard A. *What are the Gospels? A Comparison with Graeco-Roman Biography*, second edition. Grand Rapids, MI: William B. Eerdmans, 2004.

Burridge, Richard. *Imitating Jesus: An Inclusive Approach to New Testament Ethics.* Grand Rapids, MI: Eerdmans, 2007.

Byrne, Peter. *Natural Religion and the Nature of Religion: The Legacy of Deism.* London: Routledge, 1989.

Calvin, John. "Institutes of the Christian Religion, IV, 13, 1-26" (1559). In *Documents of Christian Worship: Descriptive and Interpretive Sources*, edited by James F. White. Louisville, KY: Westminster John Knox Press, 1992.

Cartwright, Nancy. "The Dethronement of Laws in Science." In *Rethinking Order After the Laws of Nature,* edited by Nancy Cartwright and Keith Ward. London: Bloomsbury, 2016.

Casey, P. M. *From Jewish Prophet to Gentile God: The Origins and Development of New Testament Christology.* Louisville, KY: Westminster John Knox, 1991.

Cater, Philip. *The Great Fiction of the Times, or Apostolic Succession, with Other Doctrines of Puseyism, Proved to be Unscriptural and Absurd.* Canterbury, 1844.

Catechism of the Catholic Church. Mahwah, NJ: Paulist Press, 1994.

Cheetham, David. *John Hick: A Critical Introduction and Reflection.* Aldershot, UK: Ashgate 2003.

Cirlot, Felix L. *Apostolic Succession: Is It True? An Historical and Theological Inquiry.* Louisville, KY: The Cloister Press, 1951.

Clayton, Philip. "Theology and the Physical Sciences." In *The Modern Theologians: An introduction to Christian theology since 1918,* third edition, edited by David Ford with Rachel Muers, 349. Malden, MA: Blackwell Publishing, 2005.

Collins, Adela Yarbro. *Mark: A Commentary.* Minneapolis, MN: Augsburg Fortress, 2007.

Conti, Fabrizio. "Preachers and Confessors against 'Superstitions': Bernardino Busti and Sermon 16 of His Rosarium Sermonum." *Magic, Ritual, and Witchcraft*, Vol. 6, no. 1 (2011): 62–91.

Cowdell, Scott. *Atheist Priest?: Don Cupitt and Christianity.* London: SCM Press, 1988.

Cupitt, Don. *Creation Out of Nothing.* London: SCM Press, 1990.

Cupitt, Don. *Taking Leave of God.* London: SCM Press, 1980.

Davies, Paul. *Cosmic Jackpot: Why Our Universe Is Just Right for Life.* Boston and New York: Houghton Mifflin Company, 2007.

Davies, Paul. *God and the New Physics.* New York: Touchstone, 1983.

de Azurara, Gomes Eanes. *The Chronicle of the Discovery and Conquest of Guinea,* as quoted in Willie James Jenning, *The Christian Imagination:*

Theology and the Origins of Race, (New Haven, CT, and London: Yale University Press, 2010.

de Botton, Alaine. "Ideas for Modern Living: Gratitude." *The Guardian.* March 14, 2010. Accessed August 5, 2016. https://www.theguardian.com/lifeandstyle/2010/mar/14/alain-botton-ideas-modern-living-gratitude?CMP=share_btn_link.

Della Rocca, Michael. *Spinoza.* London and New York: Routledge, 2008.

Denworth Lydia. "The Secret Social Power of Touch." *Scientific American Mind*, Vol. 26, no. 4 (2015).

Donahue, John R. and Daniel J. Harrington, S. J. *The Gospel of Mark.* Collegeville, MN: The Liturgical Press, 2002.

Dowd, Michael. *Thank God for Evolution.* New York: Viking, 2008.

Dummett, Michael. *Truth and Other Enigmas.* London: Duckworth, 1978.

Edwards, James R. *The Gospel According to Mark.* Grand Rapids, MI: Eerdmans: Leicester, England: Apollos, 2002.

Eichrodt, Walter. *Theology of the Old Testament.* London: SCM Press, 1967.

Eltis, David. "Introduction to the Methodology" on the *Trans-Atlantic Slave Trade—Understanding the Database,* at https://www.slavevoyages.org/voyage/about (accessed July 2, 2019).

Fasholé-Luke, E. W. "Christian Unity: St. Cyprian's and Ours." *Scottish Journal of Theology* Vol. 23, no. 03 (August 1970): 316.

Ferguson, E. "Laying on of Hands: Its Significance in Ordination," *Journal of Theological Studies* Vol. 26, no. 1 (April 1975): 2.

Ferguson, Everett. "Sacraments in the pre-Nicene Period." In *The Oxford Handbook of Sacramental Theology,* edited by Hans Boersma and Matthew Levering, 126. Oxford: Oxford University Press, 2015.

Fergusson, David A. S. *The Cosmos and the Creator: An Introduction to the Theology of Creation.* London: SPCK, 1998.

Finlay, Anthony. *Demons: The Devil, Possession and Exorcism.* London: Blandford Press, 1999.

George, Timothy. "Thin Places." *First Things.* February 2, 2015, found at https://www.firstthings.com/web-exclusives/2015/11/thin-places (accessed August 24, 2019.

Giles, Kevin. *Jesus and the Father: Modern Evangelicals Reinvent the Doctrine of the Trinity.* Grand Rapids, MI: Zondervan, 2006.

Gold, Ann Grodzins. *Fruitful Journeys: The Ways of Rajasthani Pilgrims.* Prospects Heights, IL: Waveland Press, 1988.

Gore, Charles. *The Ministry of the Christian Church.* Waterloo Place, UK: Rivington, 1889.

Gortner, David T. *Varieties of Personal Theology: Charting the Beliefs and Values of American Young Adults.* Farnham, UK: Ashgate, 2013.

Goulder, Michael and John Hick. *Why Believe in God?* London: SCM Press, 1983.

Graham, Elaine. "Redeeming the Present." In Elaine Graham, *Grace Jantzen: Redeeming the Present*. Farnham, UK: Ashgate, 2013.

Greene, Preston. "Are We Living in a Computer Simulation? Let's Not Find Out." *The New York Times*, August 10, 2019.

Griffin, David Ray. *Christian Faith and the Truth Behind 9/11: A Call to Reflection and Action.* Louisville, KY: Westminster John Knox Press, 2006.

Griffin, David Ray. *Religion and Scientific Naturalism: Overcoming the Conflicts*. Albany, NY: State University of New York, 2000.

Griffiths, Paul J. *Decreation: The Last Things of All Creatures.* Waco, TX: Baylor University Press, 2014.

Guillory, Margarita Simon. *Spiritual and Social Transformation in African American Spiritual Churches: More than Conjurers.* New York: Routledge, 2017.

Hall, Noel. "Apostolic Succession." *Scottish Journal of Theology*, Vol. 11, no. 2 (1958): 123.

Hardy, Edward R. *Early Christian Fathers . Vol. 1*, edited by Cyril C. Richardson. Philadelphia: Westminster Press, 1953.

Harris, Rev. Raymond. *Scriptural Researches on the Licitness of the Slave-Trade Shewing its Conformity with the Principles of Natural and Revealed Religion Delineated in the Sacred Writings of the Word of God*. Liverpool: printed by H. Hodgson, Pool-Lane, 1788.

Hawkins, Barney. *Episcopal Etiquette and Ethics: Living the Craft of Priesthood in the Episcopal Church*. New York: Morehouse Publishing, 2012.

Hebblethwaite, Brian. *The Essence of Christianity: A Fresh Look at the Nicene Creed*. London: SPCK, 1996.

Helm, Paul. *The Providence of God.* London: IVP, 1993.

Hick, John. *Faith and Knowledge*. Ithaca, NY: Cornell University Press, 1957.

Hick, John, ed. *The Myth of God Incarnate.* London: SCM Press Ltd., 1977.

Hick, John. *An Interpretation of Religion: Human Responses to the Transcendent.* New Haven, CT: Yale University Press, 1989.

Hick, John. *Evil and the God of Love*. New York: Harper & Row, 1966.

Hooker, Morna D. *The Gospel According to St. Mark*. London and New York: Continuum, 1991.

House of Bishops Occasional Paper. *Apostolicity and Succession*. London: Church House, 1994.

Doe, Norman. "Ordination, Canon Law and Pneumatology: Validity and Vitality in Anglican-Roman Catholic Dialogue." *Ecclesiastical Law Journal*, Vol. 8, no. 39 (2006): 407.

Hume, David. *Of Superstition and Enthusiasm*. Raleigh, NC: Generic NL Freebook Publisher, n.d. Accessed July 28, 2016.

Hurtado, Larry W. *How on Earth Did Jesus Become God? Historical Questions about Earliest Devotion to Jesus*. Grand Rapids, MI: Eerdmans, 2005.

Hurtado, Larry W. *Lord Jesus Christ: Devotion to Jesus in Earliest Christianity*. Grand Rapids, MI: Eerdmans, 2003.

Hyman, Gavin. *The Predicament of Postmodern Theology: Radical Orthodoxy or Nihilist Textualism?* Louisville, KY: Westminster John Knox Press, 2001.

Institute for Women's Policy Research at https://iwpr.org/issue/employment-education economic-change/pay-equity-discrimination/ (accessed August 23, 2019).

James, A. Gordon. "Apostolic Succession." *The Expository Times*, Vol. 70, no. 6 (March 1959): 166.

James, Susan. *Spinoza on Superstition: Coming to Terms with Fear*. Budel, Netherlands: Uitgeverij DAMON, 2014.

James, William. *Will to Believe: And Other Essays in Popular Philosophy*. Auckland, NZ: The Floating Press, 1912.

Jantzen, Grace, Jeremy R. Carrette, and Morny Joy. *Death and the Displacement of Beauty*. London: Routledge, 2004.

Jantzen, Grace. *Becoming Divine: Towards a Feminist Philosophy of Religion*. Bloomington, IN: Indiana University Press, 1999.

Jantzen, Grace. *Death and the Displacement of Beauty: Foundations of Violence*. London and New York: Routledge, 2004.

Jantzen, Grace. *God's World, God's Body*. Louisville, KY: Westminster John Knox, 1984.

Jantzen, Grace. "Flourishing: Towards an Ethics of Natality." *Feminist Theory*, Vol. 2, no. 2 (2001).

Johnston, Albert Edward. "The Laying on of Hands: Its Origin and Meaning." *The Irish Church Quarterly*, Vol. 4, no. 16 (1 October 1911): 317–18.

K. E. Kirk. "The Apostolic Ministry." In *The Apostolic Ministry: Essays on the History and the Doctrine of the Episcopacy*, edited by K. E. Kirk, 15–16. London: Hodder & Stoughton, 1947..

Keble John. "Adherence to the Apostolical Succession the Safest Course." In *Tracts for our Times: Nos.1–46. Records of the Church, nos. I–XVIII*, edited by John Keble, John Henry Newman, Edward Bouverie Pusey, William Palmer, Richard Hurrell Froude, and Isaac Williams. 7. J. G. F. & J. Rivington, 1839.

Klein, Elizabeth. *Augustine's Theology of Angels*. Cambridge: Cambridge University Press, 2018.

Knight, John Allen. *Liberalism versus Post liberalism: The Great Divide in Twentieth-Century Theology*. New York: Oxford University Press, 2013.

Lane, William L. *The Gospel According to Mark.* Grand Rapids, MI: Eerdmans, 1974.

Laplace, Pierre-Simon. *A Philosophical Essay on Probabilities,* translated by Frederick Truscott and Frederick Emory. London: Chapman and Hall, 1902.

Lebreton, Jules. *History of the Dogma of the Trinity: From Its Origins to the Council of Nicaea, i. The Origins,* transalted by Algar Thorold. London: Burns Oates and Washbourne, 1939.

Leeming, S. J., Bernard. *Principles of Sacramental Theology.* London: Longmans, Green and Co., 1958.

Leith, John H. *Creeds of the Churches,* third edition. Atlanta, GA: John Knox Press, 1982.

Lescroart, Mark. "The Healing Power of Touch." *Scientific American Mind,* Vol. 22, (July/August 2011): 7. Published online: June 23, 2011.

Lewis, C. S. (Clive Staples). *Mere Christianity.* New York: Harper One, 2012 edition.

Lindbeck, George A., *The Nature of Doctrine: Religion and Theology in a Postliberal Age.* London: SPCK, 1984.

Luther, Martin. "Babylonian Captivity of the Church" (1520). In *Documents of Christian Worship: Descriptive and Interpretive Sources,* edited by James F White. Louisville, KY: Westminster John Knox Press, 1992.

Luther, Martin. *Luthers Werke,* 7:596, quoted in Bridget Heal, "The Virgin Mary in Protestant Nuremberg." In *Religion and Superstition in Reformation Europe Studies in Early Modern European History,* edited by Helen L. Parish and William G. Naphy, 26. Manchester: Manchester University Press, 2002.

Luc Racaut. "A Protestant or Catholic superstition? Astrology and eschatology during the French Wars of Religion." In *Religion and Superstition in Reformation Europe Studies in Early Modern European History,* edited by Helen L. Parish and William G. Naphy, 154. Manchester: Manchester University Press, 2002.

Mabillard, Amanda. "Worst Diseases in Shakespeare's London." In *Shakespeare Online.* August 20, 2000. http://www.shakespeare-online.com/biography/londondisease.html.

MacIntyre, Alasdair C. *After Virtue: A Study in Moral Theory.* Notre Dame, IN: University of Notre Dame Press, 2007.

MacIntyre, Alasdair. *Whose Justice? Which Rationality?* London: Duckworth, 1988.

Mackenzie, K. D. "Sidelights from the non-episcopal communions." In *The Apostolic Ministry: Essays on the History and the Doctrine of the Episcopacy,* edited by K. E. Kirk, 461–91. London: Hodder & Stoughton, 1947.

Mackey, Rochelle B. "Discover the Healing Power of Therapeutic Touch." *The American Journal of Nursing,* Vol. 95, no.4 (April 1995).

Macquarrie John. *Principles of Christian Theology*, revised edition. London: SCM Press, 1977.

Markham, Ian S. *Against Atheism: Why Dawkins, Hitchens, and Harris Are Fundamentally Wrong*. Malden, MA: Wiley-Blackwell, 2010.

Markham, Ian S. *Do Morals Matter*, second edition. Oxford: Wiley Blackwell, 2018.

Markham, Ian S. *Go Into All the World: Faith and Engagement*, edited by Shireen R. Baker. Alexandria, VA: VTS Press, 2011.

Markham, Ian S. "Richard Burridge's Achievement." *First Things*. January 2014.

Markham, Ian S. *Truth and the Reality of God: An Essay in Natural Theology*. Edinburgh: T & T Clark, 1998.

Markham, Ian S. "Modern Theology: 9. Providence." *Farmington Papers*, October 1997.

Markham, Ian S. *Understanding Christian Doctrine*, second edition. Oxford: Wiley Blackwell, 2017.

Martin, Dale B. *Inventing Superstition: From the Hippocratics to the Christians*. Cambridge, MA: Harvard University Press, 2009, ProQuest ebrary. Web. July 26, 2016.

Martos, Joseph. *Doors to the Sacred: A Historical Introduction to Sacraments in the Catholic Church*, revised edition. Liguori, MO: Liguori/Triumph, 2001.

Matthews, W. R. "Apostolic Succession." *The Expository Times*, Vol. 70, no. 11 (January 1959): 340.

Mawson, T. J. "Freedom and the Causal Order." In *Rethinking Order After the Laws of Nature*, edited by Nancy Cartwright and Keith Ward. London: Bloomsbury, 2016.

Mbiti, John S. *Introduction to African Religion*, second edition. Portsmouth, NH: Educational Books, 1994.

McDougall, Dorothy C. *The Cosmos as the Primary Sacrament: The Horizon for an Ecological Sacramental Theology*. New York: Peter Lang, 2003.

McFague, Sallie. *Models of God: Theology for an Ecological, Nuclear Age*. Philadelphia: Fortress Press, 1982.

McGrath, Alister E. *A Scientific Theology, Volume 1: Nature*. Edinburgh and New York: T&T Clark, 2001.

McGrath, Alister E. *A Scientific Theology: Reality, Volume 2*. London and New York: T&T Clark, 2002.

McGrath, James F. *The One True God: Early Christian Monotheism in Its Jewish Context*. Urbana, IL: University of Illinois Press, 2009.

McRandal, Janice. *Christian Doctrine and the Grammar of Difference: A Contribution to Feminist Systematic Theology*. Minneapolis, MN: Augsburg Fortress, 2015.

Milbank, John. *Theology and Social Theory.* Oxford: Basil Blackwell, 1990.

Moloney, Francis J. *The Gospel of Mark: A Commentary.* Grand Rapids, MI: Baker Academic, 2012.

Moltmann, Jürgen. *The Crucified God.* London: SCM Press, 1974.

Moltmann, Jürgen. *The Trinity and the Kingdom: The Doctrine of God.* San Francisco: Harper and Row, 1981.

Montgomery, John Warwick. *Fighting the Good Fight: A Life in Defense of the Faith.* Eugene, OR: Wipf & Stock, 2016.

Murphy, Nancy C. "Does Prayer Make a Difference?" In *Cosmos as Creation: Theology and Science in Consonance,* edited by Ted Peters, 240. Nashville, TN: Abingdon Press, 1989.

Nichols, OP, Aidan. *Holy Order: Apostolic Priesthood from the New Testament to the Second Vatican Council.* Dublin: Veritas Publications, 1990.

Nineham, D. E. *The Use and Abuse of the Bible: A Study of the Bible in an Age of Rapid Cultural Change.* Library of Philosophy and Religion. London: Macmillan, 1976.

Noll, Mark A., "Evangelicalism and Fundamentalism." In *Science and Religion: A Historical Introduction,* edited by Gary B. Ferngren. Baltimore, MD, and London: The John Hopkins University Press, 2002.

Nyamiti, Charles. "The Doctrine of God." In *A Reader in African Christian Theology*, edited by John Parratt, 59. London: SPCK, 1987.

O'Connell, Robert J., S. J. *William James on the Courage to Believe.* New York: Fordham University Press, 1984.

Olupona, Jacob K. *African Religions: A Very Short Introduction.* Oxford: Oxford University Press, 2014.

Osborne, Kenan B. *Sacramental Theology: A General Introduction.* New York: Paulist Press, 1988.

Padgett, Alan G. "Practical Objectivity: Keeping Natural Science Natural." In *The Blackwell Companion to Science and Christianity,* edited by B. Stump and Alan G. Padgett. Oxford: Wiley Blackwell, 2012.

Parish, Helen, and William G. Naphy, eds. *Religion and Superstition in Reformation Europe.* Manchester, UK: Manchester University Press, 2002.

Peters, Ted (ed.). *Cosmos as Creation: Theology and Science in Consonance.* Nashville, TN: Abingdon Press, 1989.

Placher, William C. *Jesus the Savior: The Meaning of Jesus Christ for Christian Faith.* Louisville, KY: Westminster John Knox Press, 2001.

Placher, William C. *Mark.* Louisville, KY: Westminster John Knox Press, 2010.

Placher, William C. *The Triune God: An Essay in Postliberal Theology.* Louisville, KY: Westminster John Knox Press, 2007.

Plantinga, Alvin. *God and Other Minds: A Study of the Rational Justification of Belief in God.* Ithaca, NY, and London: Cornell University Press, 1967.

Plantinga, Alvin. "The Evolutionary Argument Against Naturalism." In *The Blackwell Companion to Science and Christianity,* edited by B. Stump and Alan G. Padgett, 106. Oxford: Wiley Blackwell, 2012.

Plato. *The Republic.* 507b–509c.

Polkinghorne, John. *One World: The Interaction of Science and Theology.* London: SPCK, 1986.

Potter, Dylan David. *Angelology.* Eugene, OR: Cascade Books, 2016.

Prusak, Bernard P. "Explaining Eucharistic 'Real Presence': Moving beyond a Medieval Conundrum." *Theological Studies,* Vol. 75, no. 2 (2014): 239.

Race, Alan. *Christians and Religious Pluralism.* London: SCM Press, 1982.

Renee, Hayes. "The Boggle Threshold." *Encounter* (August 1980): 92–96.

Roberts, John Russell. "Quantum Mechanics: Scientific Perspectives on Divine Action." *CTNS & Vatican Observatory/UNP* (1993).

Rorty, Richard. *Contingency, Irony, and Solidarity.* Cambridge: Cambridge University Press, 1989.

Ross, Susan A. *Extravagant Affections: A Feminist Sacramental Theology.* New York: Continuum, 1998.

Runyon, Theodore. "The Word as the Original Sacrament." *Worship* no. 54 (November 1980): 500.

Ruse, Michael. *Science and Spirituality: Making Room for Faith In the Age of Science.* Cambridge: Cambridge University Press, 2010.

Sampson, Tyler. "Scripture, Tradition, and Resourcement: Toward an Anglican Fundamental Liturgical Theology." *Anglican Theological Review* Vol. 96, no. 2 (2014): 318.

Schillebeeckx, Edward. *Christ the Sacrament of the Encounter with God.* New York: Sheed & Ward, 1963.

Schmemann, Alexander. *The World as Sacrament.* London: Darton, Longman and Todd, 1966.

Scruton, Roger. *Spinoza.* London: Phoenix Paperback, 1998.

Searle, Mark. "Infant Baptist Reconsidered." As reproduced in Maxwell E. Johnson, *Living Water, Sealing Spirit: Readings on Christian Initiation.* Collegeville, MN: The Liturgical Press, 1995.

Searle, Mark. *Alternative Futures for Worship,* vol. 2: *Baptism and Confirmation.* Collegeville, MN: The Liturgical Press, 1987.

Sedgwick, Timothy F. *Sacramental Ethics: Paschal Identity and the Christian Life.* Philadelphia: Fortress Press, 1987.

Sedgwick, Timothy F. *What Does It Mean to Be Holy Whole?* New York: Church Publishing, 2018.

Simons, Menno. "Foundations of Christian Doctrine" (1539). In *Documents of Christian Worship: Descriptive and Interpretive Sources*, edited by James F. White. Louisville, KY: Westminster John Knox Press, 1992.

Sixtus V bull, *Coeli et Terrae* (1586) as quoted in Ibid., 155.

Smith, Steven B. "Spinoza's Paradox: Judaism and the Construction of Liberal Identity in the Theologico-Political Treatise." *Journal of Jewish Thought & Philosophy*, Vol. 4, no. 2, (1995): 209.

Sonderegger, Katherine. *Systematic Theology. Volume 1, The Doctrine of God*. Minneapolis, MN: Fortress Press, 2015.

Sosa, Ernest. *Knowledge in Perspective.* Cambridge: Cambridge University Press, 1991.

Spinoza, Baruch. "The Theological-Political Tractate." In *Spinoza: Complete Works (translated by Samuel Shirley)*, edited by Michael L. Morgan, 388. Indianapolis, IN: Hackett Publishing Company, 2002.

Spong, John Shelby. *Here I Stand: My Struggle for a Christianity of Integrity, Love, and Equality.* New York: Harper One, 2001.

Stenmark, Lisa L. "Feminist Philosophies of Science." In *The Blackwell Companion to Science and Christianity*, edited by B. Stump and Alan G. Padgett, 86. Oxford: Wiley Blackwell, 2012.

Stenmark, Mikael. "How to Relate Christian Faith and Science." In *The Blackwell Companion to Science and Christianity*, edited by B. Stump and Alan G. Padgett, 68. Oxford: Wiley Blackwell, 2012.

Stob, Paul. *Rhetoric & Public Affair: William James and the Art of Popular Statement*. East Lansing, MI: Michigan State University Press, 2013.

Stout, Jeffery. *Ethics after Babel: The Language of Morals and Their Discontents*. Princeton, NJ: Princeton University Press, 2001.

Stroud, Barry. "The Charm of Naturalism." *Proceedings and Addresses of the American Philosophical Association*, Vol. 70 (1996):2.

Sullivan, Francis A. *From Apostles to Bishops: The Development of the Episcopacy in the Early Church*. Mahwah, NJ: Paulist Press, 2001.

Swinburne, Richard. *Revelation: From Metaphor to Analogy.* Oxford: Clarendon Press, 1992.

Taylor, Charles. "A Philosopher's Postscript: Engaging the Citadel of Secular Reason." In *Reason and the Reasons of Faith*, edited by Paul J. Griffiths and Reinhard Hütter, 340. New York and London: T&T Clark, 2005.

Taylor, Charles. *The Secular Age*. Cambridge, MA: The Belknap Press of Harvard University Press, 2007.

Telford, W. R. *Mark*. Sheffield, UK: Sheffield Academic Press, 1995.

The Episcopal Church. *Book of Common Prayer and Administration of the Sacraments and Other Rites and Ceremonies of the Church, together with the Psalter or Psalms of David.* New York: Church Publishing, 1979.

Thomas, Keith. *Religion and the Decline of Magic: Studies in Popular Beliefs in Sixteenth- and Seventeenth-Century England.* London: The Folio Society, 2012—originally published in 1971.

Torrance, Alan J. "Auditus Fidei: Where and How Does God Speak? Faith, Reason, and the Question of Criteria." In *Reason and the Reasons of Faith,* edited by Paul J. Griffiths and Reinhard Hütter, 44. New York and London: T&T Clark, 2005.

Torrance, T. F. *Space, Time and Resurrection.* Grand Rapids, MI: Eerdmans, 1976.

Turner, Cuthbert Hamilton. *Apostolic Succession.* London: Church Literature Association, 1945.

United Nations Statistics at https://unstats.un.org/unsd/gender/chapter4/chapter4.html. Accessed August 23, 2019.

Volpe, Medi Ann. *Rethinking Christian Identity: Doctrine and Discipleship.* Oxford: Wiley Blackwell, 2013.

von Harnack, Adolf. *History of Dogma,* translated by Neil Buchanan. Boston: Little, Brown, & Co. 1896–1905.

Ward, Keith. *Christ and the Cosmos: A Reformulation of Trinitarian Doctrine.* Cambridge: Cambridge University Press, 2015.

Ward, Keith. *Christ and the Cosmos.* Cambridge: Cambridge University Press, 2016.

Ward, Keith. "Concepts of God and the Order of Nature." In *Rethinking Order After the Laws of Nature,* edited by Nancy Cartwright and Keith Ward. London: Bloomsbury, 2016.

Ward, Keith. *Religion and Revelation: A Theology of Revelation in the World Religions.* Oxford: Clarendon Press, 1994.

Ward, Keith. *The Battle for the Soul.* London: Hodder and Stoughton, 1985.

Ward, Keith. *The Christian Idea of God: A Philosophical Foundation for Faith.* Cambridge and New York: Cambridge University Press, 2018.

Ward, Keith. *Divine Action.* London: Collins Flame, 1990.

Ward, Keith. *God, Faith & the New Millennium: Christian Belief in an Age of Science.* Oxford: Oneworld, 1998.

Ward, Keith. *Religion and Community.* Oxford: Oxford University Press, 2000.

Webb, Stephen H. *Jesus Christ, Eternal God: Heavenly Flesh and the Metaphysics of Matter.* Oxford: Oxford University Press, 2012.

Wiles, Maurice. *God's Action in the World.* London: SCM Press, 1986.

Williams, Charles. *He Came Down from Heaven.* London: Heinemann, 1938.

Williams, Peter. *The Case for Angels*. Carlisle: Paternoster Press, 2002.

Williams, Rowan. *Meeting God in Mark*. Louisville, KY: Westminster John Knox Press, 2014.

Wilson, E. O. *On Human Nature*. Cambridge, MA: Harvard University Press, 1978.

World Health Organization at https://www.who.int/news-room/fact-sheets/detail/violence-against-women. Accessed August 19, 2019.

Worship: Descriptive and Interpretive Sources, edited by James F. White. Louisville, KY: Westminster John Knox Press, 1992.

Wrede, William. *Das Messiasgeheimnis in den Evangelien*. 1901, translated into English as *The Messianic Secret* 1971.

Zagzebski, Linda. *Virtue Epistemology: Essays on Epistemic Virtue and Responsibility*. Cary, NC: Oxford University Press (US), 2001.

Zwingli, Ulrich. "Commentary on True and False Religion" (1525). In *Documents of Christian Worship: Descriptive and Interpretive Sources*, edited by James F. White. Louisville, KY: Westminster John Knox Press, 1992.

Zwingli, Ulrich. "Of Baptism." In *Documents of Christian Worship: Descriptive and Interpretive Sources*, edited by James F. White. Louisville, KY: Westminster John Knox Press, 1992.

Zwingli, Ulrich. "On the Lord's Supper." In *Documents of Christian Worship: Descriptive and Interpretive Sources*, edited by James F. White. Louisville, KY: Westminster John Knox Press, 1992.

Index

Abraham (patriarch), 101
accidents, 118, 129, 130
Agnosticism, 1, 11, 75
Anabaptist, 131
anarchismus , 7
anafühl , x, 1, 7, 95, 117, 118, 169, 170, 175, 190
ancestor, 4, 26, 28–29, 29, 30, 31, 175
angel, xi, 1, 5, 12, 18, 23, 24, 46, 55, 56, 62, 64, 66, 93, 130, 163, 164, 165, 166, 167, 167–169, 169–170, 170–171, 172, 175, 184, 186, 187
Anglican, xi, 106, 122, 142, 143, 144, 148, 153, 154–155, 157, 158, 171, 180
Anglo-Catholic, 143, 144
animist, 17, 62
annunciation, 166
anthropic principle (anthropologists), 27, 28, 193
anti-realist, 66
Apocalypticism, 96, 108
apologetics, 17, 151; new, xiv, 180–181, 183, 184, 186
apostle, xi, 98, 104, 140, 141, 142, 145, 146, 148, 149, 149–150, 151, 152, 154, 157, 158, 159, 168, 186
Apostles' Creed, 186
apostolic succession, xi, 23, 56, 62, 135, 140, 141, 142–143, 143, 144, 145, 148, 152, 155, 156, 159, 180, 184, 186, 187

Aquinas, Thomas, 19, 53, 81, 84, 129, 168, 169, 176n9, 193
archangel, 167, 168
Archimedean, 64, 83
Aristotle, 22, 36, 81, 84, 85, 129, 180, 193
Armbreecht, Ann, 189
ascension, 129, 173, 174
Astuti, Rita, 25, 28, 29, 30
atheism, ix, 1, 5, 51, 68, 76, 173, 200, 217; protest, 97
Augustine of Hippo, 53, 81, 107, 125, 129, 144, 170, 171, 193
authority, xi, 21, 22, 35, 46, 56, 63, 66, 82, 84, 87, 91, 96, 106, 107, 109, 110, 110–111, 111, 112, 121, 141, 142, 148, 149, 150, 152, 154, 157, 165, 166, 169, 187; teaching, 109, 111

Babylon *or* Babylonian, 5, 104, 129, 170
Ballou, Jacqui, vii, 182, 183
baptism *or* baptize, x, 104, 110, 111, 112, 118, 119, 120, 121, 122, 124, 126, 126–127, 127, 129–130, 130, 131, 132, 135, 150, 153, 156; infant, 124, 127, 130, 131
Baptist, 120, 131, 153, 154, 155, 170
Barbour, Ian, 41, 42, 45, 48
Barnes, Julian, 4, 5, 7
Barr, James, 46, 194
Barth, Karl, 79, 80, 104, 105, 168, 194
Bates, Matthew, 92

Bauckham, Richard, 93
Bhaskar, Roy, 47–48, 48, 49
beauty, 72, 123, 189, 198
Bible, x, xi, 10, 22, 24, 46, 62, 104, 106, 119, 126, 130, 146, 147, 165, 172, 201
big bang theory, 3, 42
bishop, 56, 127, 139, 140, 141, 142, 143, 144, 146, 148, 149, 150, 150–151, 152, 154, 155, 156, 157, 157–158, 173
Black Codes, 182
Bloch, Maurice, 25, 28, 29, 30
Boesch, Donald, 103
Bonhoeffer, Dietrich, 79
Bonino, Serge-Thomas, 163, 170
bonum commune, 170
bonum privatum, 170
Bostrom, Nick, 185
Brooke, John Hedley, 36
Brummer, Vincent, 71
Brunner, Emil, 43
Buddha, 69
Buddhism *or* Buddhist, 11, 70, 153
Burridge, Richard, vii, 105, 109
Bryson, Bill, 3, 4

Calvin, John, 87, 101, 130, 131
Cartwright, Nancy, 53, 195, 200, 201, 204
Casey, Maurice, 92, 93
Catechism, 127, 128
Cater, Philip, 141, 142
catholic, 61, 135, 139, 140, 151, 184
causal agent, 26, 55
causal determinism, 38
causation, 12, 22, 23, 23–24, 24, 25, 31, 32, 38, 39, 40, 42, 43, 53, 54, 55, 62, 117, 118, 124, 126, 127, 146; agent, 53; bottom up, 53; divine, 42, 43; empirical, 12; physical, 39, 55; self-, 43; spiritual, 22, 23–24, 24, 25, 31, 32, 42, 54, 55, 62, 117, 118, 124, 126, 127; top-down, 53, 55
Celtic, 189
Chalcedon, 94, 95
Cheetham, David, 70
children, 27, 43, 69, 126, 127, 128, 131, 167, 179, 183
Christ, xi, 9, 79, 87, 93, 94, 97, 98, 101, 105, 119–120, 121, 122, 124, 125, 128, 129, 130, 131, 133, 134, 139, 141, 142, 145, 148, 154, 157, 163, 164, 166, 174, 182
Christology, 87, 96, 99, 109, 110, 112, 125
church, ix, x, xi, xii, xiv, 1, 6, 9, 10, 12, 19, 20, 21, 22, 24, 42, 46, 61, 66, 68, 70, 75, 77, 78, 82, 92, 94, 98, 100, 104, 105, 106, 107, 109, 117, 118, 120, 121, 122, 123, 124, 127, 128, 129, 134, 135, 139, 140, 141, 142, 143, 144, 145, 147, 148, 149, 149–151, 151, 152, 153, 156, 157, 158, 159, 160, 164, 169, 171, 173, 175, 179, 180, 182, 183, 184, 186, 187, 190
Christian, xi, xi–xii, xiv, 3, 6, 9, 11, 12, 21, 22, 24, 27, 32, 35, 36, 39, 43, 46, 47, 49, 54, 55, 62, 64, 66, 69, 71, 72, 77, 78, 79, 80, 81, 82, 85, 86, 87, 91, 92, 93, 93–94, 95, 96, 97, 98, 99, 102, 103, 104, 105, 106, 107, 112, 117, 118, 119, 120, 122, 124, 126, 127, 128, 129, 132, 135, 140, 142, 143, 144, 145, 150, 152, 153, 154, 155, 158, 163, 164, 164–165, 165, 166, 167, 168, 169, 172, 173, 174, 181, 182, 183, 184, 186, 187
Christianity, 9, 12, 18, 24, 32, 41, 47, 49, 61, 66, 70, 72, 74, 77, 78, 79, 80–81, 81, 92, 93, 103, 106, 142, 146, 149, 173, 182, 183, 190
Church of England, 145, 156, 157
Cirlot, Felix, 143
Clayton, Philip, 38, 40, 43
clergy, 25, 141, 142, 145, 151
cognitive intent, 69
coherence, 28, 35, 36, 77, 81, 86, 98, 117, 153, 164, 168, 175, 187
Collins, Adela Yarbro, 110
Collins, C. John, 43
colors, xiii, 190
commission, 141, 142, 143, 146, 149, 152, 156, 157, 158
confer *or* conferred *or* conferring, 19, 63, 123, 127, 157
confirmation, 121, 156, 157, 165
Congar, Yves, 122
Congregation for the Causes of Saints, 173
consecrate or consecration, 20, 118, 128, 132, 133, 134, 139, 142, 156, 157, 158
Consonance, Theology and Science in, 42

consubstantiation, 130. *See also* real presence
contemporary skeptic, xii, 107, 184
conversion, 66, 78–79, 80
cosmology, 39–40, 70, 172, 174; African Traditional, 26
Council of Churches, 143
creatio ex nihilo, 49, 180
creationism. *See* scientific creationism
creator, 10, 12, 17, 43, 80, 82, 94, 95, 104, 163
creed, 10, 49, 81, 101, 102, 145, 186
criterion, 63, 71, 73, 102, 122
critical immanentism, 78
critical realism, 47, 49, 69, 91
cultural sexism, 180
culture-relative revelation, 82
Cupitt, Don, 66, 67, 68, 69, 195
Cyprian, 151

Dante, 168
Darwin, Charles, 36
Davies, Paul, 56n9, 64, 195
Dawkins, Richard, x, 25, 36, 37, 38, 40, 200, 217
deacon, 127, 143, 150, 180
deism, 1, 6, 8, 9, 10, 12, 13, 17, 24, 30, 31, 32, 35, 39, 40, 43, 61, 72, 190, 195
deisdaimonia, 18
deist, 6, 8, 9, 10, 11, 17, 40, 68
demon, 5, 12, 18, 37, 38, 46, 107, 109, 110–111, 112, 163, 165, 166, 169, 170–171, 175, 187; *See also* unclean spirit
Denton, Melinda Lundquist, 9, 10
Descartes, Rene', 36
determinism, 37, 38, 43, 52
devil, 20
Dionysius, 168
divine action, 42, 43, 54, 55, 100, 124, 126, 127, 167, 174, 202
divine agency, 21, 48, 49, 53, 92, 126
Doe, Norman, 157
Donahue, John, 108, 110
double agency, 43
Dowd, Michael, 45
dream, 28, 29

ecclesiastical authoritarianism, 41, 42

ecclesiology, xi, 150, 155, 180
ecumenical *or* ecumenism, 77, 78, 140, 142, 143, 144, 145, 146, 153, 184, 186, 190
Edwards, James, 110
Eichrodt, Walter, 39
Einstein, Albert, 39, 61
Enlightenment, 1, 20, 45
epiclesis, 134
episcopal *or* episcopacy *or* episcopate, 141, 143, 144, 145, 148, 152, 157, 159
Episcopal, 139, 152, 186
episkopous, 149
epistemological *or* epistemology, 63, 69–70, 70, 78, 85, 86, 111; mediational, 63; virtue, xiii, 66, 85, 86, 167, 168, 170
eschatological *or* eschatology, 69, 109, 122, 124, 150
essence, 9, 95, 104, 109, 114n48, 133, 176n3, 197
ethics, 71, 85, 86, 147, 160n1, 195, 197, 198, 202, 203, 217. *See also* morality
Eucharist, 23, 56, 118, 119, 120, 121, 122, 124, 125, 126, 128, 129, 130, 131, 132, 133, 134, 135, 145, 146, 150, 154, 190. *See also* Holy Communion
evangelical, 11, 46, 47, 49, 102, 140, 144
evangelism, x, 81
evil, x, 3, 19, 32, 111, 164, 165, 170, 171
evolution, 1, 20, 40, 42, 45, 95, 164, 165, 172, 196, 202; cosmic and biological, 164
exegesis *or* exegete, 79, 92, 104, 105, 164, 166
exorcise *or* exorcism, 109, 110, 170, 171, 187
exousia, 110, 111, 112

facts, 50, 54, 64
faith, x, xi, xii, 1, 4, 5, 7, 8, 18, 21, 24, 25, 27, 30, 39, 40, 42, 47, 49, 54, 61, 66, 74, 75, 80, 93, 103, 120, 124, 127, 128, 129, 130, 131, 141, 143, 147, 149, 152, 153, 154, 163, 172, 180, 182, 187, 190
fall (into sin), 170
false *or* falsity, 1, 6, 18, 25, 31, 39, 64, 66, 67, 77, 117, 148, 169, 173
Farer, Austin, 43

Fashole-Luke, E. W., 151
feminism *or* feminist, 50, 71, 73, 74, 103, 123, 180, 181
Ferguson, Everett, 119, 196
Fergusson, David, 42
first council, 149
Foucault, Michael, 72
free will, 8, 52
Frei, Hans, 77
fundamentalism *or* fundamentalist, 46, 153, 173, 184

gefühl , 7
George, Timothy, 189
Giles, Kevin, 102, 103
Gilkey, Langdon, 41, 42
Godhead, 94, 95, 99, 130
Gold, Ann Grodzins, 27, 28
Gore, Charles, 142, 143
Gospel, 96, 105, 107, 108, 109, 111, 112, 121, 141, 142, 150, 164, 166, 169, 174, 181, 187, 190
Goulder, Michael, 12, 144
grace, xi, xii, 31, 47, 87, 117, 119, 120, 121, 122, 123–124, 124, 125, 127, 129, 131, 132, 134, 139, 140, 141, 142, 144, 145, 146, 154, 155, 156, 157, 159, 160; means of, 124, 140
Graeco-Roman biography, 109
Graham, Elaine, 72, 73
Greene, Preston, 185
Griffin, David Ray, 48
Griffiths, Paul, 168, 169, 170, 171
Gueranger, Dom Prosper, 186
Guillory, Margarita Simon, 183

Hall, Noel, 144
Harrington, Daniel, 108, 110
Harris, Raymond, 181
Hayes, Renée, 2, 3
Hawkins, Barney, vii, viii, 139, 140, 152, 160
heaven, 5, 10, 39, 69, 82, 101, 110, 112, 127, 129, 167, 168, 172, 173, 174, 175, 181, 187, 189
Hebblethwaite, Brian, 96, 164, 165
Hebrew Bible, 126, 146
hell, 22, 75, 82, 112, 186
Herbert, Edward, 8

hermeneutic of recognition, 147
Hick, John, 11, 11–12, 66, 68, 69–70, 71, 75, 76, 82, 195, 197
Hindu, 27, 153
Holy Communion, 120. *See also* Eucharist
holy orders, xi, 123, 135, 142, 157, 180, 186
holy water, 19, 75, 172
homosexual, 105
Houlden, Leslie, 108, 144
human agency, 32, 43, 53, 55
humanism, 6
Hume, David, 8, 21, 22, 47, 198
Hurtado, Larry, 92, 93, 94, 198

idealist, 51, 54
Ignatius of Antioch, 150
immaculate conception, 153
Immanuel, 8, 104
imperialism, 12, 24, 153, 154
incarnation, 12, 43, 82, 87, 91, 92, 94, 94–95, 95, 96
inclusion, xi, 152, 179, 180, 183
indiscernibility of identicals, 95
indigenous religious traditions, 13, 25, 35
individualism, 7
intelligent design, 42, 47
Irenaeus, 101, 140, 151

James, Susan, 23, 33n22, 33n25
James, William, 66, 74, 75, 76, 86, 201, 203
Jantzen, Grace, 57n28, 66, 71, 72, 73, 73–74, 84, 86, 197, 198
Jesus, xi, xiv, 6, 9, 12, 25, 35, 47, 56, 69, 70, 77, 78, 79, 80, 82, 87, 92, 93–94, 94, 95–96, 96, 97, 98, 101, 103, 104, 105, 106–107, 107, 107–108, 108–109, 109–110, 110–112, 118, 121, 121–122, 127, 128, 129, 130, 131, 132, 133–134, 134, 135, 139, 142, 145, 146, 148, 149, 152, 153, 154, 155, 163, 165, 166–167, 169, 170, 171, 173, 174, 180, 181, 182, 184, 185, 187, 190
Jew *or* Jewish, 10, 22, 62, 92–93, 93, 96, 99, 107, 108, 109, 120, 126, 149, 182
Jim Crow laws, 182
Johnson, Albert, 156
John the Baptist, x, 55, 112

Index

Judaism, 72, 92, 93, 94, 96, 99, 153, 170, 203
Julian of Norwich, 103
justice, 66, 67, 71, 72, 73, 74, 86, 102, 179, 180, 183

Kant, Immanuel (Kantian), 8, 11, 51, 70
kai euthus, 108
Keble, John, 141
kenotic, 95, 96
Kierkegaard, Sören, 79
Kirk, Kenneth, 156
Knight, John Allen, vii, 77, 78
knowledge, 23, 29, 38, 45, 46, 52, 63, 72, 73, 76, 80, 82, 84, 85, 86, 87, 100, 106, 109, 111, 112, 132, 166–167
knowing, 7, 8, 42, 47, 48, 50, 62, 63, 64, 66, 76, 78, 80, 83, 84, 85, 86, 87, 91, 96, 106, 117, 173; tradition-constituted, 76

Lane, William, 111
language, 11, 12, 31, 41, 45, 49, 67, 69–70, 71, 77, 78, 81, 83, 84, 91, 92, 103, 105, 117, 140, 144, 145, 152, 153, 164, 184, 186, 188n15, 190, 203
Laplace, Pierre Simon, 37, 38, 40, 199
Lebreton, Jules, 92
Leenhardt, F.J., 132
Leibniz's Law of Identity, 95
Leeming, Bernard, 119–120, 120
Lewis, Ayres, 105
Lewis, C. S., 43, 92, 199
liberal, xi, 9, 11, 106, 144, 183, 184, 186
Lindbeck, George, 66, 77, 78
literalism, biblical, 41
liturgical renewal movement, 186
liturgy, 93, 122, 139, 144, 145, 159, 186
Locke, John, 6, 8, 9
logic, 3, 63, 83, 84, 99, 143, 182
Lord's Supper, 93, 128, 154
love, xi, xiii, 12, 22, 53, 54, 86, 96, 98, 99, 101, 103, 120, 124, 133, 141, 168, 170, 185, 186, 190
Luther, Martin, 20, 87, 129, 130, 131, 199
Lutheran, 155

MacIntyre, Alasdair, xiii, 63, 64, 67, 78, 80–81, 83, 199

Mackey, Rochelle, 159
Macquarrie, John, 92, 98, 106
mainline, xi, 10, 11, 77, 144, 153, 190
marriage, 75, 120, 121, 122, 183
Martyr, Justin, 150
mainline, xi, 10, 11, 77, 144, 153, 190
Martin, Dale, 17, 18
Martos, Joseph, 132
Marxism, 7
materialistic reductionism, xi, 25
materialism, xi, 25, 41, 51, 52, 185; scientific, 25, 41
Mawson, T. J., 53, 55
McFague, Sallie, 180
McGrath, James, 47–48, 49, 92, 93
memorial, xi, 6, 128, 131, 154
Messiah, 107–108, 108, 111, 153
messianic secret, 107, 108
metaphysical, 11, 62, 66, 67–68, 73, 82, 85, 97, 99, 153, 185
metaphysics, 47, 67, 97, 106, 107
metanoia, 79
Methodist *or* Methodism, 144, 154, 155
Milbank, John, 66, 80, 81
Milton, 168
miracle *or* miracles, 3, 11, 12, 23, 43, 46, 47, 127, 129
modalism *or* modalist, 100, 103
Moltmann, Jürgen, 96, 97, 97–98, 98, 99
momentous, 74, 75
moral, xiii, xiv, 2, 6, 9, 10, 17, 19, 21, 46, 67, 71, 77, 82, 85, 97, 164, 181, 190
Moralistic Therapeutic Deism, 9, 10
moral, therapeutic deism, 190
multiverse theory, 8, 153
music, xiii, 190
Muslim, 11, 62, 69, 120, 154
mysterion, 119
mystery, 2, 7, 30, 39, 40, 52, 53, 67, 69, 94, 97, 104, 108, 110, 119, 122, 125, 131
mythological, 46, 69–70

natural religion, 6, 8, 9
naturalism, 45, 47, 51, 54, 58n56; theistic, 48
Natural Theology, 8, 41, 85, 87
new age crystals, 56, 62, 67
Newton, Isaac, 36
Newman, John, 141

New Physics, 39, 40, 64
Nichols, Aidan, 147, 148
Nineham, Denis, 144, 147
nonmaterial agency, 56
non-realism *or* non-realist, 66, 82

Ockham's Razor, 165
Old Testament, 43, 56n11, 92, 93, 104, 125, 151, 152, 156, 170, 193, 194, 196. *See also* Hebrew Bible
Olupona, Jacob, 26
ontological, 38, 51, 77, 78, 139, 146, 152, 159
ontology of violence, 81
option, xiii, 1, 2, 10, 28, 40, 42, 43, 44, 45, 46, 47, 48, 49, 53, 54, 62, 64, 66, 74–75, 75, 76, 80, 81, 82, 83, 84, 92, 93, 99, 100, 143, 154, 182, 185; live, 74; forced, 74
ordain *or* ordination, 56, 102, 118, 121, 139, 141, 143, 144, 144–145, 148, 152, 154, 155, 156, 157, 158, 159, 159–160, 180
original sin, 12, 127, 170
orthodox, 6, 9, 47, 49, 62, 73, 97, 144, 152, 154, 155, 179
Osborne, Kenan, 119, 121, 122
Oxford Movement, 141

Padgett, Alan, 63
pagan, 43, 169
pantheism, 71
parallel universe, 64, 174
Pascal, Blaise, 75
Pascal's Wager, 75
Peacocke, Arthur, 41, 43
Percy, Martyn, vii, 171, 172
perichoresis, 100
personalism *or* personalist, 50, 124
personal idealism, 51, 54
Peters, Ted, 41, 42, 45
philosophical materialism, 51
physics, 2, 36, 38, 39, 39–40, 64, 84
Placher, William, 94, 101, 103, 107, 186
planet, 19, 36, 37, 42, 103, 190
Plantinga, Alvin, 54, 79
Plato, 22, 72
Platonism *or* platonistic, 49, 81

pluralism *or* pluralist, 3, 11, 30, 68, 70, 99, 104, 106, 150, 164
Polkinghorne, John, 38
postliberal, 77, 78, 80, 83
pray *or* prayer, xi, 6, 10, 59n71, 67, 86–87, 118, 132, 134, 145, 149, 154, 155, 157, 167, 172, 174, 175, 186, 190, 201, 204
Presbyterian, 144, 154
presbyters, 140, 143, 149, 150, 151, 152
priesthood, 5, 21, 140, 148, 152, 154, 157
Principle of Indeterminacy, 52
prosopopoeia, 92
Protestant, 10, 20, 126, 129
providence, 4, 6, 7, 12, 21, 43, 47, 142, 152, 173, 197, 200
Prusak, Bernard, 129
psychology, 158

Quakers, 72
quantum measurement event, 55–56
quantum mechanics, 8, 38, 39, 52, 53, 55, 56, 61, 64, 202
Qur'an, 62, 153

racism, 181, 183
Radbertus, Paschasius, 129
rationality, 52, 63, 64, 73, 81, 83, 83–84, 91, 164, 165, 168, 170, 199
realism, 47, 49, 66, 67, 69, 72, 78, 81, 82, 91
realist, xii, 49, 66, 69, 117, 184; critically, 49, 117, 184
real presence, 130. *See also* consubstantiation
reason. *See* rationality
redlining, 182
Reformation, 8, 20, 22, 129, 173
reductionism *or* reductionist, xi, xii, xiii, 3, 8, 12, 25, 30, 32, 37, 38, 45, 47, 61, 62, 117, 163, 184
Reincarnation, 3, 28, 62
reliabilism, 85
religion or religious, 1–2, 3, 4, 5, 6, 7, 8–10, 10, 11, 12, 13, 18, 19, 21, 22, 23, 24, 25–26, 27, 31, 32, 35, 36, 39, 40–41, 42, 43, 45, 46, 47, 48, 49, 54, 55, 56, 61, 62, 66, 67, 68, 69–70, 70–71, 72, 73, 74, 75, 76, 77–78, 81, 82, 83, 84, 87, 93, 111, 119, 130, 141,

146, 153, 155, 172, 175, 181, 183, 184, 185
resurrection, 3, 12, 43, 47, 54, 82, 95, 98, 108, 132, 142, 154, 166, 168, 173, 174, 187
revelation, xi, xiv, 35, 41, 43, 54, 56, 61, 62, 79, 80, 81–82, 83, 87, 91, 94, 95, 104, 105, 106, 117, 119, 146, 152, 168, 184, 185, 187
ritual, 29, 30, 121, 133, 183
Robert, John, 158
Roman Catholic, xi, 10, 11, 20, 21, 22, 47, 49, 61, 62, 77, 118, 119, 120, 121, 123, 124, 126, 127, 128, 130, 131, 139, 140, 142, 143, 147, 148, 151, 153, 154, 155, 157, 163, 172–173, 183, 186
Rorty, Richard, 66, 67
Ross, Susan, 123
Runyon, Theodore, 124
Ruse, Michael, 45, 46–47, 48

sacrament, xi, 6, 20, 62, 118, 119, 120, 121–124, 124, 125, 126, 129–130, 130, 131, 132, 133, 134, 135, 141, 143, 144, 145, 146, 152, 154, 154–155, 156, 157, 159, 184, 186; original, 124; primordial, 122, 131; sacramental, xi, 6, 20, 117, 118, 119, 120, 121, 122, 122–124, 124, 125, 126, 131, 132, 134, 135
sacrifice *or* sacrificial, 18, 21, 98, 125, 128, 132, 156, 157, 169
Saepius officio, 157
Sagan, Carl, 174
saint, xi, 1, 5, 6, 9, 12, 62, 64, 66, 163, 164, 172, 172–173, 174, 175, 184, 186, 190; cult of the, 172, 173, 175
salvation, 43, 101, 127
Sampson, Tyler, 122
Satan, 45, 86, 110, 171
Schillebeeckx, Edward, 131
Schmemann, Alexander, 124
science, xi, xiii, 1, 2, 7, 8, 12, 17, 22, 23, 24, 25, 29, 30, 32, 35–36, 36, 38, 39, 40, 40–41, 42, 43, 45
scientific creationism, 41, 42
scientism, 41, 42, 45
Searle, Mark, 124
second coming, 153

secular, 1, 31, 40, 80, 81, 84, 147, 184
secularism, 1, 43
secularization, 5
Sedgwick, Timothy, vii, 120, 189
sex, 73, 102, 103, 105, 119, 120, 163, 167, 179–180, 194
shrine, 25, 27, 28, 31
Simmons, Menno, 131
simplicity, 50, 108
sin, 87, 124, 125, 127, 156, 170, 181, 183
skepticism, xii, 1, 2, 3, 4, 5, 21, 107, 124, 153, 164, 168, 175, 184
slavery, 19, 105, 126, 181–182
Smith, Adam, 6
Smith, Christian, 9
social imaginary, 117
social sciences, 47, 48, 173
Sonderegger, Katherine, vii, 99
Sosa, Ernest, 85
soul, 5, 36, 69, 72, 75, 94, 142, 168, 180
spiritual, ix, x, xi, xi–xii, xiii, xiv, 1, 8, 10, 11, 12, 21, 22, 23–24, 25, 31, 32, 35, 39, 40, 42, 44, 45, 46, 48, 50, 51, 54, 55, 56, 61, 62, 68, 91, 107, 111, 112, 117, 118, 124, 126, 127, 129, 131, 134, 135, 140, 155, 156, 157, 158, 159, 160, 163, 166, 167, 168, 169, 170, 171, 172, 183, 184, 186, 187, 190; causation, 22, 23, 24, 25, 31, 32, 42, 54, 55, 62, 117, 118, 124, 126, 127, 155, 158, 190; realm, xi, xii, xiii, xiv, 12, 24, 32, 35, 39, 45, 54, 56, 61, 62, 91, 107, 111, 112, 135, 159, 163, 166, 169, 171, 183, 186, 190
spirituality, xi, xiv, 39, 46, 47, 62, 117, 183, 184, 186, 189; global, 39
spiritually infused, x, xi, 6, 20, 25, 26, 28, 30, 31, 32, 35, 35–36, 36, 40, 41, 43–45, 46, 47, 48, 49, 50, 51, 53, 55, 61, 62, 64, 68, 91, 106, 107, 112, 117, 121, 126, 134, 139, 140, 144, 152, 155, 157, 160, 166, 184
Spinoza, Baruch, 21, 22–23, 24
Spong, John Shelby, 174, 180, 203
Stalin, 3
Stenmark, Lisa, 50
Stenmark, Mikael, 45
Stroud, Barry, 51

substance (of sacraments), 118, 128, 129, 130, 133
suffering, 97, 108, 109
Sullivan, Francis, 148, 150, 152
supernatural, 18, 20, 51
supersession *or* supersessionist, 63, 64
superstition, xi, 13, 17–18, 18, 19, 20, 20–21, 21, 22, 22–24, 25, 30, 31–32, 32, 35, 56, 61, 118, 190
Swinburne, Richard, 71, 81, 82, 83, 203

Taylor, Charles, x, 1, 30, 63, 117, 184
Tertullian, 118, 119, 121, 151
theism *or* theist, 1, 7, 22, 40, 48, 51, 53, 54, 56, 81, 97, 153, 184
theodicy, 43, 94, 164, 165
theological reasoning, 62, 91, 92, 93, 104, 106, 163, 164, 184
Theological Traditioned Truth, 82, 83, 85, 86, 87, 91, 96, 99, 102, 106, 117
theological traditionalism, xi
theology, 9, 11, 11–12, 20, 40, 41, 42, 46, 47, 48, 48–49, 49, 53, 64, 66, 68, 74, 80, 81, 84, 85, 86, 87, 97, 99, 102, 105, 106, 107, 117, 119, 121, 122, 124, 127, 129, 144, 147, 151, 163, 164, 165, 166, 179, 181, 183, 187; process, 48–49
thin place, 189, 189–190, 190
Tillich, Paul, 132
Toland, John, 9
toleration, ix, 30
Torrance, Alan, 66, 78, 79, 80, 87, 174
Tractarian, 140, 141, 142, 144
traditional, xi, 6, 9, 12, 17, 18, 22, 24, 25, 26, 32, 43, 62, 71, 73, 93, 98, 117, 119, 144, 157, 174, 179, 180, 181, 182, 183, 184, 185
tradition of enquiry, 62, 63, 64, 66, 165
tradition-constituted, 63, 64, 76, 78, 81, 83
transcendent, 2, 6, 7, 11, 12, 68, 69, 74, 76, 81, 84, 87, 93, 95, 100, 103, 110, 183, 184, 189
transfinalization, 132
transformation, 53, 61, 72, 79, 80, 117, 124, 183
transhistorical, 43
transignification, 132
transubstantiation, 20, 118, 128–129, 133

Trinity, 11, 91, 92–93, 95, 96, 97, 98, 99, 100, 101–102, 102, 103, 104, 106, 119, 120, 128, 133, 150, 163, 164, 173, 180, 184, 186, 194, 196, 199, 201; Social, 96, 99, 101, 120
truth, 1, 12, 20, 22, 25, 38, 39, 41, 43, 46, 63, 64, 66, 67, 68, 69, 70, 71, 72, 73, 74–75, 75, 76, 77, 78, 78–79, 80, 81, 82, 82–83, 83–84, 84, 85, 85–86, 86–87, 87, 91, 96, 99, 102, 106, 108, 111, 117, 141, 142, 144, 152, 153, 159, 164, 173, 175, 184, 186, 187, 190, 196, 197, 200, 217; categorial, 77; deductive, 63; intrasystematic, 77; ontological, 77–78; scientific, 46
Turner, Cuthbert, 140
Two-Languages theory, 42

unclean spirits, 109, 110, 112, 166. *See also* demon
universe, ix, x–xi, 1, 3, 4, 6, 7, 10, 12, 25, 26, 27, 28, 30, 35–36, 36, 37–38, 38, 39, 40, 41, 42, 43–45, 46, 47, 48, 49, 50, 51, 53, 54, 55, 56, 62, 64, 68, 69, 71, 86, 91, 94, 95, 98, 104, 106, 107, 112, 117, 121, 124, 126, 134, 139, 140, 144, 152, 155, 157, 158, 160, 164, 165, 166, 174, 183, 184, 185, 190

value *or* values, 30, 31, 50, 63, 66, 67, 69, 71, 73, 91, 95, 144, 146, 159, 168
verification, 69
Virgin Birth, 3, 101
von Harnack, Adolf, 92
Voodoo, 183
vox populi, 173

Ward, Keith, 36, 37, 38, 39, 50, 51, 52, 53–55, 71, 83, 84, 90n76, 99, 100, 101, 103, 132, 133, 134, 158, 162n44, 174, 195, 200, 204
Webb, Stephen, 101
western symbolic, 72, 74
Whitehead, A.N., 43, 48, 49
Wiles, Maurice, 43
Williams, Charles, 112
Williams, Peter, 165
Williams, Rowan, 107, 108

Wisdom (of God), 91, 101, 112; Eternal, 94
Wittgenstein, 41, 78
Word, x, xi, xiv, 7, 18, 35, 56, 61, 79, 93, 94, 96, 98, 100, 101, 102, 104, 105, 106, 107, 124, 131, 132, 133–134, 134, 152, 155, 163, 164, 165, 166, 167, 169, 170, 173, 174, 184; eternal, xi, xiv, 35, 56, 61, 93, 95, 96, 98, 101, 104, 105, 106, 107, 132, 133, 134, 163, 164, 166, 167, 169, 170, 173, 184; written, 104, 106, 164, 166
Word of God, 62, 94, 98, 101, 104, 105, 112, 149, 152, 181

worldview, xi, xii, 7, 9, 10, 12, 22, 26, 27, 29, 30, 31, 36, 37, 39, 40, 46, 49, 61, 64, 67, 77, 83, 118, 153, 164, 167, 169, 184
worship, xi, 19, 20, 21, 27, 67, 69, 92, 93, 99, 125, 131, 133, 147, 156, 167, 168, 190, 195, 199, 202, 203, 205
Wrede, William, 107

Yarbro Collins, Adela, 110, 115n66, 195

Zagzebski, Linda, 85
Zurara, 181
Zwingli, Ulrich, 131

About the Author

Ian S. Markham is dean and president of Virginia Theological Seminary and a priest in the Episcopal Church. He holds a PhD in Christian ethics from the University of Exeter. He is the author of numerous books for church and classroom, as well as *Against Atheism: Why Dawkins, Hitchens and Harris are Fundamentally Wrong* (Wiley-Blackwell, 2010); *Engaging with Beduizzaman Said Nursi: A Model for Interfaith Dialogue* (Ashgate, 2009); *Understanding Christian Doctrine* (Blackwell, 2007); *A Theology of Engagement* (Blackwell, 2003); *Truth and the Reality of God* (T&T Clark, 1998); and *Plurality and Christian Ethics* (Cambridge University Press, 1994).

www.ingramcontent.com/pod-product-compliance
Lightning Source LLC
Chambersburg PA
CBHW050904300426
44111CB00010B/1366